An Uneasy Relationship

Modern Jewish History
Henry L. Feingold, *Series Editor*

An Uneasy Relationship

AMERICAN JEWISH LEADERSHIP AND ISRAEL, 1948–1957

ZVI GANIN

 Syracuse University Press

Copyright © 2005 by Syracuse University Press
Syracuse, New York 13244–5160

All Rights Reserved

First Edition 2005

05 06   07   08   09   10   6   5   4   3   2   1

Title page: Prime Minister David Ben-Gurion *(left)* and Jacob Blaustein, president of the American Jewish
Committee, August 23, 1950. Courtesy of the Blaustein Library, The American Jewish Committee.

The paper used in this publication meets the minimum requirements of American
National Standard for Information Sciences—Permanence of Paper for Printed
Library Materials, ANSI Z39.48–1984.∞™

Library of Congress Cataloging-in-Publication Data

Ganin, Zvi.
An uneasy relationship : American Jewish leadership and Israel, 1948–1957 / Zvi Ganin.
p. cm.—(Modern Jewish history)
Includes bibliographical references and index.
ISBN 0–8156–3051–4 (alk. paper)
1. Israel and the diaspora. 2. Jews—United States—Attitudes toward Israel. 3. Jews—United States—
Politics and government—20th century. 4. Jews—United States—Identity. 5. Zionism—United States—
History—20th century. I. Title. II. Series.
DS132.G36 2004
320.54'095694'0973—dc22
                                    2004016565

Manufactured in the United States of America

To the memory of Morton K. Blaustein,
who did not live to see this study completed.

Contemporary Jewish history is based
on two miracles and one catastrophe.
The catastrophe was the Holocaust
in Europe, and the miracles were
the realities created in Eretz Yisrael
and in the United States.

—MOSHE SHARETT,
Israeli Foreign Minister, 31 July 1950

Contents

Illustrations

Zvi Ganin is the author of *Truman, American Jewry, and Israel, 1945–1948* and *Kiryat Hayyim, Experiment in an Urban Utopia* (in Hebrew). He has written extensively on American Jewish and Israeli history. After receiving his Ph.D. from Brandeis University in modern Jewish history, he taught in this field at Beit Berl College in Israel. He is currently working on a history of American-Israeli diplomatic relations.

Acknowledgments

I SHOULD LIKE TO ACKNOWLEDGE the following scholars who pioneered the study of the relationship between Israel and American Jewry: the late Ben Halpern, Naomi W. Cohen, the late Daniel Elazar, Allon Gal, Yosef Gorny, Charles S. Liebman, Howard M. Sachar, Ernest Stock, and Melvin I. Urofsky.

I am indebted to Professor Henry L. Feingold of Baruch College, City University of New York, for his invaluable assistance in helping me launch this project.

It is a genuine pleasure to acknowledge the help I have received in the course of preparing this book. I am deeply grateful to Dr. Morton K. Blaustein, the late president of the Jacob and Hilda Blaustein Foundation, and to Mr. David Hirschhorn and the members of the Blaustein family. Morton Blaustein was a tower of strength, facilitating my research and giving generously of his time to shed light on his father's fascinating and significant career. Alas, he is no longer here to see the book in print. Special acknowledgment is also due to the late Dr. S. Zalman Abramov of Jerusalem, a jurist and a scholar who served as midwife to the book. Without the sustained interest and support of all of these people, I could not have completed this endeavor.

I am also indebted to my good friends Professor Jehuda Reinharz and Sylvia Fuks Fried of Brandeis University for their interest, hospitality, and assistance, and to the present and past deans of my college, Professors Aaron Zeidenberg and Mordecai Zur, for their kind support. Sadly, my beloved teacher and friend, the late Professor Ben Halpern of Brandeis University, who followed this work from its inception, did not live to see its completion.

One of the most rewarding aspects of working on this book was the opportunity given to me to do research in several archives and libraries in America and Israel whose staffs were most hospitable and helpful. I am particularly grateful to Cyma Horowitz, director of the Blaustein Library of the American

Jewish Committee in New York, and Michelle Anish; also to Helen Ritter, records manager of the American Jewish Committee, and Ruth Rauch. Their patient and cheerful help over several years of research greatly facilitated my work. Selma Hirsh and Bert Gold were most generous and helpful in elucidating the role of Jacob Blaustein and the American Jewish Committee in American-Israeli relations.

Sincere thanks are also due to Bernard Wax and the late Dr. Nathan Kaganoff of the American Jewish Historical Society, Waltham, Massachusetts; Dr. Benedict K. Zobrist, director, and Elizabeth Safly, librarian, of the Harry S. Truman Library, Independence, Missouri; the director, Dr. Abraham J. Peck, and staff of the American Jewish Archives, Hebrew Union College, Cincinnati, Ohio; and the archivists at YIVO, New York; the National Archives, Washington, D.C.; the Eisenhower Library, Abilene, Kansas; and the State Historical Society of Wisconsin, Madison.

My thanks must also go to my good friends Yehoshua Freundlich and Yemima Rosenthal, editors of the superb *Documents on the Foreign Policy of Israel*; to Gilad Livneh of the Israel State Archives, Jerusalem; to Meir Avizohar, director, and Leanna Feldman, Hana Pinshaw, and Yael Rosenfeld, staff members of the Ben-Gurion Archives at Sde Boker, all of whom were most helpful; to Baruch Tor-Raz, director of the Israeli Labor Party Archives, Beit Berl; to Yoram Mayorek, director of the Central Zionist Archives, Jerusalem; and to Nehama A. Chalom and Ofra Perlmutter of the Weizmann Archives at Rehovot.

I am also indebted to Ayala and Saadia Gelb, Mordecai Gazit, Selma Hirsh, Morris Fine, and Deborah Dash Moore for their critical remarks; to Judy and Leo Diesendruck, Fradle and Barry Freidenreich, and Laurence J. Silberstein for their encouragement; to Judy Krausz for her care in editing the manuscript; to Eldad Salzmann for his meticulous typing of the manuscript; and to Perlina Varon for typing the index.

Finally, I wish to acknowledge my profound indebtedness to Yaffa, my wife and—in this instance—research assistant, and to our children, Maureen and Eldad, Naomi and Roni, whose devotion, understanding, and support helped to bring this undertaking to fruition.

Needless to say, such imperfections as remain, including errors and shortcomings, are my own.

Introduction

THE STATE OF ISRAEL, as the great scholar of Jewish mysticism Gershom Scholem put it perceptively, "was born prematurely, under decisive historical circumstances which did not allow for any choice,"[1] so that the three collaborators in the miracle of its birth on 14 May 1948—the Yishuv (the Jewish community in Palestine), the Zionist movement, and American Jewry—were not quite ready for the new reality of Jewish sovereignty. With the British security umbrella gone, the Yishuv had to take on a life-and-death military struggle with the Palestinian Arabs, and subsequently with all the neighboring Arab states, single-handedly. The worldwide Zionist movement, for its part, had to redefine itself in light of the realization of its long-sought goal. The third element, American Jewry, found itself in a paradoxical situation arising out of the tension between myth and reality, with Israel viewed simultaneously as a solution and as a problem, and as both a unifying and a divisive symbol. On the one hand, the new state was a source of intensified Jewish self-identity and pride. On the other, there was a realization of Israel's vulnerable military and economic position; ideological conflicts over the nature of its national persona; disappointment with unfulfilled expectations of cherished images; a profound identity crisis within the ranks of American Zionists over the loss of their role as champions of a cause that had been realized so successfully; and concern that Israel's domestic and foreign policies might affect vital American Jewish sensibilities and interests adversely.

Israel, for its part, was to be greatly disappointed by the failure of America's Jews, and of the Western Diaspora entirely—particularly the leaders of the Zionist movement—to participate in the Zionist goal of the ingathering of the exiles as *olim* (new immigrants) once the gates of the homeland had opened.

This book focuses on leaders, for the inherent divergences among the three elements that collaborated in the miracle of Israel's birth were personified in the political, ideological, diplomatic, and personal struggles of a small group of dynamic leaders who influenced and shaped policies.

The first and second parts of the study are devoted mainly to the Jewish arena and constitute an examination of the interplay between the Israeli and the American Jewish leadership. They describe and explain the solutions adopted by these leaders to the new problems that arose in Israel, in the Zionist movement, and in the American Jewish community during the formative first years of Israel's existence.

The idea of a Jewish state was by no means espoused by the entire American Jewish community until the early 1940s. The affiliated Jewish community, which consisted of no more than one-fourth of the estimated Jewish population of five million,[2] was roughly divided into three uneven groups: Zionists, non-Zionists, and anti-Zionists, with the Zionists forming the majority. Most members of the Zionist parties enthusiastically supported the Biltmore program (1942), which called for the establishment in Palestine of a Jewish commonwealth or state.[3] The non-Zionists were generally associated with such organizations as B'nai B'rith and the American Jewish Committee, and with Reform synagogues. These groups were not affiliated with the world Zionist movement and maintained a neutral, and sometimes negative, position on the question of Jewish nationalism and statehood, although they tended to cooperate with the Zionists in the humanitarian aspects of building the Jewish national home (such as housing, health, and education) and supported the right of Jews to immigrate freely to Palestine. The anti-Zionists insisted that Jews constituted a religious entity alone, and not an ethnic group as well, and actively opposed both the idea of a Jewish state and the activities of the Zionist movement.

The Zionists played a major role in the political struggle to gain President Harry S. Truman's backing for a Jewish state in Palestine. The two largest mainstream groups, the Zionist Organization of America (a men's organization) and Hadassah (a women's organization), and two smaller groupings, the Labor Zionists and the religious Zionists, had a total membership of over 700,000 in 1948.[4] Led by Rabbi Abba Hillel Silver of Cleveland, the American Zionist movement became the largest mass movement in American Jewish life in the 1940s. Moreover, in cooperating with the much smaller, but highly influential, body of non-Zionists, led by such personalities as Joseph M. Proskauer and Jacob Blaustein, it created the consensus in the Jewish community necessary to elicit the massive political and financial help that was rendered to the Yishuv, without which the State of Israel could not have been established.

However, previous solutions quickly became current problems in the new Israeli context. The leaders involved in the emerging triangular relationship between the Jewish state, the Zionist movement, and American Jewry soon had to tackle fundamental questions concerning the relationship between Israel and the Diaspora, and the Zionist movement specifically; the danger of dual loyalty; the relevance of Zionist ideology and the future of the Zionist movement; control of the fund-raising purse; representation of the Jewish community vis-à-vis Israel; and the conduct of political efforts on behalf of Israel in Washington.

The main actors in this drama of debates, conflicts, and eventual solutions were an impassioned group. In Israel the central figure was David Ben-Gurion, the pragmatic prime minister, radical Zionist, and charismatic, strong-willed leader, seconded by Moshe Sharett, his scholarly and moderate foreign minister. An outstanding personality in the world Zionist movement was the brilliant but sometimes reckless Zionist leader Nahum Goldmann. The American Zionist scene was dominated by the forceful and controversial Reform Rabbi Abba Hillel Silver of Cleveland, along with his close friend and astute political ally Emanuel Neumann. The non-Zionists of the American Jewish Committee were led by a trio: Judge Joseph M. Proskauer, formerly a passionate anti-Zionist; his heir apparent, Jacob Blaustein of Baltimore, a man of action; and John Slawson, the powerful executive director of the American Jewish Committee (AJC). The critical collection of funds was dominated by the irascible Henry Montor, a fund-raising genius. The anti-Zionist camp was led by Lessing J. Rosenwald of Philadelphia, who served as president of the American Council for Judaism (ACJ), and by Reform Rabbi Elmer Berger, the Council's driving force as executive director. Lastly, mention should be made of a group of brilliant young Israeli diplomats who were influential behind the scenes: Abba Eban, the Israeli ambassador in Washington and at the United Nations; Teddy Kollek, Ben-Gurion's confidant and troubleshooter; and Avraham (Abe) Harman, who headed the Israel Office of Information in New York and after 1953 served as consul general there.

The third part of the book deals with the advocacy role played by pro-Israeli leaders vis-à-vis the executive branch in Washington in trying to impress policy makers that Israel was sui generis in the international community, and that it must not be treated solely on the basis of strategic interests. The effect these advocates had on the political relationship between the United States and Israel during the cold war era will be examined, along with the assertion that the non-Zionists had become somewhat more effective than the Zionists in this effort.

Israel, poor in natural resources, small in size, and surrounded by hostile Arab states, could not maintain itself and absorb millions of Jewish refugees from all parts of the world without outside help. Such help could come mainly from one source: the United States. But from the period of President Truman's involvement in the creation of Israel and onward, most U.S. foreign and defense policy makers regarded the Zionist enterprise as a heavy burden that complicated America's relations with the strategically located and oil-rich Arab states. This is where American Jewry's role became crucially important. The deep concern for Israel's survival on the part of this community, and the political pressure it applied, occasionally helped overcome governmental ambivalence toward the vital needs of the struggling young Jewish state.

Nevertheless, with the creation of Israel in May 1948 and with Truman's upset victory at the end of that year, American Jewish political activity on behalf of Israel underwent significant changes. The Zionist ranks were in disarray, and the American Zionist movement as a potent political force declined. This development, however, was offset by the rise in influence of the non-Zionists, epitomized in early 1949 by the ousting of Abba Hillel Silver and Emanuel Neumann from their leadership positions (although not from continued personal initiative on behalf of Israel) and by the emergence of Jacob Blaustein, the new president of the American Jewish Committee, as an intermediary between Washington and Jerusalem.

While all these personalities were deeply moved by the drama of Israel's emergence and were conscious of the vital need to assist it, their activities on behalf of the Jewish state were highly individualistic, reflecting not only the disparate nature of their characters and the way they viewed their roles, but, more broadly, the pluralistic and decentralized nature of American society and, accordingly, of the American Jewish community. These leaders sometimes had divergent views on Israeli policies and on possible solutions to the Arab-Israeli conflict. The third part examines the extent of their impact on Israeli foreign and defense policy and on the nature of American-Israeli relations.

Tension between the State of Israel, the Zionist movement, and American Jewry developed immediately with the emergence of the new state. The problematic role of the Zionist movement aside, it was only natural that two disparate Jewish societies—Israeli and American Jewish—could not always comprehend the different directions followed by one another. Hence a danger arose, as the British Zionist Federation aptly warned soon after the founding of the state:

> The State of Israel has solved the problem of Jewish homelessness. . . . On the other hand, instead of uniting and consolidating the Jewish people all over the world, there is real danger that the existence of the State may split them into two camps—Israeli and Diaspora Jews—each speaking a different language, thinking along different lines, living in a different atmosphere and absorbing a different culture.[5]

Despite this tension, and the potential danger stemming from divergent realities, interests, and ideologies and from the clash of personalities, no unbridgeable gap developed by which "Zionism would then have created the Jewish state but lost the Jewish people."[6] In the final analysis, this danger was averted because a small group of leaders (and a few Israeli diplomats), notably Blaustein and Ben-Gurion, were keenly aware of both Israel's precariousness and the mutual dependence of the American Jewish and Israeli communities, and eventually worked out a viable and creative modus vivendi.

Abbreviations

ACJ	American Council for Judaism
ADL	Anti-Defamation League of B'nai B'rith
AJC	American Jewish Committee
AZC	American Zionist Council
JA	Jewish Agency
JDC	Joint Distribution Committee
JTA	Jewish Telegraphic Agency
NCRAC	National Community Relations Advisory Council
NEA	Bureau of Near Eastern, South Asian, and African Affairs, U.S. Department of State
NSC	National Security Council
UJA	United Jewish Appeal
UN	United Nations
UPA	United Palestine Appeal
WZO	World Zionist Organization
ZOA	Zionist Organization of America

PART
I

Two Divergent Centers

1

The Specter of Dual Loyalty

1

FOR MOST AMERICAN JEWS the creation of the State of Israel was by no means a foregone conclusion. Only five years before the proclamation of the Jewish state, the eminent Rabbi Louis Finkelstein, chancellor of the Jewish Theological Seminary in New York, had asserted at a meeting of the American Jewish Committee that "there isn't one possibility in one hundred that there will be established in the course of the next twenty-five years what is called a Jewish state in Palestine. . . . This cannot possibly be done in our time."[1] However, if the creation of Israel in May 1948 put an end to the historic controversy about the practicality of the idea of a Jewish state, it also actualized the imminent tension between Israel and American Jewry on another old issue: the specter of dual loyalty. This issue would become of paramount importance to the American Jewish Committee, as it would to its rivals, the anti-Zionists on the one hand and the Zionists on the other.

From its inception in 1906, in the wake of widespread pogroms in Russia, the American Jewish Committee aimed to serve as the authoritative spokesman of American Jewry with the dual task of preventing "the infraction of the civil and religious rights of Jews" and of "alleviat[ing] the consequences of persecution" in America and abroad.[2] Composed of upper-class descendants of German Jewish immigrants—mostly lawyers and businessmen who were also members of Reform congregations—this elitist group viewed the Zionist idea as a threat to the very essence of its belief in the emancipation and integration of Jews in America. They rejected the notion of an ethnic component of Jewish identity and wholeheartedly supported the position enunciated in a resolution adopted by the American Reform Movement in 1898: "We are unalterably opposed to political Zionism. The Jews are not a nation, but a religious community. . . . America is our Zion."[3] In any event, Zionism was long considered a chimera, a fantasy, "a poet's dream," according to Louis Marshall, president of the committee and the dominant figure in it until his death in 1929.[4]

Still, despite friction between the committee and the American Zionist movement, by the 1920s, with the development of the Zionist undertaking in Palestine, Marshall, backed by several wealthy and influential members of the committee, was prepared to support the enterprise on a nonideological philanthropic basis. With the publication of the Balfour Declaration in 1917, which created a British-Zionist entente, Marshall and the committee charted a middle course, known, oddly, as non-Zionism, that supported the humanitarian and philanthropic aspects of the Zionist enterprise while totally rejecting the goal of transforming it into a sovereign Jewish state.

The committee remained a small, self-appointed body throughout the 1930s and, despite a strong anti-Zionist wing, was mainly preoccupied with growing domestic anti-Semitic activity by profascist extremists such as Father Charles E. Coughlin and pro-Nazi American groups. Nevertheless, the vigorous support of American Zionists for the Jewish national home in Palestine, with its emphasis on the ethnic component of Jewish identity, was viewed by the organization as a serious threat to the cherished achievements of political emancipation and to the status that Jews had attained in American society.[5]

Judge Joseph M. Proskauer, who was to play a formative role in shaping the committee's policy toward Zionism, was elected to the presidency of the committee in 1943 when European Jewry was being decimated and when covert and overt anti-Semitism was rife even in the United States. Proskauer, born to a German Jewish family in 1877 in Mobile, Alabama, and raised in a Reform Jewish ambience, had had unforgettable anti-Semitic encounters in his boyhood in Alabama as well as later in New York City following his graduation from Columbia University Law School. "It did not take me many days to discover," Proskauer recalled, "that the doors of most New York law offices in 1899 were closed, with rare exceptions, to a young Jewish lawyer."[6] Proskauer, subsequently to become a New York State Supreme Court justice, was a formidable figure: articulate, penetrating, endowed with political acumen, ambitious, and also vain. Leader of the assimilationist anti-Zionist wing of the committee, he viewed Zionist agitation for the establishment of a Jewish commonwealth, or state, in Palestine as "a Jewish catastrophe."[7] He was troubled about the implications of political Zionism for the status of American Jewry, convinced that "from every point of view of safety for Jews in America there has got to be an open, vocal Jewish dissent from nationalism and political Zionism." [8]

The aftermath of World War II and the Holocaust, however, brought about great change. In the encounter between ideology and reality, non-Zionism had become obsolete. The leadership of the committee asserted in May 1947:

> We must now decide what we can do that will serve the best interests of the hundreds of thousands of Jews [survivors of the Holocaust] who desperately need and desire to go to Palestine; that will safeguard the Jewish interest in Palestine; and that will put an end to the [British-Jewish] crisis of bloodshed and violence . . . that exists at present in Palestine and that may have the gravest repercussions both on the status of the Jews throughout the world and on the prospects for peace among the nations. [9]

Meanwhile, developments at the United Nations indicated that the time for a decision concerning the political fate of Palestine was fast approaching. In May 1947 the committee crossed the Rubicon at last and officially abandoned its opposition to the establishment of a Jewish state. At a historic meeting, [10] the executive committee adopted a resolution stating that if other preferred solutions (such as continuation of the British Mandate, or a UN trusteeship) were found untenable, and should the United Nations opt for an immediate political solution, the committee recommended the Zionist solution of partitioning Palestine into a Jewish and Arab state "in a manner which would give scope for further Jewish immigration and would provide equality to all citizens in any of the divisions that may be created." [11]

The change was not only ideological. The leaders of the committee actively cooperated with the Zionists in the political struggle conducted at UN headquarters in Lake Success and in Washington over the fate of the UN partition resolution. Specifically, Proskauer utilized his contacts at the State Department, while his second-in-command, Jacob Blaustein, used his influence at the White House and in the Democratic Party.

In March 1948, with the Jewish forces in Palestine suffering a series of serious defeats at the hands of the Arabs, Secretary of State George C. Marshall and Secretary of Defense James V. Forrestal, who had opposed partition all along as inimical to American national interests in the Middle East, succeeded in reversing Truman's policy of support for partition. This reversal was accompanied by an intensive campaign by American diplomats for a truce in Palestine and for a plan to put the country under temporary UN trusteeship, thereby forestalling the anticipated proclamation of the Jewish state.

Proskauer, gravely distressed at the bloodshed in Palestine, was active in this campaign, urging Moshe Shertok (later Sharett), head of the political department of the Jewish Agency, which was then based in New York, and Ben-Gurion to accept the American truce proposal.[12] But the State Department scheme was eventually—and dramatically—overturned by President Truman.[13] Proskauer's repeated pleas to Ben-Gurion to accede to the American scheme had become irrelevant. The Israeli leader was convinced that it was now or never, and, choosing not to miss the train of history, proclaimed the establishment of Israel on 14 May 1948. He had concluded that the Jewish state would have to come into being not by fiat in Washington's corridors of power, nor at the United Nations, but through force of arms on the field of battle against huge odds and at tremendous risk.

The leadership of the committee had given much thought to the implications of this historic development. Proskauer and Blaustein met with Jewish Agency leaders in February 1948 requesting to be consulted about the name of the state, the constitution, and the projected governmental system.[14] Blaustein, addressing an audience in Baltimore, discussed several possible ideas, remarking that "it appears to me now that 'The Jewish State' or 'Judea,' for obvious reasons, would be undesirable. The name 'New Judea' might be somewhat better. The name 'Eretz Israel' has been considered." He himself preferred "Zion."[15]

The committee also devoted considerable thought to the constitution of the emerging state. "It must be democratic and based on a Bill of Rights without any link between Church and State," said Blaustein. "Arabs and Christians, representing minorities, must be assured equal and civil rights in fact as well as in theory." Its government, he hoped, would "perhaps [be] modeled on the American presidential system."[16]

Blaustein's and the committee's blueprint for the constitution and governmental system of the Jewish state, while understandable in the American context, displayed considerable naïveté and a lack of firsthand contact with the political realities of the Yishuv. This lack of familiarity would later be rectified through Blaustein's subsequent visits, as well as by the opening of an American Jewish Committee office in Israel in 1961. Plainly, the committee hoped to influence the Israeli leadership to create an American-style constitutional democracy on the eastern Mediterranean shore. But they overlooked the fact that societies and their political institutions are organic developments. For example, the Israeli electoral system of proportional representation that was decided upon was inherited from the old Zionist Congress tradition, as well as from the system of Jewish self-government set up under the British Mandate.

Blaustein also had definitive views on the implications of the emerging state vis-à-vis the future role of the Jewish Agency and the Zionist Organization of America. The Jewish Agency, Blaustein declared, "should go out of existence shortly after the state actually comes into being, handing its functions over to the provisional government of the state." [17] Similarly, he felt, with the Zionist goal of a Jewish state about to be realized, the Zionist Organization of America (ZOA) and its umbrella body, the World Zionist Organization, should be dissolved as well.

Blaustein predicted that with the existence of the state, the old ideological "division of Jews into Zionists, non-Zionists, and anti-Zionists could then probably disappear." [18] Instead of this traditional triangle he favored the creation of a new, nonideological organization, called, perhaps, "American Friends of Palestine" (or substituting the final choice of name for the new state), which would confine its activities to "securing material and moral support for the newly created state" and which could serve as a model for Jews in other countries as well. The nonideological and nonpolitical character of his proposed "American Friends" would, he felt, attract Jews of all kinds to its ranks, irrespective of their previous attitude toward Zionism, thereby contributing greatly to a more harmonious American Jewish community.[19] Although Blaustein's plan failed to take into account the deeply felt ideologies and organizational needs of the various segments of the organized Jewish community and therefore was ultimately shelved, it did indicate the need for a reappraisal of the Israel-Diaspora relationship in the wake of the new political reality.

2

The executive of the American Jewish Committee met in Chicago in October 1948 to thrash out its stand on Israel. It was a large gathering, including a sizable number of representatives from chapters all over the country. Addressing the body, President Proskauer declared that Israel, by its very existence, had ended the old controversy on the idea of the Jewish state, and that, moreover, it "presented the . . . Committee with one of the greatest opportunities in its entire history for rendering service to Jewry." He thus signified not only the committee's recognition of the historic importance of this event, but also its preparedness to render support to the struggling state, which at that very moment was still at war with its Arab neighbors and was also contending with the political repercussions of the assassination in Jerusalem of Count Bernadotte, the Swedish UN mediator for Palestine, by Jewish extremists.

Regarding the implications of the birth of Israel, Proskauer stated somewhat enigmatically that "its existence creates new problems for us," but also that it had brought some highly beneficial dividends "to the position of Jews in America. The heroic and successful resistance of the Israelis to Arab aggression has been a great blessing to Jews everywhere, and should go far toward killing the stereotype that Jews lack courage." Proskauer went on to delineate the areas in which the committee could play a role, while also defining its limitations. For example, the committee could not influence the activities of the Jewish extremists responsible for the murder of Bernadotte, but, on the other hand, "it was possible for us to exert some influence within the American Zionist movement with a view to discouraging attempts by American Jews to dominate Israel." [20]

Three significant resolutions were adopted by the Chicago meeting after animated discussion. The first urged the Truman administration to continue backing the implementation of partition that would provide an adequate area for Israel to absorb a large influx of immigrants; grant the new state de jure recognition and financial aid; and support its admission to the United Nations. The other two resolutions, not immediately released to the press, called upon the State of Israel to ensure adherence to Western democratic "political structures and practices" and urged Israeli leaders to refrain from making any statement suggesting that Israel sees itself as "the spokesman for Jews the world over, or for any Jewish community outside the State of Israel." [21]

These resolutions paved the way for the final act in the process of bringing the committee into harmony with the existence of the Jewish state—the adoption of a new Statement of Views in January 1949. The statement, while reiterating the committee's historic commitment to combating bigotry, prejudice, and discrimination, and to continuing its efforts in the fields of human and civil rights, contained a new section expressing its official attitude toward the State of Israel:

> We hold the establishment of the State of Israel to be an event of historic significance. We applaud its recognition by our own and other governments.

We look forward to Israel's assumption of its full place among the family of nations as a government guaranteeing complete equality to all its inhabitants, without regard to race, creed or national origin. . . . Citizens of the United States are Americans and citizens of Israel Israelis; this we affirm with all its implications; and just as our government speaks only for its citizens, so Israel speaks only for its citizens. Within the framework of American interests, we shall aid in the upbuilding of Israel as a vital spiritual and cultural center and in the development of its capacity to provide a free and dignified life for those who desire to make it their home.[22]

The adoption of the 1949 Statement of Views coincided with a change of guard at the committee when Proskauer retired from the presidency and was succeeded by Jacob Blaustein. This changeover was not a routine one, for the younger man embodied several firsts for the organization: he was the first president of East European descent, he was not a New Yorker, and, in contrast to many of his predecessors, he was not a jurist. Moreover, his biography read like a veritable Horatio Alger story.

His father, Louis Blaustein, had arrived in the United States from Lithuania in his early teens and became a horse-and-buggy peddler in the farming region of eastern Pennsylvania. Moving to Baltimore in 1888, where Jacob was born in 1892, Louis sold kerosene in the streets of the city from a buggy, accompanied by the young Jacob in the early years of the century. Eventually, they established the American Oil Company, which would become one of the largest oil companies in the United States, with 26,000 employees by the early 1950s. Later, the business diversified into trading, shipping, and real estate. Summing up the family's achievements in 1964, Jacob Blaustein emphasized:

While our operations have spread to far-flung areas, here and abroad, *Baltimore is our home* [emphasis in original]. Here my father came over three quarters of a century ago, a virtually penniless immigrant; here we have raised our families; here we have founded most of our business enterprises; here have been and are our executive offices; and here we have participated in the various community philanthropies and cultural projects. We continue [to be] part and parcel of Baltimore.[23]

Blaustein and his family were members of a Reform congregation in Baltimore, the Oheb Shalom Temple. He became active in the American Jewish Committee in the early 1940s, serving as chairman of the General Committee. A non-Zionist outlook was a natural perspective for this highly ambitious first-generation American Jew for whom Baltimore was both home and the fountainhead of great success. However, unlike Proskauer, Blaustein was not a dyed-in-the-wool anti-Zionist, nor was he inclined to react to American-Israeli crises in apocalyptic terms.

He was a serious and thorough person, totally committed to accomplishing his goals. The following vignette by John Slawson, the astute executive vice president of the committee for a quarter of a century, describing his first meeting with Blaustein, aptly illuminates typical aspects of Blaustein's personality:

> It was in 1943 . . . in the Pennsylvania Railroad station [in New York City]. That was about the only place one could catch up with Jacob, and we were to discuss my coming to the American Jewish Committee. Before I knew what was happening, I found myself on the train continuing our discussion, with the intention of getting off at Newark. Instead, I found myself going on to Philadelphia, then at dinner with him, and then on to Baltimore. This was during the war. . . . I had difficulty going back to New York. After a great deal of effort, I managed to obtain an upper berth, into which I crawled and where I lay awake most of the night wondering what manner of man this was. As I contemplated, it suddenly dawned upon me that he knew a great deal about me, but I knew very little about him.[24]

Blaustein's work capacity was legendary. People marveled at the scope of his activities, which could be accomplished only by working a sixteen-hour day, as he did throughout his adult life. These activities included supervising his business empire; flying to Chicago to attend weekly meetings of the board of directors of Standard Oil of Indiana; traveling from Chicago to New York and Washington to attend to his duties as president of the American Jewish Committee, as senior vice president of the Conference on Jewish Material Claims Against Germany, and as board member of various U.S. governmental bodies; and frequently traveling abroad on various missions—all this before the jet age.

It was normal for him to call up members of his staff or colleagues at the committee late at night, as Selma Hirsh, his gifted assistant, related, "just checking on something in an item I had sent him, did I mean this or did I mean that. But he was always very gracious." The people who surrounded him were conscious that the essence of the man lay in his deep commitment to what he was doing, "so you could never be angry with him for calling at midnight, because you knew damn well when you hung up the telephone he was going to work for three more hours and you were going to sleep!" Hirsh commented. [25]

His attention to detail was unrivaled, evident in studying his correspondence. "If you prepared material for him he never took it at face value," Selma Hirsh recalled. "He would ask questions virtually line by line: 'how do you arrive at this' and 'why do you say that'? He internalized everything that you prepared for him. He never just read a paper." These traits, combined with stubbornness and perseverance, made him a demanding boss, an effective leader, and a formidable negotiator.[26]

As president of the committee between 1949 and 1954, and continuing thereafter as a dominant figure in the organization's work until his death in 1970, Blaustein was responsible, among his other duties, for its policies toward Israel. He had been involved in the struggle for the creation of the State of Israel, but once that goal had been achieved, and with the admission of Israel to the United Nations probable, the committee initiated a major education campaign designed to enlighten the American public regarding the nature and promise of the new Jewish state. Politically, Blaustein explained, Israel was a democratic state like America, and the Israeli War of Independence paralleled the 1776 Revolutionary War. On a humanitarian level, the development of the country's land and water resources would improve the standard of living of the Arab minority too. Blaustein expressed the hope that when the invading Arab armies withdrew and the guns were silenced, Jews and Arabs would be able to live together peacefully as they had in the past.[27] Although he delineated the limits of the committee's involvement in the fate of Israel, clearly the new state had become a significant concern of the erstwhile defense organization. Little did the new president envisage, however, that from then until his death he would devote a major part of his time and energy to ensuring the oldest democracy's continued support of the emergent new democracy in the Jewish state.

3

A radically different position was taken by the American Council for Judaism, which stood at the other end of the spectrum, beyond the Jewish consensus on Israel. Even before Israel's establishment the council, founded in 1943 by a group of Reform rabbis and wealthy lay persons of German Jewish descent, warned that such a state would be a serious obstacle to Jewish integration in America. The establishment of the state elicited panic and fury by the council over the damage it could do to the position and well-being of American Jewry. The organization, while small, was influential in the South, especially in Texas, and in the West, especially in San Francisco. Contending that it was illegitimate for American Jewry to demonstrate favorable concern for the State of Israel, the American Council for Judaism reinvigorated its previous anti-Zionist campaign with an anti-Israeli emphasis, publicizing its interpretation of Zionism and Israel through press releases, public speeches and debates, letters to selected groups of policy makers and opinion molders, magazine articles, and publications of its own.[28]

Concern about the question of dual loyalty was expressed by Alfred M. Lilienthal, one of the chief exponents of anti-Zionism in America, in a widely publicized *Reader's Digest* article in 1949, alongside a rebuttal by Rabbi Abba Hillel Silver in the same issue. Lilienthal wrote:

> Judaism was a religious faith which knew no national boundaries. . . . By contrast, Zionism was and is a nationalist movement organized to reconstitute Jews as a nation with a separate homeland. Now that such a state exists, what am I? Am I still only an American who believes in Judaism? Or am I—as extreme Zionists and anti-Semites alike argue—a backsliding member of an Oriental tribe whose loyalty belongs to that group?[29]

In this view, with its strange equation of Zionism and anti-Semitism, the Zionist movement was engaged in an immense and sinister conspiracy "to cement nationalities between Israel and all persons of Jewish faith." Thus, when the Israeli flag was hoisted on 14 May 1948, Israel's first independence day, Lilienthal recalled:

> I had no impulse to dance in the street with hysterical joy, as did so many in New York and London. For I was born and remain an American. I have no ties with, no longings for, and feel no responsibilities to Israel. And I believe that the future happiness of the Jews in America depends on their complete integration as citizens of this—our true—country.[30]

If Jews, Lilienthal warned, were to divide their love normally given to their native land, "it can lead only to disaster." This statement reflected not just the fear on the part of the members of the council that Israel's birth en-

dangered their primary mission—total integration into American society—
but also confirmed the vehement opposition by some American Jews to the
notion that any historic ethnic bond existed between Israel and American
Jewry.

Although numerically very small, the council was influential, largely as a
result of its symbiotic relationship with the American Jewish Committee—
until the early 1950s. Typically, the president and main financial backer of the
council, Lessing J. Rosenwald, had also served on the executive committee of
the American Jewish Committee for several years. He was the son of Julius
Rosenwald, who was one of the founders of Sears, Roebuck and Company.
Lessing, born in Chicago in 1891, succeeded his father as chairman of the
board of Sears in 1932, serving in that capacity until 1939. Apart from his
business and philanthropic activities, Lessing became famous as a collector of
rare books and prints. Several other members of the council also served simultaneously on the executive committee of the American Jewish Committee, a
useful connection. Moreover, the council members were affluent and socially
prominent. They also enjoyed the support of Arthur Hays Sulzberger, the
publisher of the *New York Times,* which gave them access to official Washington and to the news media.

Possibly their greatest asset, however, was Reform Rabbi Elmer Berger,
executive director of the council. Born in Cleveland, Ohio, in 1908, in a home
that was only marginally Jewish, he imbibed anti-Zionist attitudes early.
"Zionism was the anomaly—and a little-known one—in my formative years,"
he recalled. "I have felt thoroughly comfortable with the tradition of anti-
Zionism all my life." [31] He was greatly influenced by Rabbi Louis Wolsey of
Philadelphia, a prominent leader of the Reform movement and an anti-
Zionist, and in 1942 left his pulpit in Flint, Michigan, to become the council's
first executive director. Throughout his long tenure, until 1968, Berger was
the driving force behind the anti-Zionist grouping in the United States. A
skilled debater, prolific writer, and tireless organizer, Berger traveled the
length and breadth of the country to recruit new blood and to establish additional chapters. He was also the chief exponent of the council's philosophy of
integration, with Judaism viewed as a religion devoid of any ethnic bond, and
he preached his gospel in innumerable lectures and articles that received wide
exposure. Behind the scenes Berger was also one of the moving forces in anti-
Israel propaganda activities in the United States. He was a board member of
the pro-Arab American Friends of the Middle East; a close collaborator of the
anti-Zionist Kermit Roosevelt, who was an influential CIA official cum oil

company executive in the Middle East; and a friend of Fayez Sayegh, research chief of the Arab Information Center in New York.[32]

The birth of Israel did not put the American Council for Judaism out of business. In May 1948, just four days after the proclamation of the Jewish state, Lessing Rosenwald told the leadership of his organization that the event "calls for an examination and reorientation of the council policy,"[33] but dissolution was not what he had in mind. Rather, the council attempted—unsuccessfully—to enlist the cooperation of such non-Zionist Jewish organizations as the American Jewish Committee, the Jewish Welfare Board, B'nai B'rith, and the National Council of Jewish Women to issue a joint statement on the relationship of American Jews toward Israel.

The council's main effort, following the proclamation of the State of Israel, focused on pressuring Washington to withhold de jure recognition of the Jewish state until Israel amended its proposed constitution. Specifically, Lessing Rosenwald, who was in contact with Acting Secretary of State Robert A. Lovett on this question, was concerned that Article 3 of the constitution might "threaten to have a serious effect upon five million American citizens of Jewish faith (and, by parallel action, upon millions of Jews who are citizens of other lands)."[34] The controversial article read as follows: "The State of Israel is designed to be the National Home of the Jewish People and shall admit every Jew who desires to settle within its territory subject to such regulative provisions as may from time to time be enacted by the Chamber of Deputies."[35]

Rosenwald's objection was that Article 3 did not describe the State of Israel as "designed" to be the "national home" of all its citizens, no matter what their religion or national origin, rather than the national home of "the Jewish people." Such phrasing, Rosenwald pointed out to Lovett, implied that the State of Israel had usurped the citizenship of millions of individual Jews all over the world who were happy with their present citizenship in their respective nations.

"Clearly and unequivocally," Rosenwald stated on behalf of the American Council for Judaism, "to us, American citizens of the Jewish faith, the United States is our national home, and our only national home. No other land, state, or nation can explicitly or implicitly be recognized as our national home, or as 'designed' to be our national home."[36] American recognition of Israel, he warned, could be taken to mean sanctioning this objectionable Israeli claim, a lamentable state of affairs that should be rectified by Israel's eliminating this "misleading or, at best, ambiguous claim." To ensure Israel's full compliance, he insisted, any further American recognition of, or aid to, the State of Israel should be made contingent upon a public Israeli commitment to amend this article to Washington's satisfaction.

Rosenwald's grievance had no basis in fact, for in using the term "the Jewish people" the State of Israel had never intended to imply usurping the citizenship of Jews anywhere. Historian Ben Halpern pointed out that

> the Palestine Mandate's recognition of the Jewish people *(not* in quotation marks; and *not* as a nation state entity, but as an historical reality with historic connections and claims) was superseded in international law upon the creation of Israel; and the "Jewish people" (in quotation marks) concept is a figment of the imagination of the American Council for Judaism and its consultants." [37]

Rosenwald and the council were shooting at a phantom target.

Evidently the State Department was of the same opinion. After a long delay and considerable prodding by Rosenwald, it informed him that Article 3 did not justify refusing Israel de jure recognition. The Israeli constitution was in fact still in draft form, the State Department explained, so that Rosenwald's request for Washington's intervention was without basis. Stating the obvious, the reply assured the complainant that the U.S. government would object to any foreign state's attempting to impose its citizenship upon American citizens without their consent.[38]

The council's failure to block de jure recognition of Israel by Washington, however, did not discourage Rosenwald and Berger. They bombarded Secretary of State Dean Acheson and the State Department Office of Near Eastern Affairs with an unending volley of complaints, memoranda, and newspaper clippings showing the pernicious effects of the presumed Israeli doctrine that "Israel is the *national* homeland of *all* Jews [emphasis in original], and [if] the government of the United States accepts that definition, it implicitly accepts a definition of Jews as a 'nationality.'" [39] While the State Department's negative response was disheartening, Rabbi Berger told his close friend Kermit Roosevelt, "even if we are still unsuccessful in having the Department reopen an investigation of this question [Jewish nationalism], I would like Satterthwaite [director of the Office of Near Eastern, South Asian, and African Affairs] and some others to know that we have something of a case and I would like to build up a record on our behalf." [40]

In fact, with the creation of the State of Israel, Berger had been transformed from an anti-Zionist ideologue into a fanatic anti-Israel activist. This position was summed up by William Zukerman, editor of the anti-Zionist bi-weekly *Jewish Newsletter*, in a letter to Berger, his collaborator and associate, in 1954: "The difference [between us] . . . stems from the larger difference be-tween us on the general Zionist Israel position. I am not opposed to Israel as you are. I think it is here and I would like to see it stay (of course, not in its present form). I have no emotional attitude to Israel, one way or the other. . . . I do not agree with [Alfred M.] Lilienthal . . . that Israel should never have been established and that so long as it is in existence it will be a thorn in the flesh of Jews outside its frontiers. You are probably inclined to the more extreme view and I am, in this respect, more moderate than you, at least, more hopeful." [41]

For the most part, the American Council for Judaism, for all its roster of affluent and influential members, was merely a nuisance both to the State De-partment and to the American Jewish community, with the exception of the period of Secretary of State John Foster Dulles's tenure and especially when Henry A. Byroade was assistant secretary of state for Near Eastern affairs (1 April 1952 to March 1955), at which time the council gained some influence. Yet the organization had a certain kind of legitimacy in that it genuinely re-flected the latent insecurity and phobias of many established Jews who viewed the Zionist conception of Jewish nationalism and the creation of the State of Israel as a grave threat to their hard-won position in American society.

4

The impact of the creation of Israel on the half-million-strong American Zionist movement was profound. Summing up the achievement of the United Nations partition resolution in early December 1947, Rabbi Abba Hillel Silver, the foremost Zionist leader of his time, projected an unmistak-able sense of elation. To be sure, he declared, a Jewish state in part of Palestine had not been the goal of the Zionist movement. Nevertheless, it represented the maximum achievable goal in the prevailing conditions and entailed "two tremendous gains" despite its shortcomings:

> [S]tatehood, recognition of the Jewish nation as a nation on earth, marked the end of *galut* [exile] for our people. With this comes the great opportunity for us to ingather all the dispersed of our people, those who need a new home

and have been waiting for it so desperately, and the possibility in a very short time of emptying the DP's camps in Europe and giving a home at last to hundreds of thousands of our people. The UN decision is, therefore, of incalculable significance for our people and for the history of mankind."[42]

Silver anticipated that the restoration of Jewish sovereignty would enable the Jewish people to build "something very great in that little country, as it did a long time ago." Israel would become not just another political entity but a source of spiritual and religious inspiration. Credit for this historic achievement, Silver pointed out, was firstly due to the Yishuv, which had created a viable and thriving Jewish community in Palestine over a period of many years. But the immediate achievement at the United Nations, Silver emphasized, emanated from the activities of the political arm of the American Zionist movement—the American Zionist Emergency Council.[43] Clearly, the Zionist leader saw in this accomplishment a vindication of his activist brand of pressure politics and the culmination of his lifelong Zionist career.

However, Silver's and American Zionism's elation at this great achievement did not last long. The UN resolution met violent resistance from the Palestinian Arabs, subsequently threatening the very existence of the small Yishuv with an invasion by all the neighboring Arab states. No less painful was the realization by American Zionists and by Zionists throughout the world that with the creation of the Jewish state, a long and familiar era in Zionist history that had been dominated by the World Zionist movement was over.

The dawn of the new era was immediately perceptible in Washington when at the end of May 1948 Dr. Chaim Weizmann, the newly elected president of the Provisional Council of the State of Israel, was invited by President Truman to be his guest at Blair House. One of Weizmann's visitors while he was there was Edmund I. Kaufmann, a prominent Jewish leader in Washington and former president of the Zionist Organization of America. Kaufmann later recalled how deeply moved he was at the sight of Israeli flags strung along Pennsylvania Avenue:

and then as I stood in front of Blair House [and] I saw the State of Israel's large flag swaying in the breeze, I had an indescribable feeling. My mind went back to 1917 when I first met Justice Brandeis, with whom I had the pleasure of working until two weeks before his passing. As I walked the steps of Blair House I had the feeling that he was placing his hand on my shoulder and saying: a job well done.[44]

Yet Kaufmann's sense of fulfillment was tempered by awareness of the implications of the new status that Dr. Weizmann and the state that he represented had assumed: "Dr. Weizmann is President of a foreign country, and while I shall have a continued interest in his country, it will be on the basis of being a friend of Israel, the same as I have been in the past a friend of all countries who have been denied the right to set up a government of their choosing."[45] Kaufmann thus found a way to deal with the nagging question of dual loyalty—the need to define the nature of the relationship between the American Jewish community and the newly born Jewish state—a question that would be faced by every concerned Jew for years to come.

Many other problematic issues emerged as well. Stormy debates arose at Zionist gatherings as to whether the tradition of singing "Hatikvah" ("The Hope"—the Zionist anthem) at meetings should be discontinued in view of the fact that "Hatikvah" had become the national anthem of Israel.[46] More basically, Zionists of all points of view increasingly questioned the rationale for the continued existence of the American Zionist movement. Because its goal—the establishment of the Jewish state—had already been ruralized, they argued, perhaps it was time to dissolve the movement and replace it with a single new organization, which would be called something like Friends of Israel.

This grassroots sense that a significant era in Zionist history had come to an end was also shared by the Zionist leadership both in Israel and in America. With the passing of the November 1947 UN resolution and the imminent proclamation of the Jewish state, the leadership faced a series of fundamental questions relating to the problem of a voluntary movement with a political goal vis-à-vis a formal government apparatus of a sovereign state.

The crisis of the Zionist movement was painfully apparent at the Jewish Agency Executive (identical with the Zionist Executive) meeting of August 1948 in Tel Aviv, while war was still raging. With the Jewish state having assumed one of the movement's major tasks—diplomatic activity and representation in the world's capitals—the Zionist representatives sought to define their present raison d'être. Veteran religious Zionist leader Shlomo Z. Shragai pointed out that while the state had been established for the purpose of implementing Zionist aims, the present lack of direction suggested that "the Zionist movement is falling apart,"[47] a criticism reiterated by another veteran religious Zionist leader, Rabbi Yehuda Leib Maimon. Nevertheless, despite the uncertain atmosphere, it was clear that the nascent State of Israel could not handle the mammoth tasks of fund-raising, *aliyah* (immigration to Israel), and settlement of the growing number of newcomers alone. In short, there was no substitute for the World Zionist Organization—Israel's most reliable friend.

The real controversy, as became evident quickly, revolved around the question of the precise division of jurisdiction and functions between the World Zionist movement and the State of Israel. Should the Zionist movement continue to engage in political activity? Who would be responsible for fund-raising? Who would be responsible for setting the monthly quota of *olim* (immigrants to Israel)—the famous "schedule"? Who would be responsible for organizing *aliyah* from the Diaspora, for transporting and integrating the immigrants, for establishing new settlements, for educational work in the Diaspora?

Dr. Emanuel Neumann, at the time president of the ZOA and Silver's closest ally and friend, pointed out at this August meeting of the Jewish Agency Executive that the Diaspora would continue to exist and would have its own concerns. In fact, the issue of dual loyalty, he explained, had already affected the status and the interests of the Zionist movement, for the U.S. secretary of the treasury had indicated his wish to abolish the tax-exempt status of the United Jewish Appeal—the voluntary organization of American Jewry for the collection of funds for Israel and for the relief of Jews in distress all over the world—while the attorney general was insisting that the World Zionist Organization register as a foreign agent. Neumann advocated the immediate adoption of a radical policy that he termed *hafradah* (separation)—a definitive political separation between the Zionist activities undertaken by the Diaspora, on the one hand, and by Israel on the other. The first act under this policy, Neumann urged, ought to be the immediate resignation of Israeli government ministers from membership in the Zionist Executive.[48] "It was unthinkable," Neumann lamented, "that Israeli ministers had not resigned right away upon assuming their portfolios in the [Israeli] government. It would be inconceivable that the WZO [World Zionist Organization] would receive instructions from the government of Israel. This would be tantamount to a Zionist Comintern. Anyhow, we will not be a party to this set-up." Neumann's ultimatum was vigorously supported by Rose Halprin, the leader of Hadassah, which was the major American women's Zionist organization, but opposed by some of the Israeli members of the Executive.[49]

What Neumann was suggesting was that the Zionist movement must become a Diaspora movement exclusively, abolishing Israel's membership in it, while the Jews of Israel would be represented at the World Zionist Congress by an official delegation from the Knesset, Israel's parliament. Although Neumann's proposal was eventually rejected, it clearly demonstrated that concern over the dual loyalty issue was not confined to the more assimilated segments of the American Jewish community. Another noted Zionist, Rabbi Israel Goldstein, who eventually immigrated to Israel, recalled in his memoirs: "We American Zionist leaders had reason to fear that anti-Zionist groups, such as the American Council for Judaism, would charge us with dual loyalty if *hafradah* were not to become a reality." [50]

No less thorny was the question of the future of the Jewish Agency and the role of the non-Zionists in support of Israel. Although the terms "World Zionist Organization" and "Jewish Agency" had long been used interchangeably (as they still are today), they are in fact two distinct legal entities. The World Zionist Organization dated back to 1897, when it was established by Theodore Herzl as a mass world movement, while the Jewish Agency was a latecomer to the Zionist scene. Its legal basis was derived from Article 4 of the British Mandate for Palestine, ratified by the League of Nations in 1922, which recognized an appropriate "Jewish agency" to represent the Jewish interest in the upbuilding of the "Jewish national home." Under its mandate, the British government recognized the World Zionist Organization as this Jewish agency. However, Dr. Chaim Weizmann, president of the World Zionist organization, quickly realized that the enormous task of making the national home a success depended on getting the financial support of the affluent non-Zionist Jews of the West—mostly Americans. These non-Zionists, for psychological and ideological reasons, refused to be associated with the movement that he headed. Six years of difficult negotiations between Weizmann and Louis Marshall, then president of the American Jewish Committee, eventually led to the establishment of an enlarged Jewish Agency in 1929, which, it was hoped, would serve as a channel for the financial and political support of an influential segment of Western Jewry in order to ensure the uninterrupted growth of the national home. Those hopes, however, were quickly dashed with the sudden death of Louis Marshall that same year, as well as by the onset of the Great Depression.

The enlarged Jewish Agency continued to hold meetings and publish reports throughout most of the 1930s, but owing to less than vigorous involvement by the non-Zionists, it became moribund. Still, as Dr. Chaim Weizmann, president of both the Jewish Agency and the World Zionist Organization, later observed, the alliance with the non-Zionists had a positive long-term effect. "The notion that the building of the Jewish Homeland was a fantastically Utopian dream, the obsession of impractical, Messianically deluded ghetto Jews, began to be dispelled by the participation of prominent men of affairs with a reputation for sober-mindedness and hard-bitten practicality." [51]

A debate on the future of the Jewish Agency was begun in the Zionist movement shortly after the establishment of Israel, with Jacob Robinson, the Jewish Agency's erudite legal adviser, advocating discontinuing it, for two reasons. First, he argued, "there is no legal basis in international relations for the Jewish Agency" because it derived its legal validity from the British Mandate, which had ceased to exist. Second, "the Jewish Agency was a legal and political fiction since 1937 (the last session of the council [of the agency]), and such a fiction cannot go on forever." [52]

Approaching the question from a totally different point of departure—the future role of the Jews in the Diaspora and the fate of the American Zionist movement—Abba Hillel Silver too was opposed to the continuation of the Jewish Agency. "For years—perhaps for generations—the State of Israel will be dependent on the Diaspora," he predicted, and therefore nothing must be done to damage the American Zionist movement—Israel's most reliable friend—which he saw as the main vehicle for harnessing American Jewish support. Recreating the Jewish Agency, Silver warned, might weaken the Zionist movement: "Let us forget the name Jewish Agency, and start to use the name the Zionist movement," he urged. "It is true that American Jewry gives the money," he argued, "but American Zionists are those who do the fundraising." [53] In the event, Silver's (and Neumann's) advocacy of assigning to American Zionism the dominant role of main link between American Jewry and Israel, under their leadership, was rejected by Ben-Gurion and the Mapai Party that he led. Yet Silver's and Neumann's position is relevant in gaining an understanding of the policy adopted by the non-Zionist American Jewish Committee toward Israel, as well as of the Blaustein-Ben Gurion Understanding that was to be signed in 1950.

Surprisingly, even Dr. Nahum Goldmann, Silver's and Neumann's archrival, agreed that with non-Zionist opposition to the idea of the Jewish state relegated to the past, the Jewish Agency was indeed superfluous. However, he counseled that because some donors might oppose channeling funds through the Zionists, the status quo should prevail for the time being and the Jewish Agency be reconstituted.

This exceedingly complex subject, reflecting the most fundamental issues involved in the relationship between American Jewry and Israel, was not resolved in 1948 and would preoccupy the American Jewish Committee, the Zionists, and the Israeli government for a long time to come.

5

Another basic issue that emerged in 1948 was the goal of the American Zionist movement and the future role of its medium for political action: the American Zionist Emergency Council. Doubts and soul-searching agitated the American Zionist ranks, in particular the membership of the largest American Zionist group, the ZOA. Daniel Frisch, an Indianapolis businessman and former Hebrew teacher who was deeply committed to Jewish education and who was soon to be elected president of the ZOA, described the situation early in 1949 accurately: "People whose devotion to Zionism stems solely from their sympathy for the roaming multitudes of our people are inclined to feel that the establishment of a Jewish state renders the ZOA superfluous." [54] Similarly, Arthur Hertzberg, the young Conservative rabbi of West End Synagogue in Nashville, Tennessee, and an ardent Zionist, lamented: "As a Zionist, I face an impasse." As he put it, he and the movement were caught "between its own slogans, platforms, and previous records, and the realities of Jewish life today." [55]

What was needed, many ZOA members felt, was a new, up-to-date definition of the purpose of the ZOA. In view of the sharp decline in the organization's membership, the transfer of the movement's political role to the State of Israel, and increasing pro-Israeli activities undertaken by non-Zionist groups (in particular in the field of fund-raising), the question had ceased to be academic and became immediate: If Diaspora Zionists did not choose to immigrate to Israel now that its gates were wide open for *aliyah,* what then was the meaning of being a Zionist? Among the variety of responses to this basic question, Daniel Frisch's four-point program and the so-called Rifkind Report best illuminate how American Zionists adjusted to the new situation.

The ambitious American-oriented program put forward by Daniel Frisch, aimed at revitalizing American Jewry by branching out and participating in "the work of existing community organizations throughout the country with the avowed purpose, in addition to serving the cause of these organizations, of keeping alive the sense of interdependence between the Jewish communities of America and Israel." [56] Frisch also urged a concerted effort to foster Jewish education, but firmly rejected the controversial Zionist concept of opposing the continued survival of the Diaspora. "I believe that what we do for Israel in the United States is as important as what we do for Israel in Zion. . . . The two most vital communities in the world are enmeshed in mutuality."

As a corollary to the effort in Jewish education, Frisch advocated an issue that was more controversial—encouraging *halutziut* (pioneering) among American Jewish youth: "We ought to be able to send to Israel American-bred young people who want to live as Jews—minus the hyphen—under the smiling skies of the reborn Israel." His fourth point was the most novel of all. Whereas Blaustein had proposed a blueprint for Israeli democracy American-style, Frisch presented an economic blueprint for the nascent state. As leader of the predominantly middle-class ZOA, Frisch viewed his movement's historic mission as helping "Israel's middle classes to take their rightful place in Israel's society of the present and the future." The ZOA, he declared, should encourage the creation of a mixed economy in Israel, with the agricultural sector based on central planning and full rein given to free enterprise in the cities. Despite Frisch's disclaimer that "we cannot and dare not attempt to interfere with Israel's internal policy," and the caveat that "our help must be unflagging and without stint, no matter what patterns prevail," [57] it is clear that the fourth point could not have been implemented without interference in Israel's economic policies. In fact, it was precisely this point that was one of the main causes of a crisis in Israel-ZOA relations that occurred not long after, resulting in the resignation of the two most prominent ZOA leaders, Abba Hillel Silver and Emanuel Neumann. [58]

The other response by the ZOA to the new Diaspora-Israel relationship was the publication of a sixteen-page report in the spring of 1949 by a "Commission on the Future Program and Constitution of the World Zionist Organization" headed by New York Judge Simon H. Rifkind and made up of a roster of the organization's veteran leaders. Cognizant of the ubiquitous concern with the dual loyalty question, the Rifkind Report tackled it head-on: "Israel is a sovereign State. Only the citizens of Israel owe it allegiance. The establishment of Israel has in nowise affected the citizenship of Jews of other lands." [59] On this score, it seemed, there was no difference between Zionists and non-Zionists.

The report also put forward a set of principles for post-State Zionism that included aiding Israel and Jewish immigration to it, and the "fostering of Jewish self-awareness." Reiterating several of Daniel Frisch's concerns, it proposed a shift of emphasis toward cultural Zionism by stimulating "Jewish cultural creativity" and encouraging "the spread of the Hebrew language and of Jewish culture among Jewish youth and the Jewish population generally."

The relationship with the non-Zionists also occupied the Rifkind Report, with coordination on the American scene recommended through the formation of "a consultative body representing all Jewish groups interested in the welfare of Israel."[60] Although this interesting idea proved premature in 1949, it was independently revived by Abba Eban in 1951 when he served as ambassador in Washington and was eventually implemented in 1954 by the chairman of the American section of the Jewish Agency Executive, Nahum Goldmann, with the creation of the Conference of Presidents of Major Jewish Organizations (the so-called Presidents' Club).

The Zionist community also turned its attention to the question of the future role of the American Zionist Emergency Council. Established in 1939 on the eve of World War II as the political and public relations arm of the American Zionist movement, it had evolved under Abba Hillel Silver's forceful leadership into an effective pressure group that recruited the support of many members of Congress, and of public opinion, for the idea of the Jewish state. Precisely ten years after its establishment, it was at an impasse, its goal achieved. Opinion within the Zionist leadership was divided about the future status of the Emergency Council, with some leaders convinced that the council had outlived its usefulness and should be liquidated, and others insisting that it still had an important role to perform, albeit in a reorganized format.

Rabbi Abba Hillel Silver, although having resigned as leader of the American Zionist movement, still carried great weight in advocating the council's continued existence in view of Israel's precarious position. "The emergency [is] not yet over," he warned. "There is no complete armistice yet, there is no peace, there are no defined boundaries, there is an explosive Arab refugee problem. The anti-Zionist forces have not demobilized. Even the Jewish anti-Zionist forces have not demobilized, but are more active than ever. Who knows what will flare up in the Near East tomorrow, or next week, or next year?" What lay in store for the Emergency Council then, Silver argued, was a tremendous amount of political work still to be done. It had taken years to build the council and accumulate contacts, prestige, political know-how, and a competent staff. Why should such an asset be liquidated? "If we direct our attention not toward how we can dismember this body," Silver concluded, "but how we can reorient it so that it can function in relation to changed conditions, we will be serving our Movement best."[61] Eventually, Silver's position prevailed. The original body was reorganized under a new name—the American Zionist Council—but continued to undertake the same political and public relations functions in Washington and throughout the country as before.[62]

However, with many of these areas dealt with by Israeli diplomatic representation, understandably the old Zionist élan and sense of purpose had dissolved. With the almost uninterrupted succession of crises that plagued Israel from its creation, this void was filled by non-Zionist leaders such as Jacob Blaustein, interceding behind the scenes in Washington, a tactic that became increasingly vital.

The rise of Israel was bound to have a profound effect on American Jewry. Although American Jews were deeply attached to the United States as their homeland, Israel would endow them with an added sense of normalcy and equality, putting them on the same footing as other ethnic groups within the American mosaic. The Irish had their Ireland, the Poles their Poland, the Italians their Italy, the Swedes their Sweden—and the Jews now had Israel. Yet this sense of normalcy, as well as pride in their critical role in helping to create the state, was tinged with concern about the possibility that the dual loyalty issue would be raised. Among the mainstream Jewish organizations, none was more concerned with this issue than the venerable and influential American Jewish Committee.

2

Skirmishes Between the American Jewish Committee and Ben-Gurion

1

ISRAEL AS A ZIONIST STATE, with David Ben-Gurion as its radical leader, presented an awesome challenge to the American Jewish Committee, as Jacob Blaustein, the new president of the committee, soon found out. With the American Council for Judaism, and its strident supporters within the ranks of the committee, scrutinizing every statement by Israeli leaders published in such major newspapers as the *New York Times* and the *New York Herald Tribune,* and in *Jewish Telegraphic Agency* news bulletins, for possible slurs regarding the loyalty of American Jews, Blaustein and the committee leadership were constantly under pressure to do something about the alleged pernicious effects of Israeli pronouncements on the position of American Jewry. An aggravating pattern of Israeli assertiveness and American Jewish reaction emerged that bedeviled Blaustein's presidency and took up enormous amounts of time and energy, culminating in the famous "Blaustein-Ben-Gurion Understanding" of 1950 and its subsequent reaffirmations.

The pattern emerged rather soon after the creation of Israel. Shortly after taking up his appointment in 1949, Blaustein complained to Eliahu Elath, the Israeli ambassador in Washington, that despite his own and Proskauer's previous talks with President Weizmann, Prime Minister Ben-Gurion, and Foreign Minister Sharett, in which they had concurred with the principle that "the Israeli Government speaks only for its own citizens and that Jews of other countries are not part or citizens of that nation,"[1] certain translations of statements by Israeli leaders were open to misinterpretation. In particular Blaustein called attention to the English translation of Weizmann's speech at the opening of the Constituent Assembly on 14 February 1949. Referring to Israel's creation following the Holocaust, the president of Israel had spoken of the State of Israel as being earned "by all the hardships, weariness, sorrow, and tribulations that have been our portion during the past seventy years, *when one-third of our nation was annihilated* [emphasis in original]." The rub, Blaustein pointed out, was in Weizmann's use of the expression "one third of our nation," whereas according to Blaustein what the president of Israel meant was "one-third of all the Jews." [2]

In the American context, the term "nation" meant a body politic. According to the second edition of Webster's *New International Dictionary,* "nation" loosely signifies "the body of inhabitants of a country united under a single independent government; a state." Thus, to American Jews the use of the term "the Jewish nation" was abhorrent, implying that all Jews ipso facto were citizens of a foreign state (Israel) and casting aspersions on their American nationality and citizenship. This confusion arose from the entirely different Hebrew usage of the terms *am* and *umah,* which denote both "nation" and "people." [3] In other words, the terms "Jewish nation" and "Jewish people" are interchangeable in Hebrew, regardless of their particular political, legal, or historic connotations. Blaustein, in a period of cold war hysteria, was concerned lest this usage by Weizmann and others result in "confusion and [the raising of] doubts and fears on the question of implied dual-allegiance among a large number of American Jews—and I refer here not only to anti-Zionists but to non-Zionists and many Zionists as well." [4] He therefore urged the Israeli ambassador to draw the attention of President Weizmann and other Israeli leaders "to the desirability of always keeping in mind the distinction in question, so as to avoid possible misunderstandings, which bring you and us headaches, and which among other things may adversely affect the obtaining of maximum cooperation (funds and otherwise) for Israel from American Jews." [5] Blaustein's complaint of "headaches" was an allusion to the membership in the American Jewish Committee of several prominent members and supporters of the American Council for Judaism (foremost among them Lessing J. Rosenwald). Israeli cooperation on this issue, Blaustein emphasized to Elath, "can go a long way toward breaking the opposition of those Jews who are still opposed to Israel." [6]

Eliahu Elath, who was in close touch with Jacob Blaustein, was fully aware of the leader's predicament. He was equally aware of the paramount importance of assuring the committee's ongoing friendliness toward Israel and did his best to mollify Blaustein's concerns. In a letter to Blaustein, Elath agreed entirely with his friend's fundamental point of departure, that it was vital "to make it clear at all times that the Israel Government speaks only for its own citizens and that Jews of other countries are not part or citizens of that State." Moreover, he emphasized, "every Jew in this country can be fully assured that Israel will not challenge his right to remain a loyal American citizen as he has been in the past. Nor would we ever agree that by supporting Israel, any Jew, be he a national of the United States or any other State, would cease to be a faithful citizen of his native country."[7]

At the same time, Elath reminded Blaustein, Israel's Zionist commitment was to help Jews in distress wherever they were. The deteriorating situation of the Jews in Arab countries, he said, was a case in point. In this connection, Elath praised the valuable contribution made by the committee in publicizing the plight of those Jews, thereby implicitly conceding that Israel in no way challenged the committee's raison d'être of working to defend and safeguard Jewish rights everywhere, not only in the United States.

Referring to the translated segment of President Weizmann's speech, the Israeli ambassador advised Blaustein to take newspaper correspondents' reports with a grain of salt, especially those of non-Jews, who "unintentionally draw little distinction between 'Jewish' State and the State of Israel, between Jews and Israelis." Neither President Weizmann nor any other Israeli leader, Elath assured Blaustein, had "any intention of creating concern to any Jew in this country, or elsewhere, by confusing terminology."[8]

Elath also conveyed to Blaustein his "grave concern" over the "growing cooperation between the American Council for Judaism and the most anti-Semitic and anti-Israeli elements in this country." He pointed out: "Some of them belong to missionary groups operating in the Middle East, while others are open or disguised agents of oil companies. . . . These people are now determined to avenge themselves for not being able to prevent the creation of Israel by disseminating vicious propaganda, using for this purpose the Arab refugees problem and the so-called, 'dual-loyalty' [issue]." Israel's victory in the 1948 war, Elath stated, temporarily halted their activities, "but now with the assistance given to them by the American Council for Judaism, they have renewed their activities with greater intensity." Elath urged Blaustein to look into this anti-Israeli-cum-anti-Semitic nexus in order to counter its harmful effects not only on Israel but also "on the vital interests of the Jewish community" in the United States.[9]

Elath's letter was in fact the first official Israeli statement explicitly defining the parameters of Israeli-Diaspora relations. In retrospect, it may be viewed as foreshadowing the Blaustein-Ben-Gurion Understanding arrived at a year later. Indeed, before long the prime minister officially invited Blaustein to visit Israel,[10] giving the American Jewish leader an opportunity to see the newly born Jewish state for himself.

2

The main purpose of the trip, Blaustein stated on the eve of his departure in March 1949, was to investigate Israel's ability to absorb the 150,000 immigrants expected to arrive there within the next eight months. He said:

> It must be remembered that Israel has not been created solely to secure the welfare of its inhabitants but also primarily as a haven for those Jews who find it necessary or desirable to go there and lead lives free from the threat or actuality of persecution. Therefore, we of the American Jewish Committee feel, as do all American Jews, that Israel must be rendered capable not only of supporting its existing population but of acquiring and maintaining facilities for extensive immigration.[11]

On the way from the United States to Paris, Blaustein developed "a painful sacroiliac condition and had to be put to bed," related John Slawson, the executive director of the committee, who accompanied Blaustein. "He was in no physical condition to go on to Israel, but there was no stopping him. We obtained a wooden board which he used to support his back during the remainder of the journey. In spite of this handicap, Jacob managed to carry out his responsibilities without interruption." He arrived in Israel along with his family as well as Slawson; Irving M. Engel, chairman of the executive committee; Simon Segal, director of the committee's foreign affairs department; and Zachariah Shuster, director of the committee's European office. During their two-week visit, Blaustein and his mission toured the country, visiting Haifa and its factories; the famous Kibbutz Ein Harod in the Jezreel Valley; the towns of Tiberias and Nazareth in the Galilee; the lush citrus town of Rehovot, location of the Weizmann Institute of Science; several kibbutzim in the northern Negev; and finally Jerusalem.

The Americans were given the opportunity to observe the unique as well as contradictory aspects of the year-old state, the miraculous and the mundane, the heroism of Israel's War of Independence that was still being fought, and the suffering inherent in the ingathering of the exiles. A radio report delivered coast to coast on NBC by Blaustein upon his return in early May showed how deeply moved he had been by his experience in Israel. Israel reminded him of the United States in 1776, he said, in that it was a small, underdeveloped country, a melting pot bubbling with a pioneering spirit, "like America . . . a humanitarian haven for the persecuted and the oppressed." The encounter with *olim* affected him especially:

> I shall never forget the newly arrived Jews from the feudal state of Yemen. These Jews, whose families for centuries had lived a secluded life in the deserts, have nevertheless managed to maintain and preserve a deep sense of religious faith. Moved by this birth of the State of Israel, they were flown in an airlift operated between Aden on the Red Sea and the Lydda airport in Israel. These Yemenite Jews, knowing nothing of the wonders of modern civilization, had clambered aboard the great shining planes without fear. . . . In the mess hall of the camp where they are now temporarily housed in Israel, there was a banner on the wall with the biblical words: "I carried you on eagles' wings." That is how they are returning to the land.

A particularly moving experience occurred at Haifa, the chief disembarkation port for immigrant ships arriving from Europe and North Africa. The American Jewish Committee delegation had gone out in a small launch and motored from one ship to another. "What a heart-warming occasion it was!" Blaustein recalled in his radio talk, his voice trembling with emotion. "As we drew close, we could see men, women and children dancing and singing on the crowded decks. . . . The second ship was loaded with Bulgarian Jews. Many of these people, we could see, were quietly weeping; others just stood silently looking toward the land. They were overcome with a solemn feeling of gratitude at having finally reached it." [12] Blaustein's exposure to the immigrant ships loaded with survivors of the Holocaust was especially significant, for he had seen these survivors before, when a delegation he led surveyed the displaced persons camps in Germany in 1946. Then "DPs by the hundreds followed us, crowded around us . . . eagerly searching for some word of hope as to when they could be moved to a permanent country of residence. Now, finally, the answer is being given to those of them who wish to go to Israel." [13]

Blaustein's visit took place when the Israeli War of Independence was drawing to a close, giving his party an opportunity to observe both the remarkable Israeli army and the unique Israeli institution of the *kibbutzim*, many of which played a decisive role in the fighting. His visit to one of Israel's most dramatic symbols of heroism, Kibbutz Negba in the northern Negev, which had been completely destroyed by Egyptian shelling but managed to defend itself against the invading Egyptian army, was another unforgettable experience.

> We inspected trenches, underground living quarters and the dispensary, and the few weapons with which the members of the Kibbutz had successfully resisted the large Egyptian force. They had managed, miraculously, with very little ammunition, to stop an attack of 8 tanks; and all the while the battle raged, they also managed to tend their orange groves, protected them as they protected life.[14]

Besides conveying the delegation's admiration for the people and government of Israel and their achievements, Blaustein, in his broadcast, also discussed the many problems revealed by the tour. The tremendous rate of immigration, which was expected to bring close to 250,000 men, women, and children into Israel in 1949, lay at the core of the country's economic crisis, he explained. Reminding his radio audience about the small size of the country, and that its total population before the War of Independence was only 640,000, he pointed out that in American terms such a huge influx "would be tantamount to the United States receiving 35,000,000 to 45,000,000 immigrants a year."[15] Moreover, he explained, there were no selection criteria for the immigrants. The gates of Israel were wide open "to the aged and the sick as freely as to the able-bodied and productive."[16] This policy of unrestricted immigration, he indicated, naturally created enormous problems: lack of housing, with tens of thousands living in tents in crowded camps, unemployment, and inflation.

In private conference with Ben-Gurion, Blaustein had expressed his fear that the policy of unrestricted immigration could lead only to catastrophe. Ben-Gurion, while agreeing with his guest as to the serious economic consequences of his policy, stood firm. "I would oppose restricting *aliyah*," he said, "because if we will not immediately save [the Jews] from the Eastern [Bloc] (such as Bulgaria and Rumania), there is no guarantee of [ever] saving them." Besides, he added, "a speedy and large increase of Jews is an urgent need contributing to our security—since there is no assurance whatever that 700,000 Jews would be able to withstand the Arab world."[17] In the event, Ben-Gurion's daring policy did prevail.

Blaustein also pointed out to Ben-Gurion that employment could be created by private investment in Israel. However, the situation in Israel, "with the government dominated by labor, and labor itself competing with private enterprise in certain industries," mitigated against American private investment. Replying, Ben-Gurion stated that even though his party aimed at creating a socialist regime, the question of immigration superseded this consideration, for the "ingathering of exiles was paramount. Without Jewish and international capital there would be no *aliyah*; it is a life or death issue for us." He therefore asked for Blaustein's help in attracting major American industrialists to visit Israel at his invitation "to work out a mutually satisfactory plan which would attract private capital investments to that country."[18]

Turning to Israel's relations with its Arab neighbors in his talk with the Israeli prime minister, Blaustein emphasized the "fundamental necessity" for a permanent peace with the Arab countries, even though this peace still seemed remote. The political status of Jerusalem was also a difficult problem, but the most likely solution, Blaustein thought, would entail leaving the Old City in Arab hands and annexing the New City to Israel, with "some form of international control being provided for the Holy Places in Jerusalem and other parts of the country." Equally thorny was the Arab refugee problem, which Blaustein correctly viewed as the biggest barrier to peace.

The delegation was especially concerned about Israel's foreign policy orientation during that cold war period. Although details are scant, it is safe to conclude that Ben-Gurion and Sharett were told by Blaustein explicitly that the support of the American Jewish community would hinge on Israel's identification with the Western camp. At the time Israel's short-lived policy of nonidentification was at its peak, and, in Blaustein's words, "Israel aspired to be permanently neutral like Switzerland." Nevertheless, he could authoritatively report on his return that "There can . . . be no doubt that the country is strongly Western-oriented, and that Communist influence is negligible."[19]

For Americans accustomed to a two-party system, Israel's internal politics were baffling. The multiplicity of parties and the resultant arrangement of coalition governments that were potentially unstable were worrisome. But Blaustein assured his executive committee that "the Coalition government is strong and effective, and its stability at the present time is beyond question,"[20] an observation that proved valid as a result of Ben-Gurion's leadership.

Blaustein had taken full advantage of the opportunity to reiterate the position of the American Jewish Committee on the sensitive issue of Israeli-Diaspora relations, and elicited from the Israeli leaders "definite assurances . . . that Israel will abstain from speaking for Jews other than its own citizens." Moreover, he had also "strongly urged against any campaign to enlist emigrants from this country. Our representatives were struck by the assumption current among Israelis who do not know the United States at first hand, that the position of American Jews is serious. Mr. Ben-Gurion and others who know this country at first hand, of course, do not share this fallacy." [21]

Summing up his impressions to the AJC Executive Committee, Blaustein stated that the enduring impression in his first encounter with Israel and its people was the Israelis' "truly thrilling spirit of determination and optimism to overcome the many serious problems." [22] Nevertheless, he well understood that the indomitable Israeli spirit alone was an insufficient condition for success. To cope with the challenge, the young Jewish state needed outside help. With American aid, Blaustein was certain, painting his vision in bold strokes, the young state on the shores of the Mediterranean would evolve into a miniature America, becoming "a positive force for democracy and for international peace and order." [23]

Whereas Blaustein seemed to have been captivated by the miracle of the young Israel, John Slawson was mainly concerned with the impact of Israel on American Jewish life, although he shared Blaustein's admiration for the "dynamic spirit" of Israel. To be sure, he said, "the statement that American Jews are Americans and Israeli Jews are Israelis is a sound statement," yet Slawson detected among some American Jews "a nervousness for what is happening in Israel, which they would not feel about the same developments in any other foreign country, thereby exhibiting a perhaps unconscious tendency to feel an identification with and some responsibility for purely domestic developments in Israel." [24] This phenomenon, he explained, might reinforce the dual loyalty issue. Undeniably, the heroism and courage of the Israelis had a beneficial effect on the image of the American Jew, but images are capricious and fickle, he pointed out, and can also produce negative results. Therefore, the American Jewish Committee, Slawson warned, faced a dilemma. It needed to "encourage such a course of action in Israel as will be acceptable to the American public. How to do this, without taking responsibility for Israeli developments, is a matter requiring the clearest thinking." [25]

Still, Slawson denied that helping Israel was tantamount to the committee's forsaking its fundamental American-centered, emancipationist doctrine. "Our own interest in Israel," he assured the skeptics, "will not divert us from our activities in behalf of the Jews in other lands or from our belief that, at least in the Western world, the emancipation of Jews is a permanent reality." In short, the American Jewish Committee had no intention of converting to Zionism, and for this very reason it decided to have a representative in Israel whose job it would be to keep the Israeli public informed about the position of America's Jews, "lest Israel become a focus of the kind of ideology to which the American Jewish Committee has been and always will be essentially antipathetic." [26]

What then would be the limits of the American Jewish Committee's relationship to Israel? It was Judge Proskauer who attempted to demarcate this nebulous area in an address to the executive committee in 1949.

> We may properly apprise the Israeli leaders of probable American reactions to a pattern to which Americans are unaccustomed, but it is not a problem with which we should become involved. We certainly have a right forcefully to discourage Israeli propaganda for immigration from America. We have both a right and a duty to proffer friendly advice regarding the tactics of the Israelis in their international relations. We do not have the right to try to impose our American concepts on them. [27]

The Proskauer policy thus endeavored to map out a compromise between the judge's own former rigid anti-Zionism and acceptance of the sovereign Jewish state. It rejected total disinterest in the State of Israel, as demanded by the American Council for Judaism, and advocated friendly concern. The question of how to implement this middle course, however, was to be the underlying cause of periodic crises in the relationship between the committee and the Israeli leadership.

3

In fact, Judge Proskauer himself soon became involved in one of these crises. The strong-willed former president of the committee, who greatly missed the excitement of his previous involvement in American-Israeli relations in Washington's corridors of power, continued to offer Israeli and American leaders his outspoken opinions as well as mediation services in times of crisis. Having been closely associated politically with Alfred E. Smith, the Irish Catholic assemblyman from New York's Lower East Side who subsequently became governor of New York and an unsuccessful presidential candidate, Proskauer had also developed good relations with several Catholic dignitaries, in particular with Francis Cardinal Spellman of New York. He had been consulted by Sharett and Eban at various times on questions relating to Catholic-Israel relations, in particular on the question of the Vatican's position toward

Jerusalem. From 1947 onward the Vatican had consistently demanded the complete internationalization of Jerusalem, its environs, and all the holy places in Palestine, according to UN General Assembly Resolution 181 of 29 November 1947, claiming it to be the only proper solution for this difficult problem. However, the State of Israel adamantly refused to countenance the Vatican demand, which might have resulted in putting 100,000 Jewish residents of the New City of Jerusalem under international control. Foreign Minister Moshe Sharett, along with Abba Eban, who headed the Israeli delegation to the UN, spearheaded Israel's diplomatic efforts at annulling, or at least modifying, this plan. Taking this strategy one step further, Ben-Gurion and the majority of the members of the cabinet, overriding Sharett's opposition, decided in late 1948 to effect a fait accompli by transferring most of the governmental offices from Tel Aviv to Jerusalem.

Sensitive to Catholic reaction, Proskauer was enraged at this move and sent off to the prime minister an explicit letter on the matter in April 1949.

> If you will let me say so, every man in leadership suffers a grave danger from the intoxication of victory, and the mark of great statesmanship, which I hope and believe you will show, is restraint and moderation, and [I hope you will] apply this particularly to what in America has developed into a critical situation, the importance of which you may not realize. . . . There is widespread Catholic indignation at your removal of some government offices to Jerusalem, and certain other conduct of yours with respect to Jerusalem.[28]

The need, said the judge, was not for "hot-headed or intrepid action, but for a very high quality of tact and diplomacy."

If Ben-Gurion was less than happy to receive this dressing down from Proskauer, his blood boiled at Proskauer's openly siding with Sharett's "pacific way," which rejected open defiance of the UN resolution and seemed to Proskauer a more efficacious and promising approach to the question of Jerusalem. In the event, Israel suffered a serious defeat when on 9 December 1949 an Australian resolution supporting the internationalization of Jerusalem was adopted by the UN General Assembly.[29] Nevertheless, although the Jerusalem question still remained an unsettled issue, Ben-Gurion's boldness was justified by events in the long run. Proskauer's influence in this matter was obviously limited, for no amount of concern or genuine willingness on his part to help could sway Ben-Gurion on this or any other matter of supreme national interest. It was to be Jacob Blaustein's un-

enviable mission to try to find the golden mean between Ben-Gurion's calculated audacity and the committee's caution.

Although the Ben-Gurion-Sharett-Proskauer row was conducted behind
closed doors, the outward calm was shattered a few days before Labor Day in
1949 when the *Jewish Telegraphic Agency* trumpeted the news summary headline "BEN GURION URGES U.S. PARENTS TO SEND THEIR CHILDREN TO ISRAEL
FOR PERMANENT SETTLEMENT." The Israeli prime minister, in an address to
an American Histadrut (General Federation of Labor) delegation visiting Israel, had appealed for mass immigration. "Today there are only 900,000 Jews
in Israel," Ben-Gurion had told the delegation, and "our next task will not be
easier than the creation of the Jewish state. It consists of bringing all Jews to
Israel. . . . We appeal chiefly to the youth of the United States and in other
countries to help us achieve this big mission. We appeal to the parents to help
us bring their children here. Even if they decline to help, we will bring the
youth to Israel, but I hope that this will not be necessary." [30]

Ben-Gurion's statement was featured in all three Yiddish dailies in New
York, eliciting outrage by Lessing J. Rosenwald, president of the American
Council for Judaism, who promptly protested to Secretary of State Dean
Acheson in Washington, supplying him with quotations of the statement.
Rosenwald charged that the statement was yet another manifestation of
Israel's policy designed to lure American Jewish youth "away from their na-
tional integration in the United States." Even more serious, Rosenwald railed,
was the fact that the statement was made by Ben-Gurion, "the responsible
head of the foreign state of Israel. If implemented," he warned, "Mr. Ben-
Gurion's statement threatens to undermine the stability of American Jews and
might well justify an interpellation in this regard to the Israeli government." [31]
Acheson, however, did not seem too perturbed about Rosenwald's complaint,
which was routinely answered by George C. McGhee, assistant secretary for
Near Eastern affairs. From the State Department's point of view, the matter
was closed.

For Blaustein, though, recently back from Israel, Ben-Gurion's statement
was no less disturbing, although he took up the cudgels with Ben-Gurion in
private. In a letter to the Israeli leader on 19 September, he reminded him that
when "I saw you in Israel earlier this year, you told us that while you would
like to see some immigration of American Jews to Israel, particularly those
with know-how—specialists, technicians . . . you did not expect and would
not indulge in any organized campaign for the immigration of American Jewish youth." [32] In Blaustein's view Ben-Gurion was guilty not just of a breach of

confidence, but also of undermining the committee's ongoing effort to create a common and favorable American Jewish approach toward Israel, as well as of providing Israel's opponents within the Jewish community—the American Council for Judaism—with more ammunition for their anti-Israel polemics. Reiterating his friendship for Israel, Blaustein nevertheless warned Ben-Gurion that if his statement indeed represented the official Israeli line, and if similar statements were to be made, then the committee would "almost certainly"[33] undertake a reassessment of its position vis-à-vis Israel and, moreover, would proceed to conduct a public campaign against Ben-Gurion's views in this regard.

The agitation following Ben-Gurion's statement turned out to be widespread. Typical of the indignant complaints sent to Eliahu Elath in Washington and to other Israeli representatives throughout the country was one from the executive director of the Jewish Federation of Buffalo deploring the fact that the statement demonstrated Ben-Gurion's lack of understanding of the American Jewish reality. The community worker stated that he was registering not just his own objections "but the objections of millions of other American Jews who feel that their lives and their destinies are bound up within the United States, and who feel that the future of their children is in this country."[34] Though his protest, as Blaustein's, was unofficial, because he cared about Israel, the executive director reminded the beleaguered Elath that such statements as the prime minister's were likely to "add fuel to the flames of the American Council for Judaism, and to those others who have been lukewarm or unsympathetic to the aims of the men who have created the State of Israel."[35]

Significantly, some of the American Zionists were also agitated. The president of the San Francisco District of the Zionist Organization of America informed Israeli Consul General Reuven Dafni in Los Angeles that the statement, which meanwhile had been reiterated in other addresses delivered by two senior Israeli officials, David Remez, minister of communications, and Eliahu Dobkin, director of the Jewish Agency's Youth and He Halutz Department, harmed the United Jewish Appeal (UJA) campaign and "is prompting grave concern among the local Zionist leadership."[36] The Zionist leader from San Francisco, which was the citadel of the American Council for Judaism, was extremely worried lest "the recent series of advertisements [emanating from] the American Council for Judaism in San Francisco . . . coupled with unexplained antagonizing statements [by Ben-Gurion, Remez, and Dobkin] might find fertile ground in this city."[37]

Reacting to the alarming news from America, Moshe Sharett initially blamed the "contretemps caused by B.G.'s statement" on the "combination of stupidity and malice known for short as the *JTA*." Beyond the irresponsibility of the *Jewish Telegraphic Agency*, Sharett added, the prime minister had been unaware of the presence of the press and had spoken "freely, loosely, expressing feelings more than thoughts, witho\ut the slightest effort at 'formulation'—an art [in] which, when he applies himself to it, he is a great master."[38] Having said this, Sharett hoped that "this storm in a teacup will not last."

But the storm would not abate. Blaustein found himself having to cope with continued agitation on the part of the old anti-Zionist wing of the committee leadership headed by Judge Proskauer. In light of Ben-Gurion's failure to reply to Blaustein's letter of 19 September, Proskauer urged presenting the Israeli government with an ultimatum. "Failing the receipt of a satisfactory reply [from Ben-Gurion] within a specific time, the American Jewish Committee would be forced to issue a statement."[39] Blaustein, however, had a cooler disposition. He was also in constant touch with Eliahu Elath and Abba Eban. Opposing Proskauer's extremist suggestion, he succeeded in convincing the leadership of the committee to go along with his line of action, which included cabling Ben-Gurion with a request to reply to his letter and holding further meetings with Elath, Eban, and Sharett (who was scheduled to arrive in New York) in an effort to resolve the crisis.

Judge Proskauer, however, was not fully satisfied with his successor's move and embarked on his own course of action. Distressed by the dual loyalty issue, concerned that the crisis might lead to a break in relations with Ben-Gurion, and by nature haunted by apocalyptic forebodings, he contacted the prime minister directly in a letter forwarded through Eliahu Elath.

Now believe me, Mr. Ben-Gurion, you are grievously in error if you think that any such activity [urging American Jewish immigration] finds any substantial response in the attitude of American Jewry. I ask you to consider, therefore, first the futility of what you are doing. But next I ask you to consider the evil effects of it on alienating support, material and spiritual, from your cause. You have furnished the American Council for Judaism with an issue on which they will be militant, unless you recede, and rightly so. . . . I am now reasoning with you and your answer to me, to my mind, is going to determine whether my attitude of reasonableness is to be thrown into the ashcan and the philosophy of the American Council for Judaism is to prevail, for obviously people like myself cannot be expected to ask [for] American contributions to funds intended in part to achieve such [an] un-American aim as the emigration of all American Jews to Israel.

In conclusion the retired judge implored the prime minister to issue a statement

modifying your position and categorically disclaiming any intention on the part of the State of Israel to interfere with the life of American Jewry. Believe me, my dear friend, time is of the essence here. This matter does not brook delay. I am telling you this, not as a threat, but as a statement of fact, which you ought to understand for your own guidance.[40]

For some unknown reason, throughout all the commotion within the American Jewish community, with Elath, Eban, and all the other Israeli diplomats frantically pressing for clarification from Ben-Gurion, the prime minister kept silent. Blaustein's letter remained unanswered as well. Later, Michael S. Comay, one of the top Israeli officials at the Foreign Office, shed some light on this curious policy. According to Comay, Ben-Gurion was furious at the reverberations of an off-the-record talk and refused to be put in the position of having "to admit, deny or explain statements which the *JTA*, or anybody else, might publicly attribute to him in another country."[41] But he was ready to make one concession. If Proskauer insisted "on getting some [official] clarification . . . his only recourse is to address himself personally to the prime minister."[42]

The suspense over Ben-Gurion's inexplicable silence was broken on 18 October when he cabled to Elath his authorized version (which was immediately published) of the kind of help Israel expected from American Jewry. Using the opportunity of addressing a visiting UJA delegation, the prime minister in a well-crafted statement appealed to American Jewry not to concentrate only on monetary assistance to the young state but also to create in effect a kind of peace corps of experts in all fields: agriculture, industry, construction, and seafaring, "taking part in the gigantic enterprise of absorption of new arrivals and the development of the country."[43] The Israeli leader had learned his lesson: no suggestion was made of sending American Jewish youth to Israel for permanent settlement, nor was the term *aliyah* from the United

States mentioned. Essentially it was an appeal to American idealism evoking the pioneer spirit of 1776 that had conquered the American wilderness and that might help bring about a similar miracle in Israel.

On receiving Ben-Gurion's version, Elath immediately sent a copy to Blaustein, commenting that the cable "makes it definitely clear that there is no desire on the part of the Government of Israel to intervene in the internal affairs of the Jewish community in the United States."[44] Hopefully, Elath noted, this would satisfy Blaustein's and Proskauer's inquiries regarding Ben-Gurion's controversial statement, "which, according to Ben-Gurion's secretary had been misquoted by [the] *JTA*."[45] (According to another version, "the JTA statement was unauthorized.")[46]

4

With the furor over Ben-Gurion's controversial statement having subsided, a postmortem took place in late October 1949 at a two-day session of the American Jewish Committee executive committee held at the Drake Hotel in Chicago, attended by over one hundred delegates from twenty-eight cities throughout the country. Blaustein found himself having to steer a tricky course between the anti- and pro-Zionist camps. Although a considerable amount of time was devoted to analyzing Ben-Gurion's first statement, what was really at stake was the viability of the Proskauer policy that advocated maintaining friendly relations with Israel while preserving the ideological purity of the committee through "unalterable opposition to any concept of world Jewish nationalism." But in the committee's view the issues of Israel and world Jewish nationalism could not be divorced from the ideological conflict between the committee and its rivals on either extreme of the American Jewish scene: the American Zionist movement and the American Council for Judaism. This triangular ideological and organizational contest animated the Chicago deliberations.

Reviewing his intensive behind-the-scenes activities in regard to Ben-Gurion's statement, Blaustein's final judgment was that "disturbing though it was, the net effect may well be salutary, as the Israeli officials have now reaffirmed their earlier assurances that they will consistently keep the position of American Jews in mind." He also believed that his policy of maintaining friendly relations with Israeli leaders, as well as of "refraining from denouncing Mr. Ben-Gurion's statement before exhausting every possible effort to induce him to take appropriate steps to counteract it," had been justified. Even

Proskauer acknowledged the merits of Blaustein's quiet diplomacy, conceding "that it would be unrealistic to expect the Prime Minister of a sovereign State to make an official retraction of the remarks attributed to him." In Proskauer's judgment Ben-Gurion's statement via his secretary that he was misquoted, his declaration to the UJA delegation, and Ambassador Elath's letter to Blaustein were "all that we could reasonably expect." Nevertheless, he cautioned constant vigilance in the event of similar incidents in the future.[47]

From the American Jewish Committee's point of view, the ZOA also displayed dangerous tendencies. During the Chicago meeting Blaustein quoted a "particularly disturbing" statement made by the ZOA's newly elected president, Daniel Frisch, referring to the ambitious program that Frisch himself had publicized in late August designed to revive his organization and to adapt its activities to the reality of the existence of the Jewish state (see chapter 1). The Israeli side of Frisch's program focused primarily on backing the Israeli middle class and strengthening cultural relations between the American Jewish community and the Jewish state. The American part of the program aimed at the democratization of Jewish communal life and the revitalization of Hebrew education.[48] These agendas raised the committee's fears "lest a program might be in contemplation for making Israel the center of Jewish life in this country and throughout the world."[49] Prompted by such fears, Blaustein and a small group of committee leaders invited several ZOA leaders to a dinner in October, during which the committee's firm opposition to Diaspora nationalism was restated, as well as its "concern lest the Zionist movement take a nationalist direction." Blaustein noted that this informal dinner produced quick results. Immediately thereafter, Frisch, addressing a Zionist rally, confronted the dual loyalty issue head-on:

> American Jews are an integral part of the American community. To them America is home. For them the establishment of Israel represents the realization of the historic inspirations of the Jewish people . . . American Jews owe their political allegiance to the government of the United States, just as the citizens of Israel owe theirs to the government of the State of Israel. The bogey of dual allegiance conjured up by some who should know better is just pure invention.[50]

However, Frisch stressed, eliminating the specter of dual allegiance did not mean severing the intimate cultural and religious bonds linking American Jewry and Israelis, which were based on "a sense of kinship mainly arising from a sense of common history and tradition." Furthermore, not only was American Jewry's aid to Israel rooted in laudable humanitarian considerations, it was also fully consonant with the American national interest of strengthening Israel "as a bulwark of democracy in that part of the world."

Continuing this theme, Frisch reemphasized that "American Jews as citizens of this country remain here by choice, looking forward toward their own future in America." He also quoted Justice Louis D. Brandeis's classic statement that "every American Jew who aids in advancing the Jewish settlement in Palestine, though he feels that neither he nor his descendents will ever live there, is likewise a better man and a better American for doing so."

Frisch addressed the committee's anxiety regarding Ben-Gurion's call for the emigration of American Jews to Israel by asserting that the ZOA had no intention of working toward large-scale emigration, although it would assist "and facilitate the integration into Israel of those who because of their American 'know-how,' technical skill or interest in agriculture, can make a special contribution to the upbuilding of the Jewish homeland and fostering democracy in the Middle East."

The committee printed long excerpts of Frisch's speech in the minutes of the Chicago session, and, even more significantly, Blaustein declared that Frisch's remarks were "also consistent with the principles of the American Jewish Committee and with sound Americanism,"[51] a statement that was accepted without reservation. Thus, less than two years after Israel's birth, an incipient ideological symbiosis between the two erstwhile rival organizations was in the making.

Whereas the issues of the Israeli and the ZOA statements were resolved to the committee's satisfaction, at least for the time being, the question of the conflict with the American Council for Judaism on the position toward Israel was becoming explosive. Although the committee, Blaustein pointed out, "shares the condemnation of world Jewish nationalism," it differed from the American Council for Judaism on two significant counts. Firstly, on the question of Zionism, the council equated Zionism and nationalism and rejected them both, while the committee hoped to modify Zionist policies toward its point of view, recognizing that although there were "nationalist pressures within the Zionist movement . . . there are counter-pressures as well." The other difference concerned the council's publicity methods, namely utilizing the general press in the campaign against Jewish nationalism. Blaustein warned the committee leadership of the danger of such methods: "In its fear lest American Jews become guilty of dual loyalty, [the council] is raising suspicion in the minds of our fellow-citizens that a substantial number of American Jews already are guilty of dual loyalty."[52]

As examples of such publicity, Blaustein cited virulent press releases from the council's annual meeting of April 1949, Alfred Lilienthal's article in the September issue of the *Reader's Digest,* and the use made of the council's press releases by well-known anti-Semites. All of these activities, Blaustein charged, had created a "violent reaction of the organized Jewish community, as represented in the National Community Relations Advisory Council [American Jewry's coordinating body for intergroup relations and for combating anti-Semitism], against the American Council for Judaism."

Blaustein's condemnation of the council's activities was reflected in a sharply worded draft resolution accusing the council of engaging in "publicity in the general press gravely and unwarrantedly charging serious dereliction on the part of a substantial segment of American Jews" that resulted in damage to "the position of the Jew in America." The resolution urged leaders of the committee to continue negotiations with the council "in the endeavor to persuade it to desist from a course which is detrimental to American Jewry." Significantly, the accusatory resolution was seconded by Judge Proskauer.

Lessing J. Rosenwald, who sat through the sessions, was clearly discomfited. Why should his organization, he protested, be singled out for condemnation while American Zionists also utilized the general press? He also admonished the committee for accepting "the assumption of Zionists that a majority of American Jews are Zionists, an assumption which the council does not accept and which it regards as essential to challenge publicly." Denying that his group had ever questioned the loyalty of a large segment of American Jews, he explained that what it really aimed at was convincing "the American public that the nationalism implicit in Zionist propaganda is repugnant to American Jews." Because the Jewish press would not publish the council's releases, their only recourse was to use the general press. In any event, he claimed, there was no distinction between the Jewish and the general press—both could be read by non-Jewish readers, "including anti-Semites." Furthermore, Blaustein's policy of quiet diplomacy vis-à-vis Israel and the ZOA, and his satisfaction at achieving "a considerable degree of unity among American Jewry toward Israel" by this means, was similarly unacceptable to Rosenwald, who found promotion of such unity "reprehensible because it encouraged the growth of Jewish nationalism."

The lengthy debate that ensued over Rosenwald's presentation pitted the council's supporters in the committee against their rather moderate opponents. Blaustein and others, however, were determined to prevent an irreparable rift within the committee's ranks and were willing to tone down the wording of the final resolution and recommend renewed conferences with the council, although Blaustein admitted "that the position taken by Mr. Rosenwald . . . had reduced his optimism" regarding the chances of reaching common ground with the council.[53] This time, Proskauer sided unreservedly with Blaustein against the publicity methods of the American Council for Judaism, but the rival organization still had many supporters among the committee membership, whose influence could not be ignored.

5

While the committee was occupied with trying to resolve these controversial issues, David Ben-Gurion, confounded by the boomerang effect of his remarks and particularly stung by Proskauer's cutting response to his statement, took the unusual step of setting down his credo on Israeli-Diaspora relations and mailing it to Proskauer. This long, frank, and remarkable letter, dated 1 November 1949, reflected Ben-Gurion's decision to spell out his position on Zionism, dual loyalty, and Israeli-Diaspora relations once and for all. Zionism, he began, was his point of departure. He was a Zionist, and continued to be so even after Israel's birth. "But I fear," Ben-Gurion wrote, "that you tend to translate Zionism into 'Americanese,' while my conception differs from that of many of the American Zionists." For Ben-Gurion a Zionist meant a Jew seized by an "inner need, and not on material grounds alone, to live a full Jewish life"[54] in the Jewish homeland, in a completely Jewish and Hebrew ambience. This definition, he said, did not mean that Jews who were not seized by such an inner need were inferior to other Jews. They were welcome to live wherever they wished, hopefully in conditions of equality, but in his view they could not be called Zionists.

Having clarified his position on Zionism, Ben-Gurion turned to the question of dual loyalty:

> The State of Israel is the State of its residents and citizens, the same as any other state. Its residents and citizens are not all Jews. They are all citizens enjoying equal rights. A Jew outside Israel owes no political or legal allegiance to Israel. Israel in no way speaks for or represents him. . . .
> There is, indeed there can be, no contradiction between an American

Jew's duty to his country, and his relation as a Jew to the State of Israel; and the last thing to be asked would be that you should do anything incompatible with your duty to America. Having built this sovereign state of ours, and dedicated to its existence as we are, we understand this no less perhaps than anyone else.[55]

Notwithstanding the convergence of their opinions on this vital issue, Ben-Gurion refused to accept Proskauer's essential thesis, namely, that the State of Israel "in any way, [was] impinging on anyone's Americanism in asking for that kind of help [American Jews with know-how that Israel needed]." Not only had America been built by the pioneering spirit of immigrants from many countries, said Ben-Gurion, but surely American Jewish assistance in developing democratic Israel would "redound to the honor and glory of every Jew in the world and of all civilized men."

Ben-Gurion reinforced his point by recounting his personal links to America. "I want you to know," he told Proskauer, "that among the people nearest and dearest to me, two are Americans—my wife and eldest daughter, who was born in America." But apart from this personal slant the prime minister recounted a more significant historical episode in his life, describing his three years in America during World War I when he (and his close friend Itzhak Ben-Zvi, subsequently the second president of Israel) was expelled from Palestine by the Turks and eventually reached America. While there, he had helped influence hundreds of American Jewish volunteers to join the famous Jewish Legion, and although they served under the British flag, these soldiers were "recruited with the consent and active approval of President Woodrow Wilson."[56]

Ingenuously disassociating himself from the statement imputed to him, Ben-Gurion categorically denied that he expected the "immigration of all American Jews to Israel. It is worse than an un-American aim. It is sheer stupidity. There is no need to convince me of the 'futility' and 'harmfulness' of such nonsense." While the people of Israel were resolved to maintain an open-door immigration policy for every Jew "whether he comes here of his own free will, or whether for one reason or another he is obliged to leave the country of his birth," this policy was by no means predicated on causing suffering to Jews in the Diaspora. "The State of Israel will not be built, has no wish to be built, on discrimination against Jews in any other country." In conclusion he invited Proskauer to visit Israel, "if it doesn't make you entirely unacceptable to the

American Council for Judaism . . . for you have been a gallant and faithful friend, and one whose help towards the constituting of the Jewish State has been very considerable." [57]

Proskauer was ecstatic with Ben-Gurion's letter. In sharp contrast to his previous admonition of the Israeli leader, the judge was now laudatory. "To me it is a document of fundamental and historic importance," [58] he replied to Ben-Gurion. He attached particular significance to Ben-Gurion's definition of a Zionist, which he considered a means for facilitating the discarding of old notions of ideology and affiliation and creating a new framework for aiding Israel. Since the "overwhelming majority" of American Zionists had no intention or wish to leave America, "to which they are profoundly and patriotically devoted," Proskauer went so far as to reiterate Blaustein's idea of creating a brand new framework, Friends of Israel, in which former Zionists, non-Zionists, and anti-Zionists could all take part. The only condition would be "that whatever is done for Israel must also be done in the interest of the United States."

In his letter Proskauer also praised Ben-Gurion's "sharp distinction between Israelis and Americans" and he backtracked as well from his opposition to American Jewish technicians and specialists going to assist Israel. The idea was all right, he said, so long as Ben-Gurion did not expect mass emigration of American Jews to Israel. In fact, Proskauer was so impressed by Ben-Gurion's démarche that he asked if he could publish the letter. "I believe you have taken a fundamental and historic position, which should be known and should redound to the interest not only of your State, but of the Jews of America and of the democracies of the world." [59]

During the same period Moshe Sharett, in a private conference with Blaustein and executive committee chairman Irving Engel in December 1949, issued a similarly reassuring statement. Allowing the leaders of the committee to quote him, Sharett solemnly declared that Israel would not interfere in "the life of American Jewry," nor did it view the Jews of the Diaspora as citizens of Israel. Blaustein, greatly satisfied with this statement, also interpreted it to mean that the Israelis "are not operating on the concept of world Jewish nationalism." [60] This interpretation may have been a bit off the mark, for although Israel never viewed the Jews of the Diaspora as Israeli citizens, there was still a fundamental difference between Israel's and the American Jewish Committee's concepts of Jewish nationalism and of America as *galut* (exile).

The year 1949, then, was drawing to a close on a hopeful note. The remarkable Ben-Gurion-Proskauer exchange and the Blaustein-Sharett understanding seemed to have concluded a period of bitter recriminations and to have heralded the advent of a new era in the relationship between Israel and the American Jewish Committee. But it soon became apparent that the underlying causes of the pattern of Israeli assertiveness and American Jewish reaction, resulting in periodic crises, were not so easily eliminated.

3

The American Jewish Community
Viewed from Israel

1

FROM THE MOMENT it was established, the young state found itself facing a triple challenge: military, diplomatic, and economic. Militarily, the country's survival hinged on its ability to repulse the combined invasion of the regular armies of five neighboring Arab states. Diplomatically, it fought to block American and British efforts in the United Nations to reduce the area of the emergent state, resist the UN General Assembly resolution recommending the internationalization of Jerusalem, and ward off American pressure for repatriation of a large number of Arab refugees. Economically, it had to overcome the grave financial crisis brought about by adhering to the sacrosanct policy of unlimited immigration, which brought hundreds of thousands of penniless immigrants—survivors of the Holocaust and Jews from Moslem countries—pouring into the fledgling state. The leadership of the new state, which had a population of only 650,000 in May 1948, recognized that Israel could not meet the challenge alone. The challenge, though, could be met by appealing to the Western Diaspora, mainly American Jewry. An insight into Israel's precarious situation at that time may provide an understanding of how the leadership of Israel, especially Prime Minister David Ben-Gurion and Foreign Minister Moshe Sharett, viewed world Jewry, what their expectations from the Western Diaspora were, and how their perception of the young Jewish state's role shaped their attitudes toward the American Jewish community and its Zionist movement.

Israel's War of Independence ended in early 1949 after about twenty months of bitter fighting, and by the end of July the last of the armistice agreements was concluded with Syria, traditionally the most obdurate Arab opponent (Iraq vacated its army from Palestine but never signed an armistice agreement). The war left 1 percent of the small Jewish population dead—six thousand fatalities—and many thousands wounded. Despite the elation at the military victory, the population was war-weary and longed for normalcy and peace.

Normalcy, however, soon appeared to be only a pipe dream. The armistice agreements, which invariably included a clause stipulating that they were a "provisional measure" intended to "facilitate the transition from the present truce to permanent peace in Palestine,"[1] remained no more than a temporary measure in the Arab view, contrary to Israeli expectations. Eliahu Sasson, director of the Middle East division of the Israel Foreign Office and the ministry's foremost expert on Arab affairs, who had logged countless hours of candid discussions with Arab statesmen and diplomats over the years, analyzed the neighboring Arab states' strategy toward the young Jewish state in late 1949 as consisting of three concurrent approaches. The first approach favored an early attack and the destruction of Israel before it became stronger militarily, economically, and diplomatically. The second approach held that victory was conditioned upon proper preparations, including the resolution of inter-Arab conflicts, reorganizing Arab military capability, improving relations with the Western powers—mainly Great Britain, which still played a dominant role in the Middle East—improving domestic economic and social conditions, and enhancing Arab unity. The third approach advocated a strategy to keep the territory and the Jewish population of Israel as small as possible so that the country would be permanently weak, dependent on its neighbors' largesse, and unable to pursue an independent foreign policy. This strategy would be achieved by keeping Israel in a state of military tension and by refusing any form of mutual cooperation, agreement, or recognition. If, after several years, Israel "passed the test," did not collapse, and became "with heart and soul" a bona fide Middle Eastern state, it might then be accepted by the other states in the region and a modus vivendi established.[2] All three approaches together constituted the Arab consensus in Iraq, Egypt, Syria, Jordan, and Lebanon.[3] The Arab mood, then, was clearly not amenable to reconciliation with the existence of Israel, and the final blow was only a question of time.[4]

Among Israel's leaders no one was more concerned about Arab strategy than David Ben-Gurion, the first prime minister of Israel, who, more than any other leader, created and molded the new state by the sheer force of his personality. A CIA profile accurately portrayed him as "a remarkably astute politician, an able leader, and a powerful personality."[5] Indeed, he was first and foremost a leader, belonging to that particular category of leaders capable of shaping societies by their exceptional willpower, their intensity of mind, and their unbending character.

In 1906, at the age of twenty, fired by the utopian socialist Zionist vision of creating a new kind of Jewish society, he came to Palestine as part of the idealistic Second Aliyah wave of immigration, working as an agricultural laborer and watchman in the Jewish farming colonies. His outstanding leadership and organizational talents became quickly apparent—a unique capability to create and utilize political power along with a healthy dose of realism and pragmatism. These traits made him the preeminent leader of the Histadrut (General Federation of Labor) during the post-World War I period, and subsequently of Mapai, which he helped make the dominant political party in the Yishuv. Later, as chairman of the Jerusalem Jewish Agency Executive (1935–48), he became the undisputed leader of the entire Yishuv.

Despite his sojourn in the United States during World War I and several visits subsequently, his name was hardly known there, except in labor Zionist circles and among the leadership of the Zionist movement, for he was eclipsed then by the famous Chaim Weizmann, his great rival, who was to become the first president of Israel. But in 1948, almost overnight, Ben-Gurion's star rose. His resolute role in the decision to proclaim the Jewish state and his bold and effective leadership during Israel's War of Independence made him the George Washington of Israel and a figure of world renown.

Charismatic, a militant Zionist, Ben-Gurion dominated the Israeli scene until his retirement in 1963 to Kibbutz Sde Boker in the Negev desert. His complex personality never ceased to perplex even his longtime colleagues (such as Moshe Sharett, Levi Eshkol, and Golda Meir) and his close aides (such as Teddy Kollek). Imbued with an egocentric, messianic drive to restore and safeguard Jewish sovereignty, he was almost totally oblivious to human relations throughout his premiership, although away from the limelight he was compassionate toward soldiers, bereaved parents, and people in distress generally. He was humorless and solitary, without close friends. Teddy Kollek, his closest aide, observed: "He was the most impersonal man I had ever known, warm and passionate—but distant."[6] Colleagues as well as opponents often resented his abrasive and dogmatic style. His obliviousness to the insults he directed at such colleagues as Moshe Sharett, Abba Hillel Silver, Nahum Goldmann, Golda Meir, and many others created innumerable crises. This deficiency was one of the major factors responsible for pent-up animosity by the leadership of his party toward him, which was to explode at last in 1963, resulting in his final resignation from his post at the age of seventy-seven.[7]

Having conducted intensive private talks with Arab leaders during the 1930s, Ben-Gurion had no illusions about the overwhelming Arab opposition to the creation and the existence of the Jewish state. "The Arabs view us as aliens," he declared in the spring of 1949. "We are few and they are many. Naturally, the many endeavor to dominate the few, and the Arabs do not wish to forget the bitter history of last year."[8] He was, of course, referring to the Israeli War of Independence, in which the small Jewish community defeated first the Palestinian Arabs and eventually the invading armies of five neighboring Arab states. Appeals to avenge this humiliating defeat were continuously aired on every Arab broadcasting station, he reminded an audience of graduates of an officers course in May, while Muslim radio preachers constantly invoked the historical precedent of the bitter struggle between the Muslims and the Crusaders, assuring their listeners that the fate of the Jewish state would be similar to that of the Crusaders, who were eventually crushed by the Muslims in the thirteenth century.

But Ben-Gurion knew that Arab hostility could not be attributed entirely to the humiliation of military defeat. Social and cultural differences between the modern democratic Jewish society and the traditional feudal Arab society also contributed to the underlying animosity. This tension was further exacerbated by the instability of the cold war and by the threat of another world war, which encouraged, Ben-Gurion warned, the "adventurers, the mischief-makers and the war-hungry among the Arabs." Ever the clear-eyed realist, the Israeli leader cautioned his people: "We should not delude ourselves that the security of Israel might be insured through truce, armistice, and the signing of peace treaties."[9]

Although Ben-Gurion molded the Israel Defense Forces, he by no means believed that Israel's security depended on military strength alone. The country's main security component, he never tired of stressing, was *aliyah*— the immigration of Jews into the young state. He was painfully aware that 700,000 Jews—the size of the Jewish population in mid-1949—engulfed by a sea of Arabs did not stand a chance. No less important were the agricultural settlements developed along the borders, which served as a first line of defense. These components, augmented by an emphasis on industrial expansion and scientific research, as well as a foreign policy oriented toward peace and toward neutrality in the cold war, would create the necessary power base to ensure the country's security, Ben-Gurion believed.

He was always sensitive to the time factor—the danger of missing the train of history. "This is the question facing us: How will this tremendous and difficult job be accomplished? How will we carry the burden. . . . [being] so small? The entire Jewish people are small. We had hardly accumulated enough wealth in Israel, but it would not suffice to absorb the huge *aliyah*. . . . [and] we have to do the job in a short time, with a small state, an undertaking never attempted before, neither by us nor by any other people." Still, he was aware that the State of Israel had one outstanding advantage that could ensure the success of the undertaking: the Western Jewish Diaspora.[10]

2

The Western Diaspora, however, far from being an allied state with defined boundaries whose resources could be efficiently marshaled, was essentially made up of voluntary associations of Jews, as well as millions of nonaffiliated Jews, of varying degrees of commitment to Judaism and Israel. Their interest, goodwill, and involvement in Israel's well-being could be recruited and sustained only by constant effort. In America this effort meant depending on a communal leadership that was capable of translating the potential resources of the American Jewish community into sustained monetary and political aid on a scale undreamed of even a few years previously. The American Zionist movement had such a leader from 1943 onward—Dr. Abba Hillel Silver, the fiery Reform rabbi from Cleveland.

Silver was born in 1893 in Lithuania, and at the age of nine was brought by his mother to America to join his father, Rabbi Moses Silver, who had settled in New York's Lower East Side. The intensely Jewish and Zionist ambience of this milieu influenced Silver and his brother to establish the Dr. Herzl Zion Club in 1904 when Silver was eleven—the first Hebrew-speaking Zionist club in America. At the age of thirteen another young Zionist, Emanuel Neumann, who was to become Silver's lifelong friend and political ally and a prominent leader of the ZOA in his own right, also joined the club. Reminiscing about this seminal experience, Neumann recalled:

We [Emanuel and his brother] both joined it on a wintry Saturday night when. . . . the club was celebrating the Bar-Mitzvah of its then president, Abba Hillel Silver. . . . Abba, about six months my senior, was a most remarkable fellow, wholly self-possessed and self-confident, who ruled the club with an iron hand. But the crowd seemed to like his strong rule and accepted his judgments without protest. The literary programs of the club, which were presented by the youngsters themselves, were conducted entirely in Hebrew.[11]

Silver attended Hebrew Union College in Cincinnati, the rabbinical center of the Americanized Reform movement, a very long way from the East European-immigrant ambience of the Lower East Side. Graduating from the college as a Reform rabbi, and accepting the pulpit of Cleveland's prestigious Tiferet Israel Congregation (known as The Temple) in 1917, completed his process of Americanization. From then on, until his death in 1963, although he held major national leadership positions in the American Jewish world, The Temple would always remain his first love and the source of his greatest satisfaction.

Silver's impressive weekly sermons at The Temple gained him national fame as one of America's outstanding orators. This fame, and the great organizational talents that he displayed during his tenure as national chairman of the United Palestine Appeal (1938–43), catapulted him in 1943 to the leadership of the American Zionist Emergency Council, the political-action arm of the American Zionist movement. Silver, along with Neumann, turned this body into a potent vehicle for lobbying in Congress and for public pressure politics, making effective use of the Jewish vote factor and of Silver's electrifying appeal to mass audiences. Meanwhile, Silver and Neumann, who supported Ben-Gurion's activist policy vis-à-vis the British government, allied themselves with Ben-Gurion in 1946 and engineered the de facto removal of Chaim Weizmann—a political moderate—from the presidency of the Zionist movement. Silver was then elected chairman of the American section of the Jewish Agency and thus, during the crucial period leading to the establishment of Israel—1946–48—became coequal to Ben-Gurion in the Zionist organizational hierarchy, as well as the most powerful American Zionist leader of his time.

Although adored by his subordinates, he was considered by his colleagues and opponents alike as a powerful but humorless leader with a domineering and autocratic character. These traits caused tensions and crises in the top echelon of the American Zionist movement and eventually a total break in his relations with President Truman.[12]

It was to be anticipated that with the creation of the State of Israel Silver

would continue to lead American Zionism, if not in the diplomatic field as before (this had naturally become the province of the young state) then in the
crucial area of fund-raising for Israel. This continuation, however, was not to
be the case. In the fall of 1948, while the Israeli army was still battling the invading Arab armies, a grave crisis erupted within the leadership of the ZOA
and the United Jewish Appeal that had wide bearing, on Silver's and
Neumann's leadership positions and more broadly on the relationship between the State of Israel and American Jewry.

A sense of the impending crisis was conveyed to the Israeli leadership by
Henry Morgenthau Jr., who visited Israel in October 1948. The former U.S.
secretary of the treasury, who served as general chairman of the United Jewish
Appeal, warned the Jerusalem Jewish Agency Executive that unless a complete
change in the control of UJA funds earmarked for Israel were undertaken he
would resign from his central leadership position. He put it bluntly:

> We want both the Government [of Israel] and the [Jerusalem] Jewish
> Agency to declare whom they wish [to control funds earmarked for Israel] in
> America. . . . But the misunderstanding in the US is the fear that certain Jews
> in the US [Silver and Neumann, who lead both the ZOA and the American
> section of the Jewish Agency] will dictate to you what you should [do] with
> the money.[13]

In fact Morgenthau urged the Jerusalem executive to carry out a veritable revolution: to transfer control of the funds destined for Israel from New York to
Jerusalem.

Morgenthau's warning followed a drastic step taken by his closest colleague, Henry Montor, the United Jewish Appeal fund-raising wizard and executive vice president of the United Palestine Appeal (UPA). An Israeli
diplomat, describing him, noted: "Henry Montor is pretty well hated in this
country. He appears to me to be a man of outwardly great charm, of some intellectual standing, of possibly less Jewish integrity and of brilliant administrative ability. [But] he loves a fight and considers success to be evaluated in
accordance with the number of scraps he has been able to get into."[14] Montor, who had long been on bad personal terms with Silver, had submitted a letter to UPA Chairman Rabbi Israel Goldstein in September 1948 accusing
Abba Hillel Silver and Emanuel Neumann of using funds raised in the United
States for Israel "as a lever with which to change or dominate the social struc-

ture of [Israel]." [15] Montor thereupon announced his immediate resignation from his dual leadership positions in the UJA and UPA.

Montor's resignation provided the impetus for a group of veteran opposition leaders within the ZOA—Louis Lipsky, Stephen S. Wise, Louis E. Leventhal, and others—to organize themselves into a Committee for Progressive Zionism that similarly proceeded to accuse Silver and Neumann of dictatorial rule, of supporting right-wing policies in Israel, of interfering in domestic Israeli politics, and of ongoing failure to maintain contacts with the Truman administration.[16] Working in alliance with this group, Montor simultaneously organized a Committee of Workers and Contributors consisting of fundraisers and community leaders who threatened to mount an independent campaign, divorced from Silver's and Neumann's control, with three aims: across-the-board responsibility by the entire American Jewish community (and not just by the ZOA) for raising funds for Israel; remittance of all funds raised in the United States directly to Israel, without any deductions for American organizations; and ultimate control for the allocation of funds collected from American Jewry resting with the Jewish Agency in Israel.[17]

Silver and Neumann categorically rejected all accusations. The main culprit behind the "wretched controversy in the UJA," they asserted, was Henry Montor, who, because of his "divisive personality" jeopardized the success of the campaign. Moreover, Silver and Neumann challenged the constitutional authority of the Jerusalem executive to intervene in an internal American Zionist dispute and impose its own decisions, thereby undermining the independence of the American Zionist movement.[18] Their supporters in the American Yiddish press, which provided a blow-by-blow record of the controversy, went even further, blaming the leaders of Mapai for "having been so blinded by their hatred of. . . . the Silver-Neumann group that they have joined forces with the Montor group."[19]

The Silver-Montor controversy, waged from September 1948 to February 1949, involved the entire leadership of the American Zionist movement and political personalities in Israel in intense political infighting. Finally, in mid-February 1949, after being outmaneuvered by both American and Israeli opponents, Silver and Neumann announced their resignation from the executive of the American section of the Jewish Agency,[20] thus ending the era of Silver's dominant leadership in American Zionism (although not of Neumann's).

From a broader historical perspective, it is clear that the widely publicized

Silver-Montor controversy and the rift within the leadership of the ZOA were just the tip of the iceberg. Behind the scenes a much more significant crisis had been brewing for some time between two dominant leaders: Ben-Gurion and Silver.

Within the context of Zionist politics Ben-Gurion, on the one hand, and Silver and Neumann, on the other, belonged to opposing camps—broadly, leftist and rightist. Yet the two American Zionist figures themselves were also politically distinct from each other. Silver had spent all his adult life leading his congregation in Cleveland and had no first-hand experience with Yishuv politics. Neumann had lived in Mandatory Palestine during most of the 1930s, serving as a member of the Zionist Executive in Jerusalem and conducting various business enterprises there. A leading member of the right-wing General Zionist Party then, Neumann had also served on the governing board of the dissident underground military organization Irgun Zvai Leumi, a fact that did not endear him to Ben-Gurion and his socialist Mapai Party.[21]

Ben-Gurion became acquainted with Abba Hillel Silver during his visits to America, in particular during World War II, and assessed him as possessing "two positive traits: courage and initiative; and two negative ones: lack of political acumen, and collegial inability; he is a boss."[22] Ben-Gurion's reservations about Silver's character notwithstanding, both leaders were united in their commitment to activism and militancy vis-à-vis the British after the end of World War II, as well as by an intense desire to remove the moderate, pro-British Chaim Weizmann from the office of president of the Zionist movement, and so formed a tactical alliance in 1946. This alliance resulted in a devastating defeat for Weizmann at the twenty-second Zionist Congress in Basle, when he failed to be reelected to the presidency of the movement. Two political developments stemming from this coup illuminated the intensity of the infighting within the Zionist movement: Silver, hoping to succeed Weizmann as president of the movement, did not achieve this ambition, inasmuch as he and Ben-Gurion neutralized each other.[23] Yet, to Ben-Gurion's chagrin, Silver reinforced his already elevated position in the Zionist hierarchy by becoming chairman of the newly created American section of the Jewish Agency, thereby technically coequal to Ben-Gurion.

Beyond tactics, however, Ben-Gurion, the consummate political leader, insisted on determining the crucial aspects of the Zionist enterprise, while simultaneously preserving his freedom of action. Consequently he never consented to an American Zionist Monroe Doctrine. Foreseeing, with the publication of the British White Paper in 1939, that Washington was destined to replace London as the determining factor in the fate of the Jewish national home, the leader of the Yishuv henceforth directed his energies to the United States in search of sources of support. He visited America frequently during World War II and thereafter, methodically and single-mindedly building up his own personal contacts in official Washington circles, with American Jewry, and within the Zionist movement. He created an especially close rapport with Hadassah leaders, particularly with Rose Halprin, president of that organization from 1932 to 1934 and again from 1947 to 1952.[24] Perhaps his greatest success during this period was the establishment of the "Sonneborn Institute" in July 1945. Ben-Gurion realized that the Jewish state could be established only by force of arms against the combined opposition of the Palestinian Arabs and the neighboring Arab states, and discreetly set about making the necessary preparations. Bypassing the organized American Zionist community, he recruited Rudolph G. Sonneborn, a wealthy New York business executive; Meyer W. Weisgal, a talented fund-raiser who was Weizmann's representative in America; and Henry Montor of the UJA, to launch a so-called "institute." It was composed of a group of seventeen millionaires who undertook to raise the necessary funds to finance the acquisition of weapons and equipment for the clandestine weapons industry in Palestine set up by the Haganah—the Yishuv's underground military organization—and the purchase of ships for the illegal immigration of Jewish refugees to Palestine.[25]

Shortly thereafter, in order to coordinate the increasingly complex activities involved in the acquisition of these materials, Ben-Gurion also established a Haganah mission in America, in early 1946. The mission undertook its own independent fund-raising and public relations projects, creating a body of supporters, "Americans for Haganah, Inc.," headed by Abraham (Abe) Feinberg, a prominent New York manufacturer and Democratic Party fund-raiser.

The increasingly active presence of Ben-Gurion's emissaries in America inevitably aggravated relations between him and Silver and Neumann. Moreover, Silver's and Neumann's unconcealed support for the Irgun Zva'i Le'umi, under Menahem Begin's command, stirred Ben-Gurion's resentment, for the entire socialist camp within the Yishuv was engaged in a fierce political and ideological struggle against what they considered the dangerous ultra-nationalist right wing.[26]

Indeed, from the end of 1947 onward, Ben-Gurion's entries in his diary, and his remarks made in public, were increasingly critical and vituperative with regard to Silver and Neumann. By January 1949 he had come to the conclusion that "it was desirable to oust Silver and Neumann from the [Jewish

Agency] Executive—for disobeying the Executive. . . . The [Silver-Montor] controversy, and if necessary, the 'Tammany Hall' leadership of the ZOA, should be done with." [27]

During this period the American embassy in Tel Aviv was also closely monitoring what it termed the "long-standing Silver-Neumann vs. Morgenthau-Montor conflict." Reporting to Washington, Richard Ford, one of the embassy's senior officials, pointed out that some Israelis interpreted it as "a major political struggle involving the future influence which world Jewry may exert on both the internal [and] political structure and the foreign policy of the newly created State of Israel." Although the Israeli public at large did not seem to have a clear idea of the reasons for the conflict, the American diplomat noted, "the most popularly held belief here is that the Mapai government of Israel, under the leadership of Mr. Ben-Gurion, wanted to get rid of Dr. Silver and his friends because of their close affiliation with the American Republican Party, and their outspoken opposition to the development of an ardently socialist framework in the State of Israel." In the broader perspective of Israeli-American relations, Ford observed that "this interjection of American politics into the Israeli scene" was inevitable in view of the young state's dependence on American financial contributions. [28]

This interpretation notwithstanding, what was really at stake in the two exceedingly complex and bitter overlapping conflicts—the Silver-Montor controversy and the Ben-Gurion-Silver-Neumann feud—aside from personal animosities was the issue of Israel as the undisputed source of Zionist decision-making in all major issues affecting political and financial aid. No Israeli political leader was about to surrender control of the American Jewish lifeline to Israel. This refusal was especially so when the potential recipients of such control—Zionist leaders such as Silver and Neumann—might conceivably exploit their position in the UPA in order to channel financial and political aid to the sister party they supported in Israel, the right-of-center General Zionists, thereby endangering the dominance of Ben-Gurion's own Mapai Party in the forthcoming Israeli elections scheduled for early 1949. [29]

Whatever Ben-Gurion's motives, it was obvious that magnanimity and gratitude for past achievements and services were as rare a commodity in Zionist politics as in politics anywhere. Indeed, Silver himself, in previous struggles against his opponents, especially the other leading American Zionist leader of the time, Rabbi Stephen S. Wise, was as capable of ruthlessness and vindictiveness as Ben-Gurion. [30] This behavior was, in fact, reminiscent of similar circumstances thirty years earlier, in a conflict between two other eminent leaders—Louis D. Brandeis and Chaim Weizmann.[31]

Silver's ouster, and his replacement by the more pliant and cooperative—from the Israeli point of view—Nahum Goldmann as chairman of the Jewish Agency Executive's American section, marked the end of the heroic era of the American Zionist movement and the beginning of a new relationship between American Jewry and the nascent Jewish state.

3

The bitter Silver-Montor controversy, as well as agitation over the dual loyalty issue in some sections of the American Jewish community, served as vivid demonstrations to Israel's leaders of the complexity of the new relationships between the Jewish state and the Western Diaspora generally, and American Jewry in particular. Ben-Gurion, Moshe Sharett, and other Israeli leaders involved in Israel-Diaspora relations recognized that dealing with emergencies such as the Silver-Montor controversy on an ad hoc basis was insufficient and that the creation of the state required a fundamental intellectual effort to define Israel's self-perception, the nature of its relations with the Diaspora and with the Zionist movement, and the implications of these relations for the formulation and conduct of its foreign policy. These questions were thrashed out in the summer of 1950 at two significant meetings: a conference of Israeli ambassadors and a smaller gathering of experts chaired by the prime minister.

The most fundamental and complex question was whether Israel, in addition to being a full-fledged member of the international community, was a Jewish state or a Zionist state. The answer determined the very essence of the state and its policies. If Israel was conceived only as a Jewish state, then it was a normal state in the sense that its population was predominantly Jewish. As Weizmann had stated succinctly in 1919 at the Paris Peace Conference, albeit in completely different circumstances, in response to a question posed by U.S. Secretary of State Robert Lansing as to the meaning of a Jewish national home, "The hope that by Jewish immigration Palestine would ultimately become as Jewish as England is English."[32] A Jewish majority would then be the determining yardstick.

But in the minds of the founding fathers, Israel was not destined to be a normal state. It was the product of the Zionist idea translated into reality by the continuous process of mass immigration of Jews from the four corners of the earth, known as the ingathering of exiles. That was its raison d'être. Israel's uniqueness, Ben-Gurion once stated, was derived from the fact that "it was not just a state for its inhabitants but for the ingathering of exiles."[33] Similarly, foreign minister Moshe Sharett defined the uniqueness of the Jewish state thus:

> Our state is unique because it constitutes a historical asset of dispersed people all over the world. To be sure there are other states, such as Ireland and Greece, which have a Diaspora, but those peoples were never as dispersed territorially or in terms of time as the Jewish Diaspora. Moreover, they never retained such a close and vital tie among their dispersed elements as the Jewish people. Also [the Irish and the Greeks] never established their countries in consequence of the process of the return of the dispersed to the mother country.[34]

In fact, the return of the dispersed, or *aliyah*, was crucial, Sharett emphasized:

> If we do not grow in numbers we will not be able to maintain our position and develop our economic and cultural capability. . . . No doubt we must assume that for a long time many Jews, perhaps even the majority of Jews, would remain in the Diaspora. Even if Israel reached a population of five million, still six million would remain outside its borders. Yet, even for the sake of *aliyah* alone we must maintain our contacts with world Jewry."[35]

The Israeli approach to the Diaspora was thus clearly determined by its perception of the Zionist mission of the Jewish state, which mandated, in Ben-Gurion's phrasing, that "the entire Jewish people—wherever they live—are the concern of the State of Israel, the first and paramount concern."[36] This concern, however, did not mean that Israel claimed political sovereignty beyond its borders. Rather, the state was perceived as the cultural and spiritual center of the Jewish people.

Although Ben-Gurion and Sharett shared this basic Zionist approach toward the Diaspora, their background, personalities, and world view could not have been more different. While Sharett, like Ben-Gurion, was born in Eastern Europe (in 1894), he was brought to Palestine by his parents at the age of ten. Sharett's family spent their first two years in Palestine in the Arab village of En Suniya near Ramallah, where the young boy mastered Arabic and acquired a sympathetic understanding of the Arab way of life and Arab folklore.

The highly talented young man embarked on a dazzling career after World War I, studying at the London School of Economics, becoming assistant editor of *Davar*, the influential Histadrut daily, and subsequently editor of its English supplement, and at the age of thirty-nine being elected to head the political department of the Zionist Executive, thus becoming the de facto foreign minister of the Zionist movement. From independence in 1948 until Ben-Gurion's resignation as prime minister in December 1953, he served as foreign minister in Ben-Gurion's cabinets, becoming prime minister (while retaining the post of foreign minister) thereafter. He continued for a short time as foreign minister after Ben-Gurion's return to office at the end of 1955, but was ousted in June 1956 when the long behind-the-scenes rift between the two over defense and foreign policy reached the breaking point.

Sharett himself, always analytical, aptly portrayed the opposite nature of their personalities: "I am quiet, reserved, careful; Ben-Gurion is impulsive, impetuous, and acts on intuition, not reason. My capital C is Caution, Ben-Gurion's is Courage. I see all the implications and consequences of an act, Ben-Gurion sees only one side, what he wants to see, and suppresses everything else." [37]

Sharett was far more sensitive than Ben-Gurion to the dilemmas for the Diaspora posed by the creation of Israel, although he totally rejected the theory that the creation of the state would cause a split within the Jewish people. The behavior of assimilated American Jews showed, he said, that "the past two years [of Israel's existence] did more for raising the Jewish sense of peoplehood and unity than did all of Zionist propaganda since Herzl." Still, he also noted that "committed and sensitive Jews now live in uninterrupted anxiety: what will Israel do today and tomorrow, what kind of declaration will it make, how will it vote at the United Nations, and how might all this affect us—assuming, mainly subconsciously, that it must have an effect." [38]

Sharett's awareness of Diaspora concerns was evident in his first speech to the UN General Assembly on 11 May 1949, when Israel was admitted to membership in the UN. Addressing the sensitive question of dual loyalty, Sharett declared that "the State of Israel claimed no allegiance from Jews in other lands. . . . Israel expressed fervent wishes for the security, dignified existence and equality of Jews everywhere. . . . Israel would regard it as a most sacred trust to keep its doors open to all Jews in need of a home." [39] The essential elements of Israeli-Diaspora relations, then, were laid down. Israel was a normal country, laying no claim to the allegiance of Jews outside its borders, but it also had a unique commitment to the Zionist mission that mandated moral responsibility to Jewish communities in jeopardy and an open-door policy for every homeless Jew.[40]

In addressing the Israeli ambassadors conference in July 1950, Sharett, ever the scholar, examined the origins of the dual loyalty issue. Historically, he pointed out, "the question had been raised by Jews—not by non-Jews. It had created some truly serious problems [in 1947–48] when the leader of American Zionism [Rabbi Abba Hillel Silver] had addressed the United Nations as the spokesmen of the Jewish Agency, but psychologically dual loyalty was basically a Jewish invention." Not only was it not a problem in the United States, he argued, but it could actually be turned into an asset, for if Washington were interested in preventing Israel from joining the Soviet bloc and adhering to the Western camp instead, the best guarantee for this development would be strengthening American Jewry's relations with Israel. "The stronger and more vibrant these relations, the harder it would be for Israel to maintain positions which might lead to the severance of Washington's relationship with Israel."[41]

Although Sharett underestimated the potency of the problem of dual loyalty for American Jewry (Zionists and non-Zionists alike), he did warn against a one-sided or generalized approach to the Western Diaspora. For example, American and British Jewry were proud of their citizenship and their culture, he explained, and Israel would be making a grave mistake if it attempted "to undermine that pride"—if it sought to instill fear of persecution in American and British Jewry as in Nazi Germany. Israel's emissaries abroad, Sharett stressed, must be acutely aware of the complexity of the Diaspora reality.

Realistically, Sharett surmised, Israel stood no chance of attracting mass *aliyah* from the countries of the Western world. The only way it would attract even a few immigrants from these countries, he believed, was through a positive approach that emphasized the full Jewish life to be lived in the young state and the challenge of participation in a great adventure.

Israel also had something else to offer the Diaspora—the Hebrew language, Sharett stated at the conference. This was a subject very close to his heart, as it was to Ben-Gurion as well. His zealous cultivation of the revived Hebrew language was legendary: he was in the habit of correcting diplomats' grammar in outgoing dispatches at the Foreign Office and of phoning radio broadcasters to admonish them about mispronunciations. He noted an interesting phenomenon: although Yiddish and Ladino, the traditional Jewish languages of the Diaspora, were disappearing as Jews adopted the languages of their native countries, Hebrew was being taught all over the Diaspora. His idea was to make Hebrew the inheritor of Yiddish and Ladino—"to make the Hebrew language the living and cultural language of Jews in the Diaspora."[42] By this he did not mean to advocate replacing the native languages of English or French, but to create bilingual communities, as in Canada.

Cultural exchange between Israel and the Diaspora would also be valuable, Sharett believed. He, like Ben-Gurion, was sensitive to the danger of Israel's becoming a provincial, Levantine country, and thought that *sabras*—the Israeli-born generation—would derive great benefit from exposure to the Western world for various periods, exposure that would also create bonds between Israelis and the Jews of the Diaspora.

Ben-Gurion, entrusted with steering the course of a state in desperate economic straits, was deeply concerned with Israeli-Diaspora relations as well. Acutely aware of the vital importance of American Jewry and its Zionist movement as Israel's only reliable ally, he sought precise information on actual conditions in America from someone he knew and trusted, and in early 1950 sent Eliezer Liebenstein (later Livneh), a leading Mapai Party intellectual and brilliant writer highly esteemed by Ben-Gurion, to visit the United States. Livneh was assigned to study American Jewry intensively, with particular attention to the state of the Zionist movement. He visited every Jewish organization, meeting lay leaders, professionals, educators, rabbis, and intellectuals and producing a perceptive analysis along with recommendations for future action.

"The condition of American Zionism," Livneh surmised, "was a cause for grave concern: within a short time it was likely to disintegrate and degenerate—despite indications of Jewish, Hebraic and Israeli oriented awakening encompassing most of American Jewry."[43] Possibly Livneh was too eager in choosing the depiction "awakening," yet it was evident that he had made a concerted effort, within his two-month study tour, to learn the subject.

He singled out three basic elements that characterized the Zionist and pro-Israel public. First, single-interest groups, such as Hadassah and Mizrachi Women, were essentially devoted to fund-raising for practical and limited goals in Israel. Hadassah, however, was a paradox, Livneh explained. On the one hand, it was the largest and most important Zionist organization, without which there was no hope of effecting a renaissance in American Zionism. But, made up as it was of the Jewish middle class, it was the most conservative ideologically of all the Zionist organizations. Hadassah members—and even leaders—did not encourage their children to immigrate to Israel, "and they would be happy if there were no *halutziut* movement in America (although they were leery of admitting it)," Livneh observed.[44]

"Political" Zionist groups—the most important of which was the ZOA—was the second element, devoted to mobilizing political support for the Yishuv and for Israel in its early stages of statehood. However, Livneh reported, they had lost their élan and were shrinking. The ZOA, deprived of its sole raison d'être and in the throes of a leadership conflict, was actually in the process of disintegration. The demise of the ZOA, he predicted, would lead to the disappearance of the entire American Zionist movement as a guiding force in Jewish life. The situation of labor Zionism, the smaller political group, was no better. Made up of an older generation, "it lacked influence among college students, and it was divorced from the realities of American Jewish life." [45]

No less worrisome was the third group, consisting of pro-Israel individuals without Zionist organizational affiliation. "Some of them became Zionists, or pro-Israel, during the struggle for the establishment of Israel, and some of them reached their influential position as a result of their support of Israel. . . . There is no doubt about the significance of their assistance to Israel during the past two years." However, Livneh pointed out, these individuals, such as Henry Morgenthau Jr. and Abe Feinberg, lacked a power base. Their influence stemmed directly from their personal relationship with Israel or from contacts at the White House. "They are not capable of leading the Zionist movement, nor are they willing to do it; moreover, based on their personal limitations, they have even formulated an appropriate ideology." Thus, Livneh related,

> in my talk with him, Abe Feinberg lamented the deficiencies of the ZOA and the other Zionists groups. Responding, I told him: "You go and assume the leadership of the ZOA." . . . His reply was illustrative: "There is no need at all for the American Zionist movement and for the ZOA—let [some organization like] 'Friends of Israel' do the financial and political job."

In short, the unaffiliated Jewish VIPs would not do the job, Livneh warned:

> The political influence of these notables at the White House depended ultimately on the power and pressure of the Zionist movement. Of course if Truman needed—according to his appraisal of Jewish pressure—"to give" something to the Jews, he would be glad to do it through his friends (in order to strengthen their influence in the Jewish public, or to pay for past debts). However, in the absence of organized Jewish public pressure, neither

Feinberg, nor David K. Niles [Truman's administrative assistant in charge of civil rights, minorities—especially Jews—and contact with New York politics] would be able to accomplish anything.

Furthermore, Livneh argued, "there are no eternal rights in politics," and President Truman and his advisers felt that past political debts to his Jewish friends had already been settled.

Even in the crucial field of fund-raising through the United Jewish Appeal, salvation would not come from the VIPs. Livneh thought that the current year, 1950, offered the last chance to raise significant sums. Morgenthau had announced that he was leaving the UJA, while the local federations and welfare funds were clamoring for a larger share of monies raised for local needs. Maintaining the Israeli share of the funds depended on taking control of the welfare funds. This control, however, could be accomplished only by a "public movement with an activist Zionist organization and ideology," Livneh believed. The sympathetic Jewish VIPs had neither the organizational backup, the inner drive, nor a movement to which they were held responsible. Once they encountered serious obstacles, they were likely to disappear from the scene. Of course the Israeli leaders, Livneh pointed out, felt much more comfortable working with such volunteers, as they did not argue about Zionist ideological issues and to a great extent accepted Israeli policy as coming from Mount Sinai. "However, our comfort points up their weaknesses. . . . That comfort, which was perhaps useful in the past, should not be indulged further," he cautioned.

Similarly, the support for Israel given by the American Federation of Labor and the Congress of Industrial Organizations, the two large pro-Israel labor organizations, could not be sustained for long, Livneh observed. These unions were helpful mainly because of their sympathy with the Jewish labor unions. But the so-called Jewish unions had long lost their Jewish membership, and within a few years even their Jewish leadership would fade away.

The key question that Livneh addressed was the future of the American Zionist movement. If, he warned, it was not transformed into a national educational movement, then it was doomed, and its financial and political capacity to support Israel would come to an end. The consequences of the movement's problems were alarming and were already visible, namely in the steep decline in the UJA's projected income for 1951 and in the share of funds allotted to Israel. Moreover, the vacuum created by the demise of the Zionist movement, Livneh predicted, would soon be filled by the American Jewish Committee, which would serve as the "decisive arbiter" vis-à-vis Israel. This non-Zionist organization would then

> determine the amount of "permissible" political and financial support for Israel. Even now the leaders of the Committee exert a great amount of influence on the local welfare funds, and endeavor to appear in the public eye as helping Israel—so long as this fits in with their "American obligations." . . . Their ambition is to appear as the representatives of American Jewry on all issues—including Israel.

Livneh admitted that he did not know "whether Zionist leaders, utilizing their position in the UJA, had attempted to pressure Israel," but he was certain that "Blaustein would not hesitate to do it. He would not be influenced by the Jewish Agency or the Zionist Congress." Livneh pointed out that his personal relationships with Blaustein, Proskauer, and the staff of the committee were exceedingly cordial, and he liked working with them. His criticism was not personal but motivated by Zionist considerations. The present alarming situation, he predicted, would result "in the paradoxical condition in which the rise of the State of Israel would bring about the disintegration of Zionism in the largest Diaspora, and the dependence of Israel on non-Zionist elements."

Lastly, Ben-Gurion's emissary drew up a plan for revitalizing American Zionism. Incorporating some of the ideas put forward by Daniel Frisch and the Rifkind Report, the plan aimed at raising the status of Zionism to become a major force in the life of the American Jewish community by developing a Hebraic-cultural and national way of life in Jewish homes and clubs. The innovative aspect of the plan was Livneh's suggestion that American Zionists "take over" key fund-raising institutions, namely federations and welfare funds.[46]

For all its innovation, however, the plan reflected Livneh's incomplete grasp of the nature of American Jewry. Although he made a genuine intellectual effort to arrive at practical solutions based on an impartial understanding of the American situation, he was—possibly unwittingly—operating according to the traditional Zionist premise of the centrality of the Jewish national home, and his definition of Zionism was still rooted in the principle of the negation of exile. "Zionism," he remarked in the report, "means the Jew's resistance to his own exile," an implied definition of America as exile vehemently opposed not only by the non-Zionists of the American Jewish Committee, but by the American Zionists themselves. On that score there was no difference between Abba Hillel Silver and Jacob Blaustein. Although Silver, in contrast to Blaustein and the non-Zionists, deeply believed in the ethnic unity of the Jewish people, viewing it as "one historic community,"[47] he nevertheless maintained that "the majority of the Jews of the world will, in the days to come, continue to live outside of the State of Israel," pointing out that this had been the case ever since the destruction of the first Temple, when the number of Jews in the dispersion far exceeded that in Palestine.[48]

Silver's future role in the Zionist movement was, in fact, one of Livneh's concern's. Although Ben-Gurion had instructed Livneh to "completely and unequivocally" block any activity leading to Silver's reinstatement in the leadership of the WZO,[49] Livneh reported to Ben-Gurion that he could see that Silver's backers had no intention of giving up this aim. Because Silver was not interested in the presidency of the ZOA, Livneh confidentially suggested to Ben-Gurion that he offer him the chairmanship of the Zionist Executive in Jerusalem. That way he could fill a major Zionist role in the Diaspora. Moreover, achieving this position would put Silver in Mapai's debt, and thus an old wound might be healed without great political risk. Ben-Gurion, however, adamantly refused to patch things up with Silver and steadfastly opposed his return to a leadership position, having apparently concluded that two monumental egos stood little chance of productive cooperation.

While Ben-Gurion, by dispatching Eliezer Livneh to the United States, chose to bypass available sources of information at the Israeli embassy in Washington and at the various consulates across the country, Moshe Sharett attached great importance to reports by Israeli diplomats, and to the perceptive appraisals by Teddy Kollek, a veteran expert on the United States who headed the American Department at the Foreign Office.

Significantly, the picture revealed in the diplomats' reports differed little from Livneh's observations. After two years of the existence of the State of Israel, Zvi Zinder, the press attaché at the Washington embassy, pointed out in March 1950 that American Jewry had grown weary of incessant appeals "for aid in every form for immigrants, for clothes, for political parties, for scientific institutions, for food, for political intervention."[50] Consequently, many sympathetic American Jews found refuge in the less committing and less demanding ambience of "non-Zionist Americanism." Moreover, the United Jewish Appeal effort had been hurt by the internecine rivalries between the Silver and Montor factions, and contributors were less forthcoming. "More and more the Jews need shots in the arms and it is becoming obvious that the UJA must spend more and more to bring in less and less," Zinder observed. Though the UJA fund-raising techniques were "magnificently executed," they were inevitably hampered by the diminuendo following the dramatic events of the Israeli War of Independence and the creation of the state. Israel's appeal had begun to lose its luster. "The patient is setting up a resistance to the toxin and a sense of desperation and frustration has gripped the whole Jewish community," stated Zinder.

Contrary to Sharett's assessment, Zinder perceived the dual loyalty issue as the "greatest obstacle" to the strengthening of American Jewish-Israel relations, and he complained bitterly about the absence of a coherent effort to offset the damage done by those who raised this issue. To be sure, he reported, Hadassah had tackled the problem head on, arguing that "it was good Americanism to support Israel in any fashion," while others stressed that "the declared foreign policy of the United States [was] to support democracy everywhere—and Israel is a democracy."[51] But Zinder was still worried.

Another problematic area with damaging consequences for Israel's image and for the UJA effort, he pointed out, was the plethora of campaigns and missions for aid:

> All of the political parties in Israel, have sent missions not once but many times to the United States to plead special causes either in funds or moral assistance. . . . They have all been available to the press and have taken a full-blown opportunity to sound off on many issues, even to criticism of the United States and its attitude. As guests here that is inexcusable and it has had serious repercussions at times.

No less incongruous, Zinder argued, was the phenomenon of Israeli parties' maintaining branches in America, which was incomprehensible in Washington or anywhere else. Moreover, "this has mitigated against a unified approach to Washington on basic issues, and has allowed the State Department to use its facilities to becloud major issues further by pointing to major divergencies in Israel's parties and to point to these parties' American representatives."

The tendency of Israeli leaders to interfere in American Jewish internal affairs was also sharply criticized by Zinder. For example, mediation efforts in the Silver-Montor controversy by Berl Locker, chairman of the Zionist Executive in Jerusalem, were viewed by many American Jewish leaders as interference in the internal affairs of American Jewry, "and they fiercely resented it," he stated. So was Ben-Gurion's "unfortunate statement" regarding American Jewish youngsters coming to Israel. "You cannot say to American Jewry, give us help, and have one hand outstretched for aid, and at the same time have a knife in the other hand to stab this or that organization or leader." What was called for, Zinder advised, was respect for American Jewish sensibilities. "They are willing to help but they don't want Israel interfering in their affairs any more than Israel wants them to interfere in its affairs. . . . In other words, mutual respect, not political recrimination, is the order of the day."

Zinder advocated a less parochial approach than Livneh's blueprint for the renaissance of American Zionism. Despite an understandable Israeli affinity for the Zionist groups, Zinder advised that "Israel cannot afford, and must not be accused of, partisanship in their favor to the exclusion of all others. Some Jews don't want to associate with the Zionists in the United States, yet are able and willing to be of help to Israel in many ways." Their influence and help should not be discounted by "cynicism and expressions of 'Johnny come lately' to the bandwagon of Israel." The appeal of Israel must be made universal to all kinds of Jews, in community centers, youth camps, parochial schools, synagogues, and welfare agencies. This conclusion did not preclude the urgent need for the revitalization of American Zionism, a goal that Zinder felt could be accomplished with the rise of a new, young, and vigorous leadership.

Notwithstanding the sharp tone of Zinder's criticism—almost an indictment—of the approach of the Israeli leadership, his conclusion was not as pessimistic as Livneh's. "The potential of good among American Jewry is tremendous, so much so that it is a shame to see it frittered away in relation to Israel through organizational rivalries, internecine warfare and lack of understanding in Israel of how to deal with them." To be sure, he observed, the Jews are tired of incessant appeals for aid to Israel, "but this does not detract from [their] desire to be helpful. They want to get off the political hook so as to save their own position here, and that is [an] understandable attitude no matter how much it is derided by the more heated Zionists and representatives of Israel." [52]

Significantly, it was Moshe Sharett who a year previously, in 1949, had cogently set forth the principles and parameters of Israel's approach to the Diaspora, and toward American Jewry in particular, in formulating foreign policy. Because Israel had ties with Jews everywhere, he explained, it had to maintain a much larger representation than the country's small size and difficult financial situation warranted. Precisely because of this financial situation, Israel's foreign minister would have to undertake fund-raising trips, an unusual task in the diplomatic context. However, beyond Israel's desperate need to raise funds, Sharett explained, the state also had a responsibility to the Diaspora:

> The time has passed since we were in need of political assistance from American Jewry. We do not need such help. We maintain our relations with the United States government on an equal footing, qualitatively speaking. Diaspora Jews are not responsible for our foreign policy, and they need not express an opinion in this regard. If there is any responsibility, it is a one-way street. We are responsible toward them, but they are not responsible for us. However, we always remember that the outside world would judge them according to us. We are aware that our behavior, attitude and policy might affect them—and we therefore take it into consideration." [53]

While Sharett's optimism in those early halcyon days regarding Israel's ability to dispense with American Jewry's political assistance may have been somewhat naïve, his observation about the effects of Israel's behavior on the Diaspora proved apt and prescient.

4

Following the ambassadors' briefing, Ben-Gurion convened a brainstorming meeting in his office in Jerusalem on the same topic—Our Approach Toward American Jewry—on 25 July 1950. [54] The fourteen people who attended were all intensely involved in various aspects of this question. Because past ideologies proved untenable in the American situation, according to Ben-Gurion's analysis, the Israeli approach to American Jewry should therefore be discussed as if those ideologies were "non-existent." What Ben-Gurion aimed at was a free and open discussion, even if it meant slaughtering sacred cows, with the goal of clarifying the potential give-and-take that existed between the two Jewish centers.

The discussion at first revolved around the dismal failure of attempts to attract American *halutzim* to come and settle in Israel. Teddy Kollek and other participants blamed the official Israeli emissaries *(shlihim)* for doing more harm than good by using the old approaches applied in Germany and Poland in the 1930s. Most of them, he complained, disliked America, or at least did not understand it, and by warning of the appearance of an American Hitler had invited mistrust and antagonism.

Abba Eban, although not American-born, had succeeded in his few years of service there in deciphering the genetic code of American Jewry. All the familiar factors encouraging *aliyah* from other countries, he declared, were completely absent in the New World, for in the Jewish perception the land of Columbus was different:

> Culturally, America's Jews feel Americans. There is doubt whether throughout the Diaspora there ever was such a Jewish community which identified so closely with the host nation as does American Jewry. And not just Jewish leaders, even the leaders of American Zionism use the terms "our country," "our nation," "our government" in relation to the United States.

Obviously, a new approach was required here, and "no amount of negative propaganda would induce *aliyah*. What was required was positive motivation, [presenting *aliyah*] not as an act of escape from the United States but rather [laying emphasis] on the attraction of Israel."

Eban made several practical suggestions. He would not relinquish the fundamental Zionist concept of the Jewish people, because this would destroy the bridge between Israel and American Jewry, but he suggested drafting a program that would take American Jewish sensibilities into consideration. "I do not believe," he said, "that I would be able to draft a program acceptable to all, even to [the formerly anti-Zionist] Proskauer and others, but it should not make them particularly upset. The slogan which might perhaps fire their imagination is: taking part in creating a new society, from top to bottom." Professionals and scientists constituted the best candidates for *aliyah*, said Eban, and they should henceforth be considered the new *halutzim*—a heroic title hitherto bestowed only on those who toiled the land.

Like Sharett, Eban stressed the need for the study of Hebrew as a critical element in identifying with Israel. It was the vital key for breaking down cultural barriers between the two societies. Moreover, Livneh's argument that Israeli initiative was the sine qua non for bringing about Zionist regeneration was supported by Eban, whereupon this dialogue ensued:

BEN-GURION: To be sure, you are not an American, but you have spent many years living in America. What [would you expect] of this triad—Israel, the Zionist movement and American Jewry—to accomplish together? In our approach toward American Jewry, should we also include the Zionist movement?

ABBA EBAN: On the one hand we should not give up on this vehicle [the Zionist movement], which in my opinion is amenable to discipline. On the other hand, our work should not be confined to this vehicle alone. It is necessary, but not exclusive.

Moshe Sharett, characteristically analytical, criticized the entire Israeli approach to American Jewry as piecemeal—attracting immigrants, recruiting investments, fund-raising, obtaining political support—and advocated a new integrative approach. "First of all," he argued, "we should accept the existence of the Jewish Diaspora as a permanent fact." There was no alternative but to "accept this reality as something positive in Jewish life, and not as something negative. If we wish to attract these people. . . . we should not start with [the assumption] that they should be ashamed of their life [in the Diaspora]—that they are an anomaly that should be ended." On the contrary, the American Jewish Diaspora had many reasons to be proud of its role in the creation of Israel. "A [Jewish] community grew in Palestine, possessing the ability to decide [its destiny]; and a very rich Jewry developed in America, possessing political influence. These two elements brought about the creation of Israel." The Jews of America should be assured that if not for their financial and political effort, the Jewish state would never have come into being. Coming from Israel, this was indeed an unorthodox approach.

Having said this, Sharett launched an incisive counterattack on Ben-Gurion's campaign—which was almost a vendetta—against the World Zionist Organization, and in particular against the American Zionist movement. The Zionist idea, Sharett insisted, should not be reduced merely to *aliyah*. "The Zionist organization was not just an organization of *olim*. . . . One ought not deny or disqualify a person's Zionism if he did not settle in Israel. It was never done in the past, and it ought not be done now." Alluding to the rigid ideological approach of the founding fathers of modern Israel—the celebrated Second Aliyah—Sharett admonished Ben-Gurion and his generation: "The members of the Second *aliyah* must get rid of a certain heritage." While in the past they had rebelled against the kind of Zionism that did not mandate "self-realization" *(aliyah)*, their historic stand ought not lead them to "make claims which actually undermined the right of the Zionist movement to exist." If not for the British Zionist organization, whose members had no intention of leaving their homes and going to live in Palestine, the Balfour Declaration would never have been achieved. And "if not for the Balfour Declaration there would be no State of Israel today." Similarly, if not for the activity of the American

Zionist movement, comprised as it was of Zionists who would not dream of immigrating to Palestine, there would not have been a Jewish state, nor the means to sustain it.

In Sharett's view, the difference between Zionist organizations and other pro-Israel ones was the same as had existed in the past. The Zionist movement had always identified totally with, and worked exclusively for, the cause of Eretz Yisrael, and then with Israel. Its help could always be counted on in times of political or financial crisis. Israel must assign the Zionist movement a major position, Sharett advised, but it could not rely on the Zionist movement alone, inasmuch as the American Jewish Committee had often been very helpful to Israel as well.

Eliahu Elath, the outgoing Israeli ambassador in Washington, was also preoccupied with the American Jewish Committee and the question of *aliyah*. Elath, who had gained a close understanding of American Jewish life, was convinced that there was unanimity between the committee and the Zionists on this issue.

> Blaustein came here [to Jerusalem], and expressed opinions with which many Zionists identified; however, they were simply too timid to express them. Not only are the Zionists the last to support *aliyah*, they put obstacles in its path, for they are concerned that an *aliyah* from America might result in their demise. . . . the point is, they claim, that Israel's viability depends on American Jewry's strength.[55]

Ben-Gurion's response to the long discussion revealed that it reinforced two conclusions that he had reached two years previously, in 1948. The first had been expressed in a letter to Abe Feinberg in December 1948 stating that "the Zionist Movement has not yet adjusted itself to the revolutionary fact that a State of Israel has emerged. The relationship between Israel and the Diaspora cannot remain the same as before the establishment of the State." The second conclusion derived from his realization that historic differences between Zionists and non-Zionists "had lost their real meaning." Because the entire Jewish Diaspora, and American Jewry in particular, desired to assist Israel, his fertile mind had already begun the search for new forms of a "permanent partnership" between Israel and world Jewry.[56] What Ben-Gurion envisaged as a precondition for permanent partnership was a new universal Jewish ideology of pro-Israelism, which would replace traditional Zionism. This new ideology, he believed, should rest on three pillars: the State of Israel, the Bible, and the Hebrew language, which together would mold the desired sense of identification with Israel.[57]

Instead of the spent Zionist ideology, which did not speak to American Jewry, the reborn Jewish state, the Bible, and the physical manifestations of the biblical prophecies, Ben-Gurion urged, could provide the required inspiration. Plays and films could also revive Jewish consciousness even among assimilated Jews. Let them learn about Moses, the exodus, the revelation on Mount Sinai, and King David—it would resuscitate their Jewish instinct, he said. Lastly, learning the Hebrew language would forge the missing link between the two societies.

Ben-Gurion envisaged the creation of a headquarters for planning and coordinating educational work in the Diaspora in order to implement his new approach. This center could initially operate from Mapai, his own party, he suggested, although later, he said, it would become a government project.[58] However, while the ambassadors' and the prime minister's meetings demonstrated that the government officials involved had analyzed the problems incisively, appropriate solutions were not devised. This was particularly true with regard to Ben-Gurion's idea of effecting a new kind of Israel-centered, state-based partnership with American Jewry, which was shelved when Ben-Gurion was forced to devote highest priority to the country's grave economic situation caused by his policy of unlimited immigration. Indeed, the massive ingathering of exiles threatened to bring about the financial bankruptcy of the young state. Economic salvation, the prime minister realized, could come only from two sources: the U.S. government and American Jewry.

5

Ben-Gurion launched one of his most daring initiatives, aimed at averting financial disaster while allowing the unlimited-immigration policy to continue, in the summer of 1950. The groundwork was prepared in a series of meetings in Jerusalem at Ben-Gurion's urgent invitation, beginning at the end of July and attended by several cabinet members—Moshe Sharett, Golda Meyerson (later Meir), and Levy Eshkol—Jewish Agency leaders, and experts such as Teddy Kollek, Eliahu Elath, Abba Eban, and Reuven Shiloah.[59] Several American members of the Jewish Agency also flew in—Nahum Goldmann, Rose Halprin, and Baruch Zuckerman—as did Henry Montor. Subsequently, Eliezer Kaplan, Israel's exacting minister of finance, and Joseph Schwartz, director general of the JDC, also participated.

The atmosphere at the meetings was tense in light of the outbreak of the Korean War several weeks previously and uncertainty about how it might affect Ben-Gurion's initiative. The prime minister was completely frank, even brutal, in describing Israel's critical situation:

> Some of us think that there must be a new start in our work. We cannot go on living from hand to mouth. . . . Some of us . . . ask for a reduction in immigration. I hear that the Joint [the Joint Distribution Committee] will not be able to pay for transport after October, and we will have to find an additional amount of three and a half million dollars, at the present rate of immigration, in order to pay for transportation. But this is the easiest thing to pay for. The main thing is the economic absorption of the people here.

The rate of immigration was increasing, and although the number of immigrants in the transit camps had decreased from 90,000 four months previously to just over 65,000, this slight improvement was deceptive, because the real crisis loomed ahead: 600,000–800,000 Jews would have to be brought in within the next few years.

These additional immigrants, Ben-Gurion stressed, lived in *galut*, in conditions of distress, and their *aliyah* to Israel demanded emergency measures:

> This includes Jewry in Eastern Europe and [Middle Eastern] countries. Their number must be between 600,000 to a million. This is the urgent problem facing the Jewish people and facing Israel. . . . You know that we passed a law [the Law of Return of July 1950, investing all Jews with the legal right to immigrate to Israel]. . . . But [even] if there were no law we [must] accept them, whether . . . there is housing [or not]. Or [whether] there is employment or not. If the Jews from Rumania [are] allowed to [get out] next year . . . we must take them in. The same thing applies to Iraq, Persia and other countries. Whether the Jews living in the [Western] Diaspora want to come or not it is their business. . . . But [the Jews] in the *galut* [are] our problem, and the number is about a million, [excluding] Russia, where, for the time being, they are not allowed to leave. And unless we make preparations and work out plans and . . . are able to implement the plans, this kind of immigration may turn into a catastrophe for them and for Israel.

The danger of a world war erupting from the Korean conflict, although discounted by Ben-Gurion, could not be ignored. This danger added urgency to his initiative, for the possibility existed that there might be only a few years of peace left to save the Jews of the *galut*. His ambitious plan envisaged taking in 600,000–700,000 Jews within three years at the rate of 200,000 or more a year, thereby nearly doubling the population, at a cost of $1.5 billion. Where would the money come from? The State of Israel, Ben-Gurion proposed, would provide 20 percent of the sum or perhaps slightly more through taxation, and hopefully the U.S. government and the Western Diaspora, including American Jewry, would be induced to provide $1 billion. Israel would then apply to Washington either for a "loan, for help [a grant], or for both."

The underlying premise of Ben-Gurion's financial plan was his expectation of aid from Washington. Although aware of the implications of the Korean conflict, he shrewdly surmised that "this help from the American government is important not only in itself . . . [but] the [response] on the part of American Jewry will be much greater if they know that the American government and the president are behind us." He announced that the unprecedented task of securing Washington's aid was to be assigned to Abba Eban, Israel's new ambassador to Washington, and to the American Jewish community.

The Israeli leader also impressed on the participants the urgent need for a revolutionary approach to solve the problem of the desperate state of Israel's economy. "You know our negative balance [of payment]—our export is something like 12 percent of our import, and the question of foreign currency is becoming more and more fatal. . . . We must make a new start, we must view the thing as a whole—the entire problem." Herein lay Ben-Gurion's best leadership qualities: tenacity, ruthless determination, and an uncanny ability to focus on the single most important task and drive this home to his audience.

> This is the second phase of establishing the State. The State was not established for the sake of [its present population]. . . . What will become of Jews in England or America? They will take care of themselves, or history will take care of them. . . . [And] the question of the status of Zionists, and so forth, we will leave to the [Zionist] Actions Committee. . . . But the real problem is a million Jews . . . for whom there is no other choice; there is no other choice for us either. We have to bring them over.

It was no accident that the first participant whose response Ben-Gurion sought was Henry Montor. True to his reputation for bluntness, Montor, after citing the worrisome figures that showed the steady decline of the UJA intake since its 1948 peak, challenged Ben-Gurion to name the groups or organizations that would undertake to raise the huge amount of money that was projected. American Zionists, he noted, were the bête noire. This dialogue then followed:

MR. BEN-GURION: Suppose state and Zionism speak in one voice—the Jewish Agency, the Government of Israel, the Zionists in America, even the Rabbi of Cleveland—[all] speak in one voice.

MR. MONTOR: If I touch upon a field which is somewhat delicate, I ask for indulgence and perhaps my original plan not to say anything would have been better. . . . I believe the Zionist movement is an impediment to the State of Israel these days. . . . You are asking that the Jews of America provide a billion dollars in the next three years. Let us leave that aside for a moment. Whether 300 million or a billion, there is no organ in the Zionist forces in America which can mobilize the Jews of America to that kind of imaginative, constructive thinking. The Zionist movement consists of groups which are concerned primarily with their own affairs. Each has its special message, special activity and each is convinced that the salvation of Israel depends exclusively upon the fulfillment of that task.

Montor was emphatic that the "mass support" for the gigantic task that lay ahead required the creation of a "new instrumentality which will establish a link between America and Israel so that American contributors will be made to feel they are not just used but are useful." Montor, who was thereby reinforcing Ben-Gurion's concept, reiterated the "Friends of Israel" idea, an overall organization encompassing all Jews regardless of their ideology, "united as an effective buttress for Israel not merely for funds but to serve as a backbone of [a] loan."

Ben-Gurion's far-reaching initiative raised several fundamental questions, Montor said. The first concerned methods to raise the staggering amount of money that was needed, whether it would be "a loan, a gift, or a combination." But the question of method could not be divorced from the controversy over the role of American Zionism, namely, which American Jewish organization was in charge with respect to Israel and could take on the responsibility of fund-raising. Lastly, there was the question of Israel's policy of neutrality in the cold war and its effect on the chances of receiving U.S. aid.

In the event, the question of determining the appropriate method for raising funds was perhaps the least difficult, although implementation was complicated. Similarly, the question of Israel's cold war policy was resolved as well. The controversy over the role of American Zionism, however, refused to die. It raged throughout the Jerusalem meetings, pitting Ben-Gurion and Montor in one camp versus Rose Halprin, president of Hadassah, and Nahum Goldmann, chairman of the American section of the Jewish Agency, in the other. Struggling under the ever-growing burden of leading Israel, and deeply concerned by the danger of an imminent world war, Ben-Gurion vented his frustration on Halprin, who had devoted her life to the Zionist cause:

> We are in a serious position and we count on you to do your duty. You in America can do a little more than you do now. . . . There may be a [world] war. . . . It will be a very serious business for everybody. For us, even if the war does not come to this country, we will die of hunger. We are surrounded by Arab countries. The only way out is the sea, and that may be blocked. We must make an effort to provide for our own food [as quickly as possible.] I know this has nothing to do with Zionist policy, but it has something to do with our survival.

The controversy gained momentum as Henry Montor lashed out at the ZOA, imploring "the Zionist movement to permit and welcome and mobilize these men [non-Zionists] who want to help the State of Israel in the ways that they choose, because the Zionist movement, for reasons which are immaterial at this moment, has no place for them." Montor reiterated the idea of creating a new medium that would allow "the link to Israel [to] become universal in America and not [remain] the monopoly of the Zionist organization."

The counterattack was led by Nahum Goldmann, who, after Silver's resignation (which he had helped engineer), had become the dominant figure in American Zionism. Goldmann derided Montor's "Friends of Israel" idea, questioning the commitment of these supporters. "If there [should] be a conflict between Israel and America," he posited, [Abba Hillel] Silver will be with Israel. I am not sure where your Friends will be." Goldmann also suggested that Montor's conceptual proposition in fact veiled a personal ambition to replace the present leadership of the Jewish Agency in New York. Dismissing Montor's proposal, Goldmann concluded that the American Zionist movement should not be dismantled, but rather must be reformed and mobilized for the fund-raising campaign ahead.

The participants did, however, address themselves to the practical issues at hand. Montor, unrivaled in fund-raising expertise, mooted another possibility for securing Washington's aid: a grant of $500 million. He explained that the concept of "grant" was used advisedly, because it was inconceivable for Israel, in its desperate economic situation, "to think in terms of a repayable loan unless it is prepared to accept the consequences of default in the years ahead." But, he warned, there was a catch. In order to enable American Jewry to support the demand for Washington's aid, "Israel has to be prepared to assume all the political consequences that grow out of such a demand." That is, Israel must be willing to forgo its policy of neutrality in the cold war and associate itself with America "politically and militarily." Unless this association happened, Montor cautioned, American Jews "will certainly hesitate. They will reason as Americans, not merely as Jews, and I think it is fair to say that most American Jews will think first as Americans and secondly as Jews. Their whole attitude to Israel will be affected [by what will] be undertaken, whether it is loans, investments or gifts." Montor's straightforward advice reinforced the growing Israeli realization, discernible even before the outbreak of the Korean War, that a neutrality policy had become untenable,[60] a message that Jacob Blaustein would convey to Ben-Gurion around the same time.

Ben-Gurion's initiative was given final shape at an emergency conference called in Jerusalem in early September 1950 (later confirmed at a larger gathering in Washington). The conference, held at the King David Hotel, was attended by forty-four American Jewish business and communal leaders, both Zionist and non-Zionist.[61] Several participants urged the Israeli government to reconsider the policy of unlimited immigration in order to avert financial disaster, but the majority realized, as Joint Distribution Committee (JDC) Director General Joseph Schwartz put it, that

> Israel could not limit immigration even if it would wish to do so. At the present time 8,500 Jews are being sent out of Rumania to Israel every month and over this the Government of Israel has no control. To be a realist is to recognize that immigration cannot be reduced, unless the Government of Israel sends ships back and thus creates an *Aliyah Beth* [illegal immigration] against the Government of Israel.[62]

The series of meetings in Jerusalem produced an innovative Four-Point Program projected for the coming three years that aimed at raising $1.5 billion in the form of: (1) intergovernmental aid, (2) UJA gift money, (3) private capital investments, and (4) a bond issue.[63] Undoubtedly the policy of unlimited immigration that necessitated the Four-Point Program was a gamble in human suffering, but it was a gamble that had to be taken. David Horowitz,

Israel's astute director general of the Ministry of Finance, explained the challenge aptly at a Hadassah National Board meeting in April 1951:

> We in Israel have substituted the theory of comparative costs by a theory of comparative suffering, which means that we don't apply the criterion of possibility. We don't apply to the policy of unlimited immigration the criterion whether these people can be soundly and economically integrated in the life of the country. . . . But whether the suffering which they will endure in the transit camps of Israel will be greater or smaller than the suffering which they would have to endure in the countries of persecution from which they come, taking into account not only the material but the psychological factors—personal safety, anguish, fear, oppression, cultural uprooting—[as well as the] physical suffering."[64]

In the end, the gamble did succeed, but at a heavy human price for the hundreds of thousands of immigrants from Eastern Europe and the Moslem countries housed in tents and shacks during their first years of absorption. Nevertheless, under the circumstances, with the trauma of the Holocaust painfully recent and the country suffering from an acute lack of capital, Israel had no choice. The oppressive Communist and Moslem countries could seal their gates at any moment. It was now or never, and Israel, and the *olim,* opted for now.

In keeping with its traditional insistence on remaining independent of organized Jewish life, the American Jewish Committee stayed away from the Jerusalem conferences, underscoring once again the divergent agendas of Israel and the non-Zionist leadership. Whereas Ben-Gurion gave highest priority to the implementation of the Four-Point Program, Blaustein remained concerned about policy statements emanating from Israel that might stoke the embers of the dual loyalty issue.

4

The Blaustein–Ben-Gurion
Understanding of 1950

1

THE EARLY SKIRMISHES between the American Jewish Committee and Ben-Gurion were not to be the last ones, showing that the process of adjustment by American Jewry to the existence of a Jewish state was by no means over. This realization was evident toward the end of 1949 when Israeli as well as American Zionist policy statements evoked new crises, impelling Ben-Gurion to take certain measures lest they jeopardize the crucial cooperation of the non-Zionists in the Four-Point Program.

An innocuous speech by Ben-Gurion in Tel Aviv in November 1949, reported in the *New York Herald Tribune,* aroused a hue and cry among non-Zionists in America. In it the prime minister warned Diaspora Zionist donors that their gifts would not give them any influence over Israel's policies, a warning that was evidently directed at Abba Hillel Silver and his followers in the ZOA after they had been accused by Morgenthau and Montors of trying to use American Jewish financial clout for just such purposes. The main thrust of the speech was that Zionists needed to adjust their thinking to the new reality of "an independent, sovereign and pioneer state,"[1] but this was not the point for an AJC member who wrote to Blaustein from Dallas, Texas. What bothered him was the prime minister's use of the expression "Israel promotes the gathering of the exiles from their dispersion," which, the Texas member alleged, proved that Ben-Gurion was going back on his assurances to Blaustein of 18 October 1949, that he would call for the immigration to Israel of only a few American Jews with special technical skills. What especially rankled the AJC member, he informed Blaustein, was Ben-Gurion's use of the term "nation" (in fact, "the national vanguard" was used to describe the

Zionist movement in its role of bringing immigrants to Israel). This use constituted an explicit justification for the long-held position of the American Council for Judaism. Enough, the AJC member cried.

> Our Committee must stop pussy-footing. The time calls for courage and forthrightness—not dissembling. . . . Now, let us not continue to damn the American Council for Judaism. The Council attempted to do the job that the Committee failed to do. Let us cooperate with the Council and forget the petty bickering and personality clashes. The Council has been right. Why not recognize this patent fact?[2]

Vigorously rising to this challenge, Blaustein referred the complainant to later letters from Ben-Gurion showing that the Israeli leader had not reneged on his prior assurance that Israel needed only "selective immigration, primarily of technicians" from America. But the main problem here, Blaustein knew, was the extreme sensitivity of many non-Zionists to Israeli pronouncements. Having gained a deeper insight into the intricacies of Israeli-Diaspora relations since his visit to Israel in March 1949, he now recommended a less excitable reaction to Israeli statements:

> I regard it as essential, as apparently you do not, to make a very clear-cut distinction between *personal attitudes* and *official policies* [emphasis in original]. I know perfectly well that there are people, some of them prominent in Israel and in the Zionist movement in this country, who hold to the concept of political world Jewish nationalism, which the American Jewish Committee has so steadfastly repudiated, and will always repudiate.

Moreover, Blaustein argued, Ben-Gurion's use of the term "nation" was legitimate. "That Israel is a nation is an incontrovertible fact. The dependence of that nation on financial aid from American Jews obviously creates problems for its officials. Their fear that the power of the purse may be used by American Zionists to interfere in Israel's internal affairs is by no means an unnatural one." Ben-Gurion was merely addressing that fear, he pointed out. "Nor am I unduly disturbed," he said, "about the other quotation regarding 'the gathering of the exiles from their dispersion.'" Indeed, "many Jews of Eastern Europe and other parts of the Old World have regarded themselves as exiles. Even in this country there are probably some Jews who do not feel secure or deeply rooted in the American environment," though the vast majority viewed themselves as Americans, and their self-image would certainly not be "affected by the mere rhetoric of such expressions as 'gathering of the exiles.' " But all were agreed that Israel should not interfere in the internal affairs of the American Jewish community. So far, he said, Israel had not done that, "and I most vehemently repudiate the allegation that the American Jewish Committee is either 'pussy-footing' or 'dissembling.' "

Lastly, addressing the matter of his perennial nemesis, the American Council for Judaism, Blaustein declared: "We shall be happy to cooperate with the Council to the extent that we can agree on the proper implementation of the ideology which we hold in common." But the committee, and he himself, would not tolerate the council's publicity methods, which called into question the loyalty of American Jews. He asked his colleague from Dallas:

> I wonder how you yourself reacted, when you read the item in the Dallas *Morning News* a couple of weeks ago on Lessing Rosenwald's speech in your city. Did you really think it helpful for the Dallas public to learn from a prominent Jew that the idea that "the Jew should separate his religion from his nationality in the same manner as other religious groups do . . . is a rather hard idea to put across"?[3]

Meanwhile, another storm was brewing. A front-page report in the *Jewish Morning Journal* by its Israeli correspondent described a celebration in December 1949 at Haifa port "where immigrants embarking from the Israeli ship 'Negba' brought the total Israeli population to one million Jews."[4] The correspondent also reported on a speech delivered on the historic occasion by Eliahu Dobkin, the Jewish Agency Executive member in charge of immigration, who "spoke with bitterness against Jews in America and other Western democracies." Where would the second million Israelis come from, Dobkin wondered, considering that Israel could not rely on immigration from the Arab countries or from behind the Iron Curtain, while "American Jews are philanthropic Zionists. They don't think of Zionism for themselves, and the redemption of the country is not for them but for others."[5] Dobkin's speech, the reporter explained, reflected the bitterness harbored by "the most important Israeli leaders" toward American Jewry's "indifference" regarding *aliyah* to Israel.

Dobkin's chastisement of American Jewry, which followed a similar rebuke a month earlier, put the Israeli embassy in Washington on the spot. The counselor at the embassy, Moshe Keren, rushed off a letter to a senior official at the Foreign Office in Jerusalem, Michael Comay, warning of the harm Dobkin's speech could do. From an Israeli point of view, he said, the speech was perfectly correct—Zionism indeed meant the ingathering of exiles. But for the overwhelming majority of American Jewry it was highly inflammatory. There was a consensus among American Jews, Keren noted, that "not only was there no reason for them to leave their homeland, but even the suggestion to immigrate to Israel seemed insulting, or even [worse] was perceived as propaganda designed to cast doubt on their loyalty to their country. American Jews are highly sensitive to any attempt—be it the most modest one—to influence them in a direction which contradicts this belief."[6] Dual loyalty, "whose validity is denied by us," was in fact a real issue, for although Israel still enjoyed great popularity and friendship, American Jewish communities were pressing for a greater share of the UJA allocations for urgent local needs long neglected because of Israeli needs.

Keren called for greater sensitivity in Israel:

> Every word uttered in Israel, in particular if pronounced by high officials, is transmitted here and receives a surprising amount of attention. Our opponents exploit every argument and pretext supplied unintentionally by us. Ben-Gurion's statement [urging U.S. parents to send their children to Israel for permanent settlement] evoked protests and articles from coast to coast; and I am afraid that such will be the case regarding Dobkin's comments.[7]

Indeed, at a meeting between Blaustein and Berl Locker in January 1950 Blaustein protested against Dobkin's "disturbing statements" urging mass immigration by American Jews to Israel.[8]

Keren had touched upon the basic question of what it was that Israel wanted of American Jewry. If Israel wished essentially to retain their financial, moral, and political support, then, in the opinion of a growing number of Israeli representatives, it must stay away from ideological polemics, which in any case were ineffective. A propaganda campaign preaching pure Zionism was a no-win situation that would undermine the very foundations of support for Israel and jeopardize the success of the United Jewish Appeal. Such a campaign, Keren and others feared, could also push the rest of American Jewry into the enemy camp.

The year 1950 started out badly in terms of relations between Israel and the American Jewish Committee. Dobkin's speech at Haifa may have reinforced the growing conviction by many members of the committee, as Blaustein put it to Ambassador Elath in late January, that "the clarification of the Ben-Gurion statement to the Histadrut may have been the result merely of expediency."[9] Blaustein himself, ever conscious of his own and his organization's standing in the Jewish community, also explained to Elath that the committee would not settle for mere statements. What was needed was some agreement on the fundamental issues affecting Israel-American Jewry relations.

Meanwhile, the American Council for Judaism was becoming more problematic in the American Jewish scene. Anger on the part of the organized Jewish community at the council's publicity policy finally reached the boiling point in late January 1950 when the National Community Relations Advisory Council (NCRAC)—the coordinating body for the American Jewish Committee, American Jewish Congress, Anti-Defamation League, and several other organizations concerned with intergroup relations—published a sharp condemnation of the American Council for Judaism in the Anglo-Jewish press. The committee, anxious to keep the intra-Jewish fight from going public, had tried to prevent this exposure, but had finally given in, adding its voice to the NCRAC condemnation of "the small but highly vocal group of Jewish individuals known as the American Council for Judaism responsible for the publication in the nation's press of reiterated statements casting doubts on the loyalty of American Jews who have demonstrated their sympathies with Israel."[10] The statement pointed out that "the overwhelming majority of American Jews, Zionist and non-Zionist alike," cognizant of their deep religious and cultural attachment with the Jews of Israel, were fully aware of their obligation to aid Israel in the tremendous task of absorbing hundreds of thousands of homeless Jews.

Leaders of the American Jewish Committee had been meeting with the council leadership throughout 1949 in an effort to influence them "to discontinue the issuance, or sponsoring, of harmful statements in the general press," in Blaustein's words. But the committee's efforts ended in failure. Although both organizations, in Blaustein's view, were united in their opposition to the concept of Jewish nationalism in the Diaspora and what they saw as its negative effects should it spread among American Jewry and elsewhere, nevertheless the committee and the council differed fundamentally on what constituted a "nationalistic" statement. In the committee's view the council's perception was so all-encompassing as to amount to "an extreme and sweeping anti-Israeli position." Further, according to Blaustein:

We frankly do not understand what the Council hopes to gain by its particular kind of publicity in the general press. They can hardly expect to influence the statements and actions of Zionists and the Israelis by such attacks. Nor can it be believed that the favor of our fellow Americans who are not Jews will be so won. On the contrary, the latter may unfortunately be tempted to conclude: a plague on all the Jewish houses.[11]

The council had in fact dropped its publicity campaign in the general press for a while after the series of meetings with the committee leadership, but in April 1950 the campaign surfaced again. Two offensive headlines that had appeared in the *New York Times* were cited by Blaustein in a report to his colleagues:

April 23: [Morris] Ernst Warns Jews of "Making" Ghetto Separatism as "Reactionary" as Anti-Semitism, Lawyer Tells Judaism Council
April 24: Zion Critics Score Exodus to Israel[12]

What was particularly obnoxious to the president of the committee was a new aspect of the council's publicity policy as described by Lessing Rosenwald: "The Council has continued to take public questions to the public that is concerned, rejecting the ghetto diplomacy of haggling in private conferences about public issues."[13] Although Rosenwald did not identify who it was who had engaged in "ghetto diplomacy," it was clear that his attack was aimed at Blaustein's and the committee's policy of quiet diplomacy. This public assault signified the final break in relations between the two organizations. Blaustein, who had long doubted the chances of modifying the council's extreme anti-Israeli policy, concluded that their rift was indeed unbridgeable. "The long and short of it is that, out of our discussion on the council's publicity methods, there emerged a crystal-clear conviction on our part that these methods are themselves only a reflection of much deeper attitudes that are at total variance with our own, namely an anti-Israel position."[14]

The council remained a lost case and a great nuisance for Blaustein until its final demise after the 1967 Six-Day War, although he did not view it in such pernicious terms as another leading member of the committee, Murray I. Gurfein, who in 1950 called the council "a threat to the position of the Jew in America."[15]

2

The final break with the American Council for Judaism temporarily damped down one problem. It did not, however, end the periodic crises in American Jewish-Israeli relations. Blaustein, apparently less enthusiastic about Ben-Gurion's letter of clarification to Proskauer of 1 November 1949 than its recipient, found himself in a dilemma. Continuously subjected to conflicting pressures within the committee regarding the relationship with Israel,[16] he simultaneously understood the reasons for the Israeli leaders' statements. In April 1950 he decided to press for a meeting with Ben-Gurion aimed at probing the prime minister's and his government's basic concepts with regard to Israeli-Diaspora relations and, subsequently, at issuing an open, official, and binding clarification of this troublesome question. He brought up the matter in meetings in Washington with Ambassador Eliahu Elath, who understood the American Jewish community's problems, and whose unenviable job included trying to put out fires kindled by unpalatable Israeli pronouncements.

Responding to Blaustein's request, Elath prepared a tentative policy draft that could be of use to the American Jewish leader in future contacts with President Chaim Weizmann and Prime Minister Ben-Gurion. The draft stated that because many "well-meaning Jews" were reluctant to extend aid to Israel because of their grave concern over the dual loyalty issue, it was highly desirable for the government of Israel "to make it perfectly clear once again [that Israel] has no intention whatever of interfering in the internal affairs of the Jewish communities abroad, nor [is it] putting them under political obligation to Israel, as only those Jews who live in Israel have such obligation."[17]

Shortly afterward Elath was transferred to London and Abba Eban took up the ambassadorship in Washington, in addition to representing Israel at the United Nations. But Elath still kept in touch with Blaustein about his projected trip to Israel and his desire for public clarification of Israeli-Diaspora relations.[18] Attending the Israeli ambassadors' conference in July 1950 in Tel Aviv, Elath impressed on Ben-Gurion the vital need for reaching an understanding with Blaustein, following which Ben-Gurion cabled Blaustein inviting him to visit Israel as his guest "to discuss matters [of] mutual interest."[19] Elath urged Blaustein to accept the invitation and visit Israel "not only for discussion [with the] Prime Minister, but also [to] study conditions [in the] country essential for proper understanding [of] our problems."[20] Blaustein did not reply immediately, "realizing that failure to secure a satisfactory clarification [of Israel-Diaspora relations] free of any quid pro quo would prove seriously embarrassing," he recalled in his subsequent report to his colleagues.[21] He decided first to obtain a consensus from the committee's leadership on his mission, which was forthcoming, "since the Israeli authorities were fully cognizant of [Blaustein's] objective and of the unfavorable repercussions should his mission fail, [so that] it was a calculated risk that should be taken."[22] In addition, Blaustein, like many others, feared that the Korean War might turn into a full-fledged world conflagration and therefore consulted with the State Department as to his projected trip to Israel. Assistant Secretary of State for Near Eastern Affairs George McGhee, Blaustein reported, "not only urged him to go to Israel, but entrusted him with the mission of communicating certain views of our government to the Prime Minister."[23] The president of the committee accepted Ben-Gurion's invitation.

Blaustein, accompanied only by the head of the AJC foreign affairs department, Dr. Simon Segal, arrived in Israel on 13 August. Despite the summer heat, Blaustein, the thorough and meticulous workaholic, put his second visit to Israel to use not only for obtaining the intended clarification of Israel-Diaspora relations, but for an extensive tour of the country as well. He was amazed by the recovery of Jerusalem after the 1948 War of Independence, recalling that on his first visit, in April 1949, "after the siege which had almost reduced the city to starvation, Jerusalem was still a ghost town. Today, eighteen months later, 35,000 new immigrants have been settled in Jerusalem,"[24] and the city was bustling with activity and economic development. The American visitors also flew over the Negev to the new port of Elath on the Red Sea. The town, which had sprung up out of the desert only one and one-half years previously, already had a small airport, housing for the first settlers, newly dug wells, and the beginnings of a fishing industry. But what was most impressive—and problematic in its economic ramifications—was the flood of immigrants "into that little country from places where they have been discriminated against and persecuted. They are coming by the thousands from the countries behind the Iron Curtain whenever they are permitted to leave. In the last few months, the largest number has come from Rumania. And they are also coming from the Near East."[25]

Blaustein was given the VIP treatment in Israel. Although in line with the committee's traditionally independent policy, he was not scheduled to take part in the forthcoming discussions with American Jewish leaders intended to pave the way for the Four-Point Program, he met with Ben-Gurion, Moshe Sharett, most of the other senior government ministers, and key figures in finance, industry, and labor during his two-week stay. Recognizing his vast experience in industry and business, Ben-Gurion and Minister of Finance Eliezer Kaplan listened to his advice on Israel's serious economic problems and projected rehabilitation programs. He also had conferences with U.S. Ambassador to Israel James G. McDonald and his deputy, Richard Ford, as well as with Ely Palmer, the U.S. member of the United Nations Palestine Conciliation Commission. For most people it would have been a backbreaking schedule, but not for Jacob Blaustein, whose capacity for working sixteen hours a day and ability to master intricate problems under any conditions were well known.

The climax of the mission was a series of extended conferences between Blaustein, Segal, and Ben-Gurion, with several ministers and aides, leading to the now-famous Blaustein-Ben-Gurion "understanding," or "exchange of views." [26]

The first conference, on 13 August, was the longest and the most important. Blaustein and Segal were invited to a lunch at Ben-Gurion's home, where they were joined by Eliezer Kaplan, Minister of Labor Golda Meir, Eliahu Elath, and Teddy Kollek. Ben-Gurion dominated the luncheon and the meeting that followed, which lasted over five hours, with the other participants occasionally asking questions or making comments, and Jacob Blaustein "raising several points and intervening at some length on a few occasions," as reported by Simon Segal. The agenda set by Ben-Gurion consisted of two main items: a candid elucidation of the prime minister's position on Israel's relations with American Jewry, and an analysis of the situation in the country.

Giving his visitors a brief account of his personal road to Zionism in Poland under the Czarist regime and his decision to come to Eretz Yisrael nearly forty years previously, Ben-Gurion acknowledged that his brand of Zionism was not shared by all Jews or even by all Zionists. Furthermore, addressing the subject of post-1948 Zionism, "there is very little distinction," he stressed, "between American Zionists and non-Zionists. The distinction is between those who choose to remain in the countries in which they are living now and those who . . . believe that their personal happiness is possible only in a thoroughly Jewish environment." The Israeli leader also emphasized that he "fully respects the decision of those Jews who do not desire to come to Israel and does not consider them for that reason as being worse Jews than himself." In fact, he continued, "most of the Jews who are [now] coming to Israel are not Zionists, and a large number probably have never heard of Herzl and the Zionist [movement]. However, they are coming because of dire need, and some also, especially the Yemenites, because of Messianic ideals."

Blaustein interjected that on the eve of his departure to Israel, during his meeting at the State Department, George McGhee had been "very much concerned that the present rate of immigration may economically break the back of Israel and that some kind of slow-up is indicated." At this, Ben-Gurion explained how totally unacceptable to Israeli public opinion, and to himself, such an idea was. Israel's very raison d'être demanded its providing "a home to the Jews who need or desire to come, and the people of Israel would go to any length to carry out this aim." This principle applied especially to the Jews behind the Iron Curtain and in the Moslem countries, whose fate as Jews was in jeopardy, he said.

Referring again to McGhee's warning, Blaustein attempted to disabuse Ben-Gurion of the wildly held notion in Israel "that America will never permit an economic collapse and that, if the situation becomes really desperate, the American Government will help either through a direct loan or through a loan from the Import and Export Bank." Under present legislation, he pointed out, there was no chance of expecting aid from the Marshall Plan. Similarly, the policy of the Import and Export Bank was to grant loans that were justified primarily on economic grounds. Thus, while McGhee had not questioned the principle of free immigration for Jews arriving from behind the Iron Curtain, he nevertheless maintained that "some regulations will have to be established for immigration to Israel of Jews from countries where they are not in immediate danger of life, like North Africa." Ben-Gurion, while not conceding as much, implied in his response that some regulation had indeed been put into effect, which had resulted in a reduction in the immigration rate.

Ben-Gurion proceeded to outline his basic view of the Diaspora, dividing world Jewry into three categories: (1) the citizens of the State of Israel, (2) "the countries of exile from which the Jews [must] emigrate, and (3) the Jews of the free and democratic countries." Because American Jewry belonged to the third category, he fully concurred with the American Jewish Committee's basic position "that any attempt to induce the American Jews to come to Israel based on the propaganda that they are not secure or free in the United States is harmful both to the American Jewish community and to Israel." Ben-Gurion reiterated that he had no intention "[of indulging] in such propaganda," and agreed with Blaustein that "this is both harmful and futile and, therefore, foolish. Everyone has a right to be foolish but one should not abuse it." However, he pointed out, he could not "control every [Jewish] Agency official or . . . prevent . . . Israeli leaders from making statements."

But there was the rub, Blaustein interposed, touching on one of the main purposes of his mission to Israel. "The source of these statements, and who was making them, is of great importance." Their effect on the American public was a function of the importance and prominence of the Israeli leaders who made them. Therefore, he explained, "a clear and unmistakable statement by Mr. Ben-Gurion himself is of great importance and would dispel the misunderstandings that have developed and would help to change the atmosphere in the United States towards Israel, as well as . . . cut the ground from under those who attack Israel, or those who are seeking a rational excuse for refusing to support Israel."

Apparently briefed beforehand by Elath on Blaustein's intention to request a public announcement, the prime minister immediately stated his willingness to "clarify the situation," giving Elath and Kollek the task of preparing "such a statement . . . for his consideration." In fact, Ben-Gurion was no novice at working out statements with the American Jewish Committee. As far back as June 1942, during his long visit to the United States, he had conducted exhaustive secret negotiations with Maurice Wertheim, then president of the committee, that had resulted in a draft known as the "Cos Cob Formula." In it Wertheim and several of his colleagues agreed to support the eventual establishment of "an autonomous commonwealth" in Palestine, at such time that the Jews would constitute a majority there, while Ben-Gurion, addressing the dual loyalty question, gave his word that the creation of such a commonwealth "will in no way affect the political or civil status and allegiance of Jews who are citizens of any other country."[27] The committee, however, eventually rejected the Cos Cob Formula, a consequence of Wertheim's weak leadership and the adamant opposition of the anti-Zionist camp led by Proskauer.

But history did not repeat itself in Jerusalem this time. In the course of long and complex negotiations, Ben-Gurion and Blaustein agreed that a clarification statement would be issued on 23 August in the form of an exchange of views. The venue for this important event was to be the stately King David Hotel, where an official luncheon was given by the prime minister in Blaustein's honor. Present were six cabinet members, the chairman of the Jewish Agency Executive, American Chief of UN Military Observers in Palestine General William E. Riley, and other dignitaries. David Ben-Gurion prefaced his carefully written statement with a warm welcome to Jacob Blaustein, whom he described as "a representative of the great Jewry of the United States to whom Israel owes so much." Ben-Gurion saw in his American Jewish guest one of "the finest examples" of the laudable American Jewish tradition of aiding and protecting Jewish communities in distress throughout the world.

The prime minister then moved on to the delicate issue at hand—clarifying "some of the problems which have arisen in regard to the relationship between the people of Israel and the Jewish communities abroad, in particular the Jewish community in the United States."[28] In essence, these problems were the historic controversial issues of American Jewry's concern about dual loyalty as well as the question of who spoke for world Jewry, and the more recent issue of the immigration of American Jews to Israel. Ben-Gurion was explicit and unequivocal on these problems:

> The Jews of the United States, as a community and as individuals, have only one political attachment and that is to the United States of America. They owe no political allegiance to Israel. In the first statement which the representative of Israel made before the United Nations after [its] admission to the international organization, he clearly stated, without any reservation, that the State of Israel represents or speaks . . . on behalf of its own citizens [only], and in no way presumes to represent or speak in the name of the Jews who are citizens of any other country.

Ben-Gurion went on to endorse a doctrine of noninterference in the internal affairs of world Jewry. "The Government and the people of Israel," he said, "fully respect the right and integrity of the Jewish communities in other countries to develop their own mode of life . . . in accordance with their own needs and aspirations." Moreover, he said, Israel fully understood that "any weakening of American Jewry, any disruption of its communal life, any lowering of its sense of security, any diminution of its status, is a definite loss to Jews everywhere and to Israel in particular." Because the success of the Israeli endeavor depended on cooperation with American Jewry, "we, therefore, are anxious that nothing should be said or done which could in the slightest degree undermine the sense of security and stability of American Jewry."

Addressing the controversial topic of the immigration of American Jews to Israel, the prime minister reiterated that Israel needed American Jews with technical and managerial know-how in order to implement its development programs speedily, but their decision to come, whether "permanently or temporarily, [is at the] discretion of each American Jew himself. It is entirely a matter of his own volition." The same applied to the immigration of *halutzim* to Israel, he said, although he was hopeful that they would come not only from the countries of exile characterized by oppression, but also from the countries of freedom and equality. Their decision to come, of course, must also be one of free choice.

Blaustein's response was twice as long as Ben-Gurion's speech. Sharing with his audience his deep impressions of Israel's "tremendous progress," as well as his gratification at the Jewish state's commitment to democracy and opposition to totalitarianism, he proceeded to analyze the meaning of Israel's birth for Diaspora Jews:

> While Israel has naturally placed some burdens on Jews elsewhere, particularly in America, it has, in turn, meant much to Jews throughout the world. For hundreds of thousands in Europe, Africa and the Middle East it has provided a home in which they can attain their full stature of human dignity for the first time. In all Jews, it has inspired pride and admiration, even though in some instances, it has created passing headaches. Israel's rebirth and progress, coming after the tragedy of European Jewry in the 1930's and in World War II, has done much to raise Jewish morale. Jews in America and everywhere can be [prouder] than ever of their Jewishness.[29]

By "burdens" and "headaches" Blaustein probably meant not only Ben-Gurion's and Dobkin's past statements, but the very essence of Israel's Zionist mission, in particular its manifestation through Zionist propaganda in America. Condemning the Israeli perception of American Jewry as living in exile, he declared: "To American Jews, America is home. . . . They believe in the future of a democratic society in the United States under which all citizens, irrespective of creed or race, can live on terms of equality. They further believe that, if democracy should fail in America, there would be no future for democracy anywhere in the world," in which case Israel's existence would also be insecure.

By the same token he strongly objected to any intention on Israel's part to interfere in the internal affairs of Diaspora communities, or to any presumption to speak in their name. Moreover, he said: "The future development of Israel, spiritual, social as well as economic, will largely depend upon a strong and healthy Jewish community in the United States and other free democracies," clearly implying that the Western Diaspora should be viewed not just as Israel's equal, but as a permanent component of Jewish existence.

Returning to the aim of his mission, he concluded by cautioning that soothing statements were not enough, and that what was needed was "unmistakable evidence that the responsible leaders of Israel, and the organizations connected with it [the Zionist movement], fully understand that future relations between the American Jewish community and the State of Israel must be based on mutual respect for one another's feelings and needs, and on the preservation of the integrity of the two communities and their institutions."

That the resolution of the ideological differences and conflicts of interest between the two sides required patience, perseverance, and, above all, willingness to compromise was attested to in an account of the Blaustein-Ben-Gurion negotiations by Simon Segal:

> It was touch and go [all the time]; we had ups and downs and until [the] last night we still did not know whether or not we will get a satisfactory statement.
> We met with Ben-Gurion twice . . . [for] eight hours. . . . The statement that we have finally got . . . is not all we have suggested. It is a compromise between our original suggestions and their proposals and they consider that they went as far as they possibly could go to meet our point of view. You may note that Mr. Ben-Gurion is definitely stating that Jews of America are not exiles and by implication, that all their campaigns of "gathering of the exiles" do not apply to American Jews. This was a point very hard for him to accept but he finally did agree.
> He also reasserts that they have no desire to interfere in the internal affairs of the Jews outside of Israel and that they respect the integrity of these communities to develop their mode of life and their indigenous (this word was very hard for them to swallow) institutions.
> The negotiations and the bickerings were quite difficult and it is only through the persistence of Mr. Blaustein that this result was finally achieved. He had to use honey and vinegar, threatened them to leave without any agreement, reminded them time and again that he was here at their invitation and came here on the assumption that they had basically agreed with our position and so on and so on from early morning until late at night. But here we are and I do not think that any other human being could have achieved more. Personally I believe that, while it does not dot all the i's and cross all the t's, it goes very far clarifying the relationship between Israel and [the] American Jewish community.[30]

Blaustein had two aims in embarking on his mission: probing Ben-Gurion's and his colleagues' thinking, and obtaining a final and definitive statement, both of which he achieved to a surprising degree. He discovered, during his long conferences with Ben-Gurion, that they were on common ground after all. The committee's fears that the prime minister might have been secretly planning to recognize the American Zionist movement as the sole spokesman of American Jewry vis-à-vis Israel were soon shown to have been unfounded. This was not a concession made to satisfy Blaustein specifically, for by late 1948 Ben-Gurion had lost faith in American Zionism as a viable instrument for aiding Israel and was seriously considering replacing the Zionist movement with a new non-ideological organization for universal pro-Israelism.

However, for Ben-Gurion, the lifelong radical Zionist who perceived Zionism as a revolution in Jewish life and who preached "not [merely] non-surrender to the *galut* [exile], but making an end of it,"[31] acceding to Blaustein's demand for a statement that America was not exile was an entirely different matter. Contrary to Segal's interpretation, Ben-Gurion did not go so far as to state this explicitly. It was equally impossible for him to yield on Israel's Zionist mission. Although at Blaustein's urging he grudgingly agreed to remove the phrase "the gathering of exiles" from his statement, he also declared: "We should like to see American Jews come and take part in our effort," by which he meant the immigration of American professionals, as well as some kind of a Jewish peace corps that would help develop the Jewish state side by side with the *aliyah* of selected *halutzim* who would join *kibbutzim* throughout the country.

Back in the United States, Blaustein and the committee described the exchange as being of "historic significance."[32] At last, Blaustein stated, it clarified the "troublesome problem of alleged dual loyalty and of the relations of Israel to the Jewish communities outside its boundaries." While some statements by Israeli leaders may be expected to deviate from the exchange from time to time, he conceded realistically, he was convinced that "the statement [by Ben-Gurion] represents the official policy of the Israeli government." Replying to a question as to how the exchange would affect the policy of the American Jewish Committee, Blaustein explained that it "would not change the [committee's] policy of helpfulness to Israel, but should allay the misgivings felt by some of our members concerning the wisdom of that policy." Herein lay the key to Blaustein's thinking. The exchange provided him with the ammunition he needed for his continuous struggle with American Council for Judaism supporters within the committee's ranks. More than that, it at last defined the parameters of Israel-Diaspora relations, a definition that was essential for his methodical mind-set. He would spare no effort to preserve the inviolability of those parameters to his dying day.

Ben-Gurion, essentially a pragmatic leader, chiefly concerned with the vital need to obtain the non-Zionists' financial and political support to implement his urgent Four-Point Program, was willing to yield to Blaustein on points that belonged to the ideological, or millenial, sphere, without compromising on Israel's raison d'être. Given his negative view of American Zionism in any case, this yielding did not entail a real concession.

Despite its significance to both Blaustein's and Ben-Gurion's agendas, the publicized exchange of views was only one facet of their mutual concerns. During their first meeting on 13 August Blaustein had also raised the question of Israel's policy of nonidentification in the cold war,[33] particularly in light of the Korean conflict. Blaustein bluntly told Ben-Gurion that although Washington had "little doubt" regarding Israel's "Western orientation," still, "some further steps might be taken which would indicate not only to the high government officials but also to the people of the United States that Israel can be counted upon." Indeed, said Blaustein, in meetings he had had with President Truman, Secretary of Defense Johnson, Secretary of State Acheson, and Mr. McGhee, he had consistently emphasized that Israel was a "bastion of democracy" as a persuasive argument for providing arms for Israel. But that assurance was not enough.[34]

In fact, under intense White House pressure immediately after the outbreak of the Korean War, the Israeli government had crossed the Rubicon, announcing on 2 July at an extraordinary cabinet meeting, held at President Weizmann's home in Rehovot, Israel's support for the "Security Council in its efforts to put an end to the breach of peace in Korea."[35] But in Blaustein's estimation it was important to dispel the notion, still widely held, that Israel was sitting on the fence, and he sought an affirmative response from Ben-Gurion to the UN secretary general's request to send "combat forces, particularly ground forces" to Korea, which had been addressed to all member states supporting UN action there.[36]

In fact, only a few days before the Ben-Gurion-Blaustein conference the Israeli government had rejected Ben-Gurion's suggestion to send a military unit—even a token one—to Korea, deciding instead to send medical aid.[37] Still, Ben-Gurion told Blaustein, he (Blaustein) was preaching to the converted, for Truman's intervention in Korea "has . . . considerably delayed, if not altogether prevented, a third World War. It was the greatest act for peace that America could have made. As far as the Israeli Government was concerned, there was unanimous approval to support the United Nations on Korea, and in the Knesset only the Communists and [the left-wing] Mapam have voted against the Government's position." Unquestionably, Ben-Gurion stressed, Israel stood foursquare with the West. But the Jewish state had another major consideration. "As long as there is still a chance of getting Jews out of the countries behind the Iron Curtain, it cannot become a part of the Western Bloc." Still, he said, in the event of a crisis, should Israel have to face the choice between "independence and Zionism on the one hand and Communism on the other, the overwhelming majority of the people, even including some groups in Mapam . . . will choose Zionism and Israel's independence." [38] In Ben-Gurion's perception of Israel's national interest, the question of *aliyah,* and in particular of saving Jews in jeopardy, would always come first in the formulation of foreign policy.

Ben-Gurion had many other pressing concerns apart from the Korean War. The day before Blaustein's departure, the prime minister unexpectedly invited him with Segal "for a strictly confidential and highly important discussion," [39] during which he requested Blaustein to discuss two critical military and economic questions with President Truman and his top officials, even though Abba Eban had also been "instructed to ascertain the views of the American Government." Ben-Gurion, traditionally suspicious of British Near Eastern designs, was anxious to know if in the event of a world war, American-British strategic planning would entrust the defense of the Near East to the British, pointing out that "the Israelis . . . would be very uneasy if this were the case." In addition, in light of "the extremely precarious" condition of Israel's economy, he wanted to know "whether the United States is prepared to give full economic support to the Israelis to enable them to increase their manpower and to expand their industrial and military potential."

Fearing the imminent outbreak of a third world war, and haunted by Israel's military and economic vulnerability in addition to the country's political isolation, Ben-Gurion went even further and raised the idea of creating an American-Israeli alliance. He entrusted Blaustein to deliver a message to President Truman to the effect that Israel stood squarely with the West not only ideologically but also in practical military terms, and "in the event of a conflict" would be committed to defend Western interests in the Near East. Aware, however, of Washington's suspicion of Israel as a neutral state, aside from its being viewed as a burden, he wished to convince Truman of Israel's real potential for enhancing America's vital interests:

> In the East, only Israel, Turkey and possibly India can be counted upon as allies of the West. Consequently, it is in the interest of the United States to strengthen Israel and to increase its manpower to the greatest possible extent. Far from being in favor of restricting immigration . . . [Israel] should be encouraged by the US so as to increase [its] military potential. . . . With a population of, say, two million [it] could mobilize an army of about 300,000 while with its present population of a little more than a million, the army strength could be at a maximum of 150,000 . . . while mathematically [this] may be incorrect, militarily 300,000 is more than double 150,000. It would be much better policy for the United States to increase the potential of Israel than, in [the] event of a conflict, to have to send American boys, materials and supplies from America to fight in the Near East.[40]

Moving on to the projected Israeli Four-Point Program, Ben-Gurion again emphasized the extreme importance of impressing "upon Washington that a strong Israel is in the interest of the United States as well." Although Ben-Gurion was evidently eager to initiate the American-Israeli alliance, when Blaustein broached the idea of the prime minister visiting the United States, Ben-Gurion considered it suitable "only after the preliminaries of a substantial loan or economic treaty with the United States were agreed upon, so that he actually would come only for the finalization of negotiations."[41] In any event, Ben-Gurion, said, he would not come before the congressional elections of November 1950 in order to avoid the appearance of interfering in domestic American politics. In the event, Ben-Gurion visited the United States in 1951, but aside from his success in launching the Israel bonds campaign, his idea of an American-Israeli alliance was destined to be cold-shouldered by both the Truman and the Eisenhower administrations.

Blaustein and Segal also had a series of issues that they were intent on raising, besides hearing the Israeli concerns. They were troubled, they told Ben-Gurion during the course of the visit, by what appeared to them Israel's peculiar educational system, which was conducted along party lines, as well as by the church-and-state issue. Regarding the educational system, there was no quarrel between them, the prime minister said, assuring them that the system was in the process of being revised and that a general educational system would be established instead, which did, in fact, occur in 1953.

The issue of the relationship between church and state, or, more accurately, the Orthodox religious establishment and the state, however, was much more complicated.[42] Although most Israelis were not religious (in the Orthodox sense), Ben-Gurion explained, coalition politics necessitated making certain concessions to the Orthodox parties. Nevertheless, he hoped that "eventually this problem will be settled to the satisfaction of the great majority." But Blaustein and Segal took exception, especially to discrimination against Reform rabbis, who were prevented from performing their functions in Israel. The prime minister explained that in view of the fact that until then there were no Reform rabbis in Israel, the question was theoretical. Nevertheless, he

> authorized Mr. Blaustein to state in the United States, although without quoting him personally . . . that "he knows it from the highest authorities in Israel that if any Reform rabbi comes to Israel he will enjoy the same rights and privileges as the Orthodox [rabbis]." He, Ben-Gurion personally, will see to it that the Reform rabbi and the congregation will have complete equality and will be able to worship according to their own beliefs.[43]

While this commitment reflected Ben-Gurion's point of view on the issue and satisfied the committee leaders temporarily, the issue was not to be resolved and remained a point of dissension in Israeli society.

Toward the conclusion of their final meeting, Blaustein discovered one of Ben-Gurion's remarkable traits: his insatiable intellectual appetite. Weighed down as he was with grave affairs of state and formidable responsibilities, the prime minister raised a last unexpected point with his American guests. Becoming "really enthusiastic and eloquent," Ben-Gurion unfolded a plan to establish "a cultural foundation in Israel for the translation of the great classical works." This foundation would, for example, "undertake to translate all the works of [Thomas] Jefferson into Hebrew, and give the general social and historical background of the era of the American revolution." Apprehensive of the danger of Israeli youth becoming provincial and out of touch with the Western intellectual heritage, the prime minister told Blaustein that he needed an investment of about 250,000 to 300,000 Israeli pounds to finance the cultural foundation. The president of the committee, impressed by Ben-Gurion's intellectual zest and genuine commitment—Ben-Gurion said that if the foundation were established, "he personally would be very happy to give up all governmental positions to become the head of it"—readily agreed to try to interest a few people in America to lend their support for this undertaking, "which might be of great cultural value in maintaining . . . Western influence in Israel."[44]

An additional outcome of Blaustein's first two missions to Israel was the beginning of an unlikely personal friendship that developed between the radical Zionist prime minister of Israel and the non-Zionist pragmatist from Baltimore. This remarkable friendship, reflected in their habit of calling each other by their Hebrew first names, was to last until Blaustein's death three years before that of Ben-Gurion.

3

Reactions in Israel to the Blaustein-Ben-Gurion Understanding were mixed. "If new proof were needed for the mature statesmanship of Israel's Prime Minister," went a laudatory editorial in the *Jerusalem Post,* "it can be found in the words which he addressed yesterday to Mr. Jacob Blaustein, president of the American Jewish Committee."[45] However, *Davar,* the Histadrut daily, traditionally a solid Ben-Gurion supporter, treated the understanding between the prime minister and the non-Zionist leader with reserve, confining itself to a factual account of the exchange of views on its front page, under the misleading headline: "We Wish to See American Jewry Immigrating, the Prime Minister Says at a Luncheon in Honor of Jacob Blaustein."[46]

Nathan Alterman, the most popular Israeli poet at the time, whose weekly "Seventh Column" in *Davar* cuttingly satirized current events, allowed himself more license. Taking up Blaustein's assertion at the King David luncheon that "American Jews vigorously repudiate any suggestion or implication that they are in exile," Alterman suggested that while the polite luncheon was not the ideal place for down-to-earth talk, the opportunity for plain speaking should not be missed. Aiming his arrows directly at Blaustein and indirectly at Ben-Gurion, the poet endorsed the validity of the Zionist conviction that America was still a *galut:*

> To them, those Jewish leaders
> With their rusty way of thinking
> Their misleading, enfeebling, anesthetizing
> pronouncements–
> Which chain the [Jewish] people to their exile

If only somebody had roared:
Stop it! Let my people go![47]

No less critical was *Haboker,* the General Zionist daily oriented toward business and free-enterprise groups. Ideologically and politically aligned with Silver and Neumann's circle in the ZOA, it took issue with Ben-Gurion, accusing him of underhanded trickery in "getting rid of gifted [Zionist] political opponents, capable of influencing developments in and outside of Israel, while attempting to obtain support from a new source—the non-Zionist leadership."[48] Similarly, *Hatzofe,* the organ of the religious Zionists, accused Ben-Gurion of undermining devoted American Zionists by his preferential treatment of Blaustein, "the leader of the assimilated Jews in America."[49]

Alone amid these harsh critics, the independent *Haaretz* sympathized with Ben-Gurion's genuine dilemma of trying to gain the support of the non-Zionists without yielding on Israel's Zionist credo. Nevertheless, while agreeing with Ben-Gurion on the need for the non-Zionists' support, *Ha'aretz* felt that the price was too high and that their aid could have been obtained without making ideological concessions and without jettisoning Rabbi Silver. Assuredly, *Ha'aretz* argued, achieving the goal of $1.5 billion for the Four-Point Program from the Zionist movement alone was totally fanciful, but there was no possible justification for continuing to boycott the proven leadership talents of Rabbi Silver at such a critical time.[50]

Abba Eban too, writing privately to the Foreign Office in Jerusalem, had some criticism. Blaustein was right, Eban said, to demand Israeli restraint in pronouncements "bound to emphasize spiritual divisions within American Jewry." On the other hand, he cautioned, a line had to be drawn. After all, Israeli appeals for the support of American Jewry flowed from pure Zionist principles, and appealing for *aliyah* from the New World was similarly justifiable. Most important: "I would have been reluctant to publicly admit that the term exile [Eban used the interchangeable word *golah,* and not *galut*] is not applicable to American Jewry." Despite American Jewry's obvious political freedom and affluence, he pointed out, "their reactions to all manifestations of Jewish experience is a typical exilic one—starting with concern for non-Jewish reaction and ending with sensitivity, tinged with pride and concern, regarding Israeli activities."[51]

Clearly, Ben-Gurion's reorientation, from exclusive reliance on American Zionism and its leadership toward a new policy of dealing directly with American Jewry—Zionists and non-Zionists alike—would encounter widespread criticism and resistance both in the Israeli polity and in the Zionist movement.

Reactions were mixed in the United States as well. Recognition of Blaustein's significant achievement was reflected in the Yiddish *Morning Journal*, the Orthodox New York daily, which carried an article entitled "Death Certificate for Dual Loyalty," by poet and critic Jacob Glatstein. Blaustein, he wrote, "has brought back from Israel a death certificate for Madam Dual Loyalty, who has been a source of distress to so many frightened Jews. These frightened Jews started screaming about dual loyalty even before the Dorothy Thompsons [the former Christian Zionist turned anti-Zionist] got around to it." Nonetheless, Glatstein doubted whether Blaustein's "guarantee" would mollify the phobias of the American Council for Judaism.[52]

A critical reaction was articulated by Dr. Samuel Margoshes, writing in the labor Zionist-oriented New York Yiddish daily *The Day,* who wondered why Blaustein had been invited to Israel by Ben-Gurion twice in the course of one year, while no similar invitations had been extended to Zionist leaders. Behind these invitations, and the Blaustein-Ben-Gurion Understanding, Margoshes suspected, lurked a quid pro quo entailing the future support of the American Jewish Committee for Israel. Margoshes also faulted Ben-Gurion for going back on his promise to Blaustein not to interfere in American Jewish affairs. "The fact is that by strengthening the American Jewish Committee, Israel's premier [will] be weakening a great many other Jewish groups in America, notably the Zionist groups."[53]

The American Jewish Congress, which was the committee's pro-Zionist rival, also attacked the Blaustein-Ben-Gurion Understanding scathingly in its *Congress Weekly,* accusing Ben-Gurion of finding it necessary "to cast Mr. Blaustein in the role of unofficial ambassador of the American Jewish community, and to address to him an elaborate political declaration, largely platitudinous, and obviously designed to appease the easily offended 'sensibilities' of Mr. Blaustein and his associates." The trade-off, the magazine claimed, was that Ben-Gurion hoped that the non-Zionists' support would "yield certain economic results."[54]

Not surprisingly, the Blaustein-Ben-Gurion Understanding was not received with open arms by all the members of the committee either. While Blaustein's achievement was highly praised by some of his colleagues—"You accomplished a wonderful—in fact amazing result,"[55] one committee member wrote him—there were plenty of complaints. An upstate New York member angrily protested at the amount of time Blaustein and the committee were devoting to Israel:

> The AJC favors grants in aid for Israel—Fine. The AJC meetings are full of Israel—Fine! But where are you leading the AJC? I thought our primary concern is with Jews in the USA and how to better our position here. What have you to say about the Peekskill riots [two anti-Jewish riots in August and September 1949, resulting from Communist-sponsored open-air concerts given by Paul Robeson]?[56] How are we going about the prevention of such anti-Semitic manifestations in the heart of a conservative area? What about the increasing dislike of Jews in rural communities? Or are we just a limb of a Zionist group? I feel we are going far afield. Starting with Wertheim [namely his agreement with Ben-Gurion in 1942], pushed much further under Proskauer, and now carried on by your good self.[57]

The religion-and-state issue in Israel was also hurled at Blaustein. Another member, fearful that "soon the time will come in America when our enemies will quote back to us intolerant statements of our Israeli friends," wanted to know whether during Blaustein's many hours of private conferences with Ben-Gurion any time at all was devoted to the religious problem. "We are engaged in a constant fight against the encroachment of churches, here and abroad. And yet we are supposed to give unstinted support to a state which is organizing a new religious totalitarianism." The complainant conceded that Ben-Gurion, "as an old Socialist, is probably not in sympathy with Jewish religious fanaticism. He is a prisoner of the coalition." But was American Jewry in a position to "strengthen his hand"?[58]

It was the distinguished historian Salo W. Baron of Columbia University who viewed the Blaustein-Ben-Gurion Understanding with the most profound insight. While praising Blaustein's achievement in Jerusalem in obtaining the "joint declaration" with Ben-Gurion, thus clarifying "the objectives on both sides of the Atlantic Ocean," Baron realized that the value of the understanding lay entirely in its implementation. While the "principles are laid down, it is extremely important to see that they be put into practice to the mutual satisfaction of Israel and American Jewry. I personally believe that this is the most important, though extremely complex, task facing Jewish communal leadership." Drawing on his historical research of the Second Commonwealth experience, Salo Baron saw a parallel between the current situation and the historic one, when "the Jewish State felt a certain responsibility for the fate of other Jewish communities, whose population . . . also far outnumbered that of Palestine. And yet, because of difficulties in securing concerted action, the interests of Palestinian Jewry often ran counter to those of the Jews of the dispersion. The ensuing tragedy which engulfed both communities is a matter of record." What was needed, therefore, the Columbia historian told Blaustein, was "action based upon study." Thorough research "in the light of both historic experience and contemporary realities" must precede the development of a detailed and serious program of action in Israeli-American Jewish relations.[59]

Eliahu Elath, Israeli ambassador to Washington, presents a Torah
Scroll to President Truman, 1 October 1949. Courtesy of the
State of Israel Government Press Office.

Jacob Blaustein, president of the American Jewish Committee, reads his
statement on the American Jewish-Israeli relationship at the historic King
David Hotel luncheon, 23 August 1950. From left to right: Prime Minister
David Ben-Gurion, Jacob Blaustein (standing), Minister of Labor Golda
Meir, Foreign Minister Moshe Sharett. Courtesy of the Blaustein Library,
The American Jewish Committee.

Prime Minister Ben-Gurion and Ambassador to Washington,
Abba Eban present a menorah to President Truman during
Ben-Gurion's visit to the U.S., 2 May 1951. Courtesy of the
State of Israel Government Press Office.

Prime Minister Ben-Gurion and Ambassador Eban chat with
President Truman at the White House, 2 May 1951. Courtesy
of the State of Israel Government Press Office.

Prime Minister Ben-Gurion meets Jacob Blaustein and other
Jewish leaders during his visit to the United States, May 1951.
Courtesy of Israel State Archives.

Prime Minister Ben-Gurion's cavalcade in Chicago during his visit
to the United States, May 1951. Courtesy of Israel State Archives.

Prime Minister Ben-Gurion and Ambassador Eban meet with Secretary of Defense George C. Marshall during Ben-Gurion's visit to the United States, May 1951. Courtesy of Israel State Archives.

Foreign Minister Moshe Sharett (right) converses with American Zionist leaders: Nahum Goldmann (center) and Louis Lipsky (second from left). Courtesy of Sharett Archives.

Moshe Sharett and Rabbi Abba Hillel Silver, 3 April 1956. Courtesy of Sharett Archives.

PART
II

Spokesmen
for American Jewry
vis-à-vis Israel

5

The Struggle Between the American
Jewish Committee and the
Zionist Movement, 1951

1

THE RISE OF ISRAEL was also bound to have an effect on American Jewish politics, whose arena was the Jewish organization, local as well as national, usually run by a small number of leaders. From World War I almost until Israel's emergence, the struggle for supremacy within this arena was most intense between two major groupings: the American Jewish Committee and the Zionists. The Zionists were the challengers, not only in terms of the idea of a Jewish state, but also in terms of the committee's historic hegemonial claim as sole custodian and spokesman of American Jewry regarding overseas relief (including to the Yishuv) and as representative in Washington.[1]

The establishment of Israel sharpened this historic struggle, specifically over two basic and related issues: who holds the purse strings for funds raised for Israel, and who speaks for the Jews vis-à-vis the Jewish state. These problems were at the root of the deep conflict between the American Jewish Committee and the Zionists over an agreement drawn up between the World Jewish Congress and the Jewish Agency in 1951, and over the granting of a quasi-sovereign status to the World Zionist Organization-Jewish Agency. In addition, a new personality on the American Jewish scene—Nahum Goldmann, chairman of the American section of the Jewish Agency Executive—was to play an important role in these conflicts.

Nahum Goldmann, born in 1894 in Lithuania and raised in Frankfurt am Main, Germany, described himself in his autobiography as belonging to a unique generation, "the last of its kind": emanating from the East European shtetl "but educated in the West and combining many features of European culture, Eastern and Western, Jewish and non-Jewish."[2] At fifteen the precocious young Goldmann had written articles on Zionist topics and was delivering Zionist speeches. In 1923 Goldmann and his close friend Jacob Klatzkin founded the Eschkol publishing house and began publishing the ambitious *Encyclopedia Judaica,* of which ten volumes in German and two in Hebrew appeared. In 1935 he entered the field of diplomacy, working in Geneva as *"un diplomate juif sans passeport,"*[3] by his own description, serving as the diplomatic representative of the Jewish Agency at the League of Nations headquarters until the outbreak of World War II. In 1940, having fled the German invasion of France, and through the intervention of his mentor, Rabbi Stephen Wise, Goldmann and his family arrived in the United States. Remarkably, the European diplomat, with his heavy German accent (it was said in jest that he spoke ten languages in German), and with no roots in America, quickly became a major figure on the Zionist scene and was appointed the Jewish Agency's representative in Washington. He was among those who championed the adoption by the Jewish Agency Executive of the partition plan for Palestine in 1946. After the establishment of Israel, Goldmann remained in America and, hand-in-glove with Ben-Gurion, maneuvered Abba Hillel Silver's resignation from the post of chairman of the American section of the Jewish Agency Executive, to be replaced by himself.

He had prodigious talents as a negotiator, an astute mind, wit, charm, talent as a raconteur, and long experience in the political and diplomatic arena, yet he was not universally liked or trusted. Abba Hillel Silver and Emanuel Neumann thought him superficial and unreliable. Proskauer and Blaustein regarded him as a sharp operator. Similar opinions were held by Ben-Gurion, Sharett, and Golda Meir. Yet all these leaders were ready to utilize Goldmann's talents so long as he was politically useful.

Goldmann could be described as a creative maverick and a perennial dissenter within the Jewish and Zionist leadership. Indeed in his book *Le Paradoxe Juif,* he contrasted himself to Israeli leaders, stressing: "I do not identify one hundred percent with any idea or movement. I always maintain a distance with my doubts and reservations; therefore I do not have a narrow view of things."[4] Declassified State Department records confirm gross indiscretions on his part in the area of Zionist diplomacy,[5] and tend to justify the less than favorable view held at the time of this highly talented personality who, while considering the Jewish people his constituency, was ever the embodiment of the cosmopolitan and rootless Jew.

Goldmann was most closely associated with the World Jewish Congress, which he founded with Rabbi Stephen Wise in 1936. The purpose of this Zionist-oriented organization, as defined by Goldmann, was "to establish the permanent address of the Jewish people" as "a real, legitimate, collective representation of Jewry which will be entitled to speak in the name of the 16 million Jews to the nations and governments of the world, as well as to the Jews themselves."[6] The congress, established at the height of the Nazi regime in Germany and during a period when pro-Nazi and anti-Semitic propaganda activity was spreading alarmingly in the United States, was viewed by the committee with apprehension. Historically, the American Jewish Committee had always opposed the very idea of a world Jewish organization. Not only did the congress imperil the hard-won achievements of emancipation, the committee believed, but, its leaders claimed, by planning to create an international Jewish parliament, Wise, Goldmann, and their supporters were fostering Diaspora political nationalism and thereby playing right into the hands of Hitler and the anti-Semites who questioned the Jews' loyalty to their native countries.[7]

The committee's opposition to Wise and Goldmann's brainchild was not based on ideological grounds alone. It correctly viewed the new organization as a rival in the highly competitive field of Jewish politics, encroaching upon one of the main purposes of the committee's existence: the defense of Jewish civil and religious rights wherever Jews lived.

In early 1951, with the Blaustein-Ben-Gurion Understanding barely concluded, an irritating new row broke out. A delegation representing the committee and B'nai B'rith complained to Blaustein that Nahum Goldmann, in his dual capacity as chairman of the American section of the Jewish Agency and acting president of the World Jewish Congress, had concluded an agreement between the agency and the congress by which the Jewish Agency, recognizing the work of the World Jewish Congress on behalf of "the Jewish people in the Diaspora," would give that organization a share of the proceeds of "united Jewish or Israel campaigns," the amount to be determined by itself and the World Jewish Congress.[8]

On learning of this complaint, Jacob Blaustein, representing the non-Zionists, together with Edward M. M. Warburg, general chairman of the UJA, and Frank Goldman, president of B'nai B'rith, sent a vigorous protest to Berl Locker, the Jerusalem chairman of the Jewish Agency Executive. Although Blaustein had received assurances that the agreement did not apply to the United States, he still considered it an affront. Whether or not it applied to the United States, he said, "it certainly is apparent to even the most unacquainted with Jewish politics that there will be a co-mingling of funds from other sources, and that in fact the World Jewish Congress will benefit, even if indirectly, by the decision as to its budgetary needs made in Jerusalem."[9] Moreover, it was inconceivable to the non-Zionist American Jewish leaders that the Jewish Agency, whose declared scope of activities was confined to work in Israel, would channel funds intended for Israel to a body engaged in political work in the Diaspora. It was only elementary, Blaustein wrote Locker, that before concluding such an agreement

> courtesy would require at least the consultation with those to whom you have entrusted the responsibility of raising funds in the United States. The American Jewish public is not going to countenance any organization being designated from Israel as the chosen instrument for protecting the rights of Jews throughout the world, and speaking in their name; and in addition, it is not going to subscribe funds which it intends for Israel in order to have them be used for the strengthening of one or another arm of [the] Jewish political scene outside of Israel.[10]

Locker must reconsider the agreement, Blaustein said, and in future the non-Zionists, who took upon themselves "the difficult task of raising the maximum funds in this country," should be consulted in advance on such policy matters. The whole affair was "an additional headache that we just had not counted on."[11] By "additional headache" Blaustein meant one more problem added to the current issues of anti-Semitic allegations that Jews were associating with Communism, and the accusations of anti-Semitic publications that Anna M. Rosenberg, appointed assistant secretary of defense, was a Communist fellow-traveler—all of which occupied the committee intensely.[12]

Meetings between the committee's leadership and Nahum Goldmann, as well as intervention by Abba Eban at Blaustein's request, resulted in a buildup of pressure on Nahum Goldmann. Meanwhile Ben-Gurion arrived in America in early May 1951,[13] and Blaustein hoped that a solution to the controversy would be found through his intervention.[14] But Blaustein had underestimated his wily opponent. Goldmann informed Berl Locker in Jerusalem that he was prepared to make only one concession—that the agreement between the World Jewish Congress and the Jewish Agency reflected the opinion of the Zionist Executive and not of the Jewish Agency.[15] He also pressured Locker not to make any promises to Blaustein "with regard to the termination of the agreement this year." As the summer wore on, he made several other minor concessions, certain, he informed Locker, that these would "keep . . . [Blaustein] quiet." [16]

Finally, exasperated and angered at Goldmann's delaying tactics, Blaustein sent an ultimatum both to him and to Berl Locker, in July 1951. Accusing Goldmann of trying to deceive him by using all sorts of abstruse arguments regarding the authority of the present executive of the Jewish Agency to commit the new executive, he informed them that if the agreement were not cancelled, the American Jewish Committee and the other concerned American Jewish organizations would be placed "in a position to govern ourselves accordingly even though it will not be pleasant." [17]

Goldman finally gave in. The agreement between the Jewish Agency and the World Jewish Congress, he told Blaustein in September, would not be renewed. [18] This capitulation, however, was more apparent than real, because he had arranged for the Keren Hayesod, the fund-raising arm of the World Zionist Organization operating outside the United States, to undertake future allocations to the World Jewish Congress "without any public announcement," he confided to Berl Locker. [19]

While the Blaustein-Goldman contest was an extension of the old rivalry between the American Jewish Committee and the World Jewish Congress, something more significant was at stake. Fundamentally, it reflected the basic insistence by the American Jewish leaders on the integrity of the UJA allocation process. As Blaustein put it to Berl Locker: "When Jews, Zionists as well as non-Zionists, contribute for the purpose for which the Jewish Agency exists, they are under the impression that they are contributing to the upbuilding of Israel exclusively, and not to organizations that are working outside of Israel." The Jewish Agency was in essence a trustee, and "as such, cannot otherwise allocate funds which were given to it for Israeli purposes exclusively." [20]

2

Four years after the triumph of the World Zionist Organization on 29 November 1947, when the historic United Nations partition resolution was adopted, the Zionist movement was still in the throes of a grave identity crisis. Emanuel Neumann, poignantly describing the ongoing sense of letdown in 1951, doubted whether his colleagues in Israel "realize to the present day the extent and nature of this crisis. For decades the Zionists in the dispersion were sustained by the Herzlian conception that they and the Movement they served were part of the Jewish State in the process of realization." What kept the Diaspora Zionists going, said Neumann, was the dual sense of participation [in] and responsibility for the exhilarating enterprise of creating the Jewish national home.

> They penetrated Jewish communities, introducing the Zionist flag, the Zionist anthem, Hebrew culture and the Zionist way of life. They subscribed and sold shares of the Zionist Bank, which is now the National Bank of Israel. . . . They engaged in political work wherever possible—the most humble Zionist was an unofficial ambassador. In short, they were not merely fundraisers and donors, but nation builders, engaged upon a great venture in practical statesmanship.[21]

Now, almost overnight, the Zionist movement "was shorn of its political prerogatives and much of its authority. This was unavoidable; but the manner in which it was done, with little regard to psychological effect, aggravated the reaction among the Zionists of the Diaspora. . . . Zionists were not only dejected, but confused, having no clear idea where and how they fitted into the new picture." At the same time, Neumann bitterly complained, alluding to the Blaustein-Ben-Gurion Understanding, the non-Zionists who in the past were hostile to the Zionist idea were avidly courted by Ben-Gurion after the creation of Israel: "They rushed onto the bandwagon, all but hurling the driver from his seat."

Neumann perceived that for the Israelis, the emergence of the state made the Zionist movement superfluous, because "every citizen of Israel, in discharging the duties of citizenship, is discharging his duties as a Zionist."[22] The Zionist movement, said Neumann, had in fact become a Diaspora movement, "the enterprise of Diaspora Jewry with relation to Israel." He advocated, therefore, the creation of a new Zionism, ideologically oriented toward both Israel and the Diaspora "for as long as there are Jewish communities in the dispersion." In view of the new reality, American Zionists who viewed themselves as carrying the main burden of the movement would not be satisfied merely with glib talk of "partnership" or "alliance" between Israel and the Zionist movement. If the movement were to discharge its obligations toward the state, the State of Israel "must assume corresponding obligations toward its partner. It must, in turn, strengthen its ally and fortify its position by giving it every encouragement and full recognition of its unique status. It must do so consciously, positively and consistently—as an integral part of its fixed policy."[23]

There were two aspects of the movement's "unique status," Neumann explained. The first was a division of jurisdiction and functions between the Zionist movement and the government of Israel—which eventually was accomplished. But the second aspect was much more far-reaching. As far back as the summer of 1948, during deliberations of the Actions Committee in Jerusalem, he had privately suggested that the WZO should assume the responsibility for "all organized effort by the Jews of the world on behalf of Israel."[24] In other words, the State of Israel should concede an area of its sovereign activity—the maintaining of direct contact with Diaspora Jewry—to the WZO.

Nahum Goldmann, although no favorite of Neumann, was also an advocate of the "special status" aspect of the WZO. In a private discussion with Ben-Gurion he portrayed the new situation of world Jewry since Israel's establishment as a house with

three storeys. . . . An intermediary storey was necessary to lend strength and act as a connecting link between the two. It is upon the occupants of the intermediary storey, viz. the Zionist Movement, that all the unpopular duties and difficult tasks which the State of Israel cannot itself carry out will be placed. . . . The most important of its functions is the maintenance of an indissoluble link between the Jewish people and the State of Israel, a link with the Jews who are not in the State of Israel but are vitally interested in it.[25]

One of the major tasks referred to by Goldmann was handling *aliyah*. However, in order to enable the WZO to fulfill this and the other tasks, Israel must recognize the WZO as the sole representative of the Jewish people. While this recognition should be done without thwarting the desire of other Jewish organizations to render assistance to the young state, Goldmann asserted, the special status was a sine qua non. "The Zionist Organization should be given status so that it may appear before the Jewish people as the recognized representative of the State, as a collaborator in the upbuilding of the State."[26]

The special-status issue was hotly debated in 1951–52 among Israeli officials and within Zionist and non-Zionist ranks, reflecting a clash of personal, political, organizational, and ideological interests. The debate reached a peak in the summer of 1951, and again in the Knesset in 1952 when it was finally resolved. Once again it pitted Jacob Blaustein and the American Jewish Committee against Nahum Goldmann and his allies within the Zionist movement and the Israeli public. Ben-Gurion was also involved, and, at Blaustein's urging, played an increasingly active, and eventually decisive, role.[27]

The American Jewish Committee reacted with great displeasure to news of preparations for submitting a draft status law to the forthcoming twenty-third Zionist Congress. Blaustein requested clarification from Eban in April 1951 as to whether the Israeli government intended "to make the Jewish Agency for Palestine the sole channel for [the] relationship with American Jewry on questions of aid to Israel." Aware of the explosive potential of the status issue, and having consulted with Moshe Sharett, Eban informed Blaustein unofficially that no change in the relationship between Israel and American Jewry was contemplated, and that the Israeli government intended to continue to maintain "the closest and most direct relationship possible with all American Jewish organizations equally." Above all, Eban assured Blaustein, "whatever arrangements may be made in Jerusalem for granting a specific status to the Jewish Agency there, [whereby it might] undertake certain semi-governmental functions in relation to immigration, [they] will not in any way affect the principles or practices of the Government of Israel in its relations with American Jewry."[28] While Eban was not authorized to publicize his letter, he asked Blaustein to regard it as a personal assurance, allowing the president of the committee to inform the leadership of his organization that there was no cause for alarm.

Nahum Goldmann, however, had something else in mind. "The Status Bill," he told Ben-Gurion, "must include a clear-cut status for the Jewish Agency *outside of Israel* [my emphasis] . . . [for] unless the Government officials are obliged to consult with the representatives of the Zionist movement on all questions concerning Israel, the position of the Zionist movement will undoubtedly deteriorate." This deterioration would result in jeopardizing the fund-raising effort, the Jewish Agency, and the Zionist movement "as a whole."[29]

Meanwhile, Ben-Gurion made a historic visit to the United States in May 1951. It was the first opportunity that the largest Jewish community in the world had to meet the charismatic leader, and his effect on them was electrifying. "SHALOM, David Ben-Gurion, Champion of Israel's Independence, Protagonist of Democracy and Social Justice—Home-Builder for the Homeless of His People—Scholar, Leader and Statesman," adulated the usually

sober biweekly *The Reconstructionist*.[30] New York City, where the young socialist leader had arrived thirty-six years earlier after being exiled from Palestine by the Turks, welcomed him with a traditional ticker-tape parade that
drew a cheering crowd of one million along the streets of the cavalcade route
bedecked with Israeli and American flags. Launching the first campaign for
the sale of State of Israel Bonds in New York, the prime minister set out on a
two-week tour of major cities with large Jewish populations, investing a concerted effort in stimulating the bonds sale. The effort was well rewarded, for
in its first year the campaign sold a total of $65 million worth of bonds, which
in addition to UJA contributions provided the wherewithal to significantly
ease Israel's desperate balance of payments problem.[31]

But Ben-Gurion's outstanding success in stimulating the bonds drive
proved to be a big disappointment for the American Zionists. In his address to
a huge audience at Madison Square Garden, the Israeli prime minister "never
once mentioned Zionism or Zionists: they were taboo," Neumann
lamented.[32] At a dinner in New York City given by Jewish leaders at the end of
Ben-Gurion's tour, Emanuel Neumann and other Zionist leaders took him to
task for his glaring omission. Stung, the prime minister replied that he had not
come to America to address Zionists exclusively, "but to [address] all of
American Jewry . . . because all Jews now had the duty and the opportunity
to cooperate in strengthening the State of Israel." Years later, Neumann's bitterness was still palpable as he recounted the incident. "I was not very happy,
for it seemed that he was writing off the Zionist movement completely."[33]

In view of the special-status controversy, a goodwill message sent by Ben-
Gurion to the annual convention of the ZOA, which was held in Atlantic City
a short time after his return to Israel, attracted considerable attention. Reporting the message, the *New York Times* wrote that in his greetings the prime
minister had outlined the main tasks of the Zionist movement as "the building
of the State of Israel and its security, the fulfillment of the Ingathering of Exiles, the enhancement of the pioneering movement, and Hebrew culture and
education."[34] While no mention had been made of a special status, past president of the ZOA Abba Hillel Silver detected in the prime minister's message
"a reaffirmation of this special status which the Zionist movement has always
had among the Jewish people in reference to the upbuilding of Israel," and
praised the statement as "evidently a complete and welcome reversal of the
position which Mr. Ben-Gurion expressed at the meeting of the Zionist leaders on the eve of his departure which created so much consternation in the
ranks of the Zionists all over the world."[35]

Although Silver had read into Ben-Gurion's message more than its text warranted, his comments, also reported in the *Times*, disturbed the non-Zionists. Blaustein complained to Eban that he had already received "numerous phone calls about this . . . and some of the quoted phrases [from Ben-Gurion's message] give me special concern." [36] Moreover, the president of the committee warned the ambassador that the non-Zionists would refuse "to canalize [their assistance to Israel] through the Zionist Movement." By granting any special status to the Zionist movement, said Blaustein, "the Government of Israel would be prejudicing its chances of assistance from other organizations or individuals. The ZOA represents only a small proportion of American Jewry both in number and in influence." [37]

The proposed status law evoked even sharper criticism from Abe Harman and Michael S. Comay, two senior Israeli diplomats who had an intimate knowledge of British and American Jewry. Nahum Goldmann's idea was untenable, Harman argued, because it would "deny the State of Israel through its representatives the right to come into direct contact with any association of Jews or individual Jews in any part of the world." Besides, he pointed out, the proposed law, even if enacted, "would not work in practice." [38] Comay also thought that the status law idea was flawed, for while conceding the validity of the complaint of the Zionist organizations that the "State [of Israel] and its representatives have undermined them," the issue, he stressed, was not ideology but the very survival of the young state, which needed help from all Jews. "There are important Jewish organizations, and hundred of thousands of individual Jews in America and elsewhere," said Comay, "who are deeply moved by Israel and anxious to play their part in building it up. But they want to deal directly with Israel and its representatives; and they do not want to accept the Zionist bodies as their middle men." It was high time, thought Comay, that Nahum Goldmann, the moving force behind the status law, was knocked off his perch. "In the States, at present . . . every important pro-Israel activity—whether UJA, Bond Drive, grant-in-aid, political help, or anything else—cuts right across the distinction between Zionist and non-Zionist. The only real anomaly in this situation is the continued existence of an American Executive of the Jewish Agency, under Nahum Goldmann." In this situation, Comay concluded,

it would be absurd to tell people like [Jacob] Blaustein in the United States, [Ewen E. S.] Montagu [president of the Anglo-Jewish Association and of the

United Synagogue] in the United Kingdom, and [Samuel] Bronfman [president of the Canadian Jewish Congress] . . . that they cannot talk to us directly, but must apply to 41 East 42nd Street [the ZOA office in New York City], or 77 Great Russell Street [the Zionist office in London].[39]

In short, the Israeli diplomats argued, the status law was a misguided initiative.

Besides Harman and Comay, who campaigned against the status law, Abba Eban, who kept in close touch with Blaustein, and Teddy Kollek, now Ben-Gurion's influential aide, who was also in contact with Blaustein, opposed it as well. Early in August 1951, just a few days before the Zionist Congress was to convene in Jerusalem, Blaustein urged Eban to convey two recent illustrations of the futility of the status law initiative to Ben-Gurion. One was that "even without such 'special status,' the President of ZOA engages in discussions in Washington on political issues" without consulting Eban, and the other was "the latest example of the tangible help I, a *non-Zionist* [emphasis in original], was able to give yesterday with our State Department in obtaining its agreement for the United Sates to co-sponsor the Resolution regarding the Suez Canal blockade."[40] Eban assured Blaustein that he would indeed reiterate to Ben-Gurion his (Eban's) "previous warnings against allocating any special status to any American Jewish organization and thus diminishing our prospects of obtaining assistance from all American Jews on a legal basis."[41] While it is difficult to accurately assess the impact of the Israeli diplomats' input, it is probable that the pressure from the Ministry of Foreign Affairs, as well as from Teddy Kollek at the Prime Minister's Office, worked to reinforce Ben-Gurion's innate opposition to the status law idea and ultimately affected government policy on this issue.

3

A convergence of controversial Israel-Diaspora issues in August 1951 combined to bring about the worst crisis yet in relations between the American non-Zionists and Ben-Gurion's government. Addressing a pre-Zionist Congress conference of the Ihud Olami (the world union of Mapai and its Diaspora supporters) in Tel Aviv on 8 August, the prime minister took the opportunity to discuss a wide range of questions to be brought up at the forthcoming congress. The creation of Israel, he told the audience, had changed the definition of a Zionist. Whereas until 1948 every Jew who paid his shekel (the symbolic membership dues) or was willing to further Zionist aims was considered a Zionist, now Jews who wished to identify themselves as Zionists would have to undertake certain duties and obligations:

> Firstly, a collective obligation of all national Zionist organizations to assist the Jewish State under all circumstances and all conditions, even if such an attitude contrasts with the views held by the respective national authorities. [Here Ben-Gurion praised British Jewry for its admirable stand against the British government White Paper policy.] Secondly, an obligation to propagate Hebrew culture among youth abroad; and thirdly, no toleration by the Movement of Zionist organizations unwilling to promote a pioneering spirit.[42]

Addressing the special status issue, the prime minister angrily declared, "the problem is not the status of the WZO, but rather the obligation of the Movement." To merit the desired status, he said, the WZO would have to undertake the three above-mentioned obligations. Only then would the State of Israel be bound to grant it a special status within Israel. The status of the WZO in the Diaspora, however, was not the business of the Jewish State. "Captivating the heart of the Jewish people was the exclusive responsibility of the Zionist movement."[43]

But Ben-Gurion did make a significant concession to the Zionists in this speech, pointing out that constitutionally, by granting a special status to the WZO-JA, the State of Israel would be obliged to recognize that body as the representative of the Jewish people within Israel and allow it "a field of activity in Israel, under the supreme sovereignty of the State."[44]

Reactions in America were swift. Edward M. M. Warburg and Joseph J. Schwartz, the two heads of the United Jewish Appeal, dashed off a cable to Nahum Goldmann, who was in Jerusalem for the Zionist Congress, demanding to know whether the first obligation of the Zionist organizations that Ben-Gurion referred to, as reported by the *Jewish Telegraphic Agency*, was correct (the *New York Times* report of the speech had not mentioned this point). "Its appearance in *JTA*," went the cable, "causing great concern and uneasiness and may affect fall campaign if not corrected." Warburg and Schwartz insisted on obtaining a "clarifying statement" from the prime minister.

A similar cable was sent by Blaustein to Ben-Gurion, referring in particular to an erroneous report by the *Times* that Ben-Gurion's government intended to grant diplomatic status to the WZO. Besides demanding immediate clarification by the prime minister, Blaustein warned Ben-Gurion that if the report of his speech was accurate, then "consequences are bound to follow both in respect to our further aid to Israel and also to a compulsion that we openly oppose these views and programs as they are inimical to the welfare of American Jewry."[45]

At first it appeared that the by now familiar pattern of pacification by Ben-Gurion in reaction to American Jewish criticism was being repeated again. "Have seen neither *JTA* nor *Times* report," Ben-Gurion cabled Blaustein. "Cannot therefore affirm or deny." He did, however, emphasize to Blaustein that his statement was "completely in accord" with the 1950 understanding between them.[46] Ben-Gurion's secretary meanwhile notified Warburg and Schwartz that the *JTA* report was inaccurate. What Ben-Gurion had actually said, the secretary cabled, was that "national Zionist organizations must agree to aid Jewish state under all circumstances and conditions even if they oppose views or dislike composition of government of Israel."[47] It turned out, however, that the *JTA* report had been accurate. According to English excerpts of the speech, the crucial paragraph—which had been omitted entirely from the circulated Hebrew version—contained the proviso that it was "the duty of the Zionist Organization . . . to assist the State of Israel in all conditions and under any circumstances . . . *whether the government to which the Jews in question owe allegiance desire it or not* [my emphasis]."[48] Ben-Gurion's statement, in fact, constituted an explicit enunciation of his radical brand of Zionism, namely the centrality of the State of Israel in the life of the Jewish people.

Abba Eban, with his awareness of American Jewry's sensitivities, understood that unless quickly dealt with, Ben-Gurion's statement could cause serious harm. Having informed Blaustein that he felt that the reactions in the United States to Ben-Gurion's statement "sufficiently grave to impel my return to Washington," he cabled the prime minister, conveying the concern of the non-Zionists. Ben-Gurion reiterated that the statement attributed to him had been "grossly inaccurate."[49]

But Blaustein and the non-Zionists would not swallow the excuse of inaccurate reporting. Blaustein's anxiety over Ben-Gurion's speech stemmed not only from an apparent breach of faith, coming as it did precisely a year after the conclusion of the solemn understanding between them, but also from the prevailing atmosphere in America since the outbreak of the Korean War. With growing cold war tension and concern about Soviet nuclear espionage, anti-Semitic agitators had intensified their attacks on the loyalty of the American Jewish community, accusing Jews of being Communists and Soviet agents.[50]

This atmosphere, coupled with the imminent convening of the Zionist Congress in Jerusalem and anticipated fireworks concerning the issues of exile and *aliyah* in relation to American Jews, resulted in increasingly insistent cables and letters by Blaustein to the Israeli prime minister.

"I am being besieged by both non-Zionists and Zionists," Blaustein wrote to Ben-Gurion, "to issue an immediate public denouncement of your August 8th statement which would, among other things, result in a marked curtailment of American aid to Israel." To prevent this reduction in aid from happening, Blaustein explained, he needed a prompt clarification from Ben-Gurion reaffirming the basic principles of the 1950 understanding, namely that Israel would refrain from saying or doing anything that might result in creating the impression of dual loyalty among American Jewry; that in using the term "ingathering of exiles" Ben-Gurion would make it clear that Jews in the Western democracies, such as the United States, do not consider themselves in exile; and that no effort would be undertaken to encourage mass immigration from Western democracies, "as distinct from facilitating the immigration of those Jews who of their own volition want to go there, and [as] distinct from American Jews with specialized knowledge and training going to Israel to aid it with its problems."

Blaustein also reiterated the committee's unequivocal objection to the granting of diplomatic status to the WZO. If any special status at all were granted to the WZO, he argued, it should be confined to resettlement and rehabilitation activities within Israel. Ideologically as well, the committee opposed the special status concept with its implication "that Jews everywhere comprise a nation which the WZO would represent in Israel." Moreover, he pointed out, "non-Zionist groups and other friends of Israel here are not naive. They will not fail to understand that despite any initial provision limiting this status of WZO to representation in Israel, it would be the forerunner of [a] special status elsewhere, as soon as it is felt that the aid which such groups and individuals can render Israel is dispensable."

The basic issue, however, was who made the greatest contribution to Israel. Rejecting American Zionist claims, Blaustein reminded Ben-Gurion that the most effective and tangible aid rendered to Israel had come from non-Zionists and individuals not affiliated with the American Zionist movement. Referring to the political and intergovernmental area specifically, he argued that the American Jewish Committee, in collaboration with the Israeli ambassadors in Washington, had "played so important a role in every stage of Israel's development." This role had been the case with respect to the UN partition resolution; recognition of Israel by the United States; Israel's admission into the UN; two major Export-Import Bank loans; the Tripartite Declaration of 1950, in which England, France, and the United States resolved to maintain a balance of arms between Israel and the Arab states; German restitution; vital American grants-in-aid to Israel; and his recent intervention with the State Department regarding the UN Security Council deliberations on the Suez Canal blockade of Israeli shipping.

Blaustein stressed that the American Jewish Committee had worked "within the framework of American interests" in all these activities. Sometimes the committee had had to persuade government officials of the logic of aiding Israel, but it never followed the course implied in the prime minister's controversial statement of 8 August, mandating Zionists to "aid the Jewish State under all circumstances, *even if such an attitude clashes with the views of their respective national authorities*" [emphasis in original]. "This kind of attitude," the president of the committee declared, "is utterly inadmissible in American Jewish life, as it is, I am sure, in the life of Israel."

Concluding his long and frank letter, Blaustein recapitulated the committee's and his own credo on the parameters of the relationship between Israel and the American Jewish community:

> As you know, we are not given to making claims or to seeking publicity on what we do. The only reason for mentioning here our aid to Israel is to point out that it is extended without interfering with Israel's internal affairs. We do not ask for special status, and we have acted with regard to Israel's affairs only when you or your representatives or our Government with your knowledge have asked us to do so. And then, I am sure you will agree, we have responded. Virtually all we ask—and that is fundamental with us—is that Israel observe the proper relationship toward Jews in other countries, and that Israel continue to develop within a democratic framework.[51]

4

Blaustein's eloquent plea reached the harried prime minister when the deliberations of the twenty-third Zionist Congress were in progress. This congress would be the first to come to grips with the implications of the new realities in the Israel-Diaspora relationship created by the birth of the Jewish state. Five years had elapsed since the previous congress had met in Basle in 1946, a period of tremendous change in Jewish life. With the decimation of most of European Jewry during the Holocaust, the center of gravity of world Jewry had moved to the New World. The British Mandate had disappeared from Palestine forever, replaced by the sovereign State of Israel, which had become a full-fledged member of the United Nations. Still recovering from the impact of the War of Independence, the new state was trying to cope with the challenge of receiving hundreds of thousands of destitute immigrants annually. A transformation had also taken place among the dramatis personae of the Zionist movement. Chaim Weizmann, relegated to the ceremonial office of president of Israel, was fatally ill. The charismatic David Ben-Gurion dominated the Israeli scene. Rabbi Abba Hillel Silver, shunted aside, had been replaced by Nahum Goldmann at the helm of the American Zionist movement.

The very building in which the congress took place in Jerusalem reflected Israel's struggle to keep pace with new realities. The roof of the brand new National Convention Center was still unfinished, the building was covered with scaffolding, and the effort to equip it as a properly functioning convention hall, including providing facilities for simultaneous translation into four languages (Hebrew, English, French, and Yiddish), had required considerable determination and improvisation.

Three central issues dominated the deliberations: the relationship between Israel and the WZO, as embodied in the special-status question; the need for an updated definition of Zionism; and the urgent appeal for *halutziut*.

Significantly, the special-status idea was supported by a broad spectrum of the congress. While Nahum Goldmann was the main proponent of the idea, he was not alone. His views were supported by the Israeli political parties of both the left and the right, as well as by many—though by no means all—American Zionists. Abba Hillel Silver impassionedly called on the congress to vote for granting a special status to the WZO as the representative of the Jewish people in the Diaspora. Although conceding that numerically the Zionists had never encompassed all the Jews of the Diaspora, he believed they merited this status because they constituted the avant-garde that had "always represented the totality of the spirit of peoplehood . . . the hope and impulse of continuity [of the Jewish people]."[52]

After a lengthy debate, the congress adopted a resolution whose most important sections were:

B. The Congress considers it essential that the State of Israel shall grant, through an appropriate legislative act, status to the WZO as the representative of the Jewish people in all matters relating to organized participation of the Jews of the Diaspora in the development and upbuilding of the country and the rapid absorption of immigrants.

C. In relation to all activities conducted in the interest of the State of Israel within Jewish communities in the Diaspora, it is essential that the Government of the State of Israel shall act in consultation and coordination with the World Zionist Organization.[53]

The resolution was a compromise. It endorsed the thesis that the WZO spoke for world Jewry in all matters regarding the Diaspora's involvement in supporting Israel, but it did not go as far as some Zionist parties, particularly the extreme left and right, advocated, namely that the special status extend beyond the borders of Israel. The majority of the congress delegates realized that the State of Israel could not grant any national status beyond its borders, could not be expected to grant diplomatic status to WZO representatives, and could not be expected to deal with the Diaspora exclusively through Zionist channels.

The second issue—the quest for a contemporary definition of Zionism—highlighted serious differences within the Zionist movement, and no unanimity on the ultimate aim of Zionism was achieved in the ensuing prolonged and heated debates. Essentially, the Israeli delegates defined the aim of the movement as "the redemption of the Jewish people through the ingathering of the exiles in Eretz Yisrael," the so-called Jerusalem Program,[54] but to the delegates from the free and democratic countries of the Western world—mostly American—this definition, which interpreted "redemption" as requiring all Jews to live in Israel and which viewed all Jews living outside Israel as living in exile, was not only totally unacceptable but repugnant.

The American Zionist counterattack on the proposed Jerusalem Program was led by the brilliant ideologue of American labor Zionism Hayim Greenberg, and by Rose Halprin, the acerbic and spirited leader of Hadassah. Greenberg dealt with the complexity of the concept of *galut*: "Wherever Jews live as a minority, where they are not politically or socially independent and are subject to the everyday pressures of another civilization and mode of life, but rely on the good graces of the non-Jewish majority, such a place is *galut*."[55] But a clear distinction must be made between types of *galut*. While both America and Iraq could be considered *galut*, he argued, they were totally different. In Iraq Jews were persecuted and victimized and had to flee for their lives, whereas the American Jewish community enjoyed both civil rights and substantial influence.

Greenberg therefore emphatically rejected the oft-repeated Israeli argument, which drew on the historical precedent of Nazi Germany, that America's Jews were deluding themselves in thinking that America was different. Many non-Jewish Americans also shared the belief that "it can't happen here," he maintained. This optimistic faith in the uniqueness of the American experience, Greenberg said, was rooted in the common belief that the American Revolution was the most successful in world history, that there had never been any counterrevolution in America, and that American patriotism was unafflicted by the poisonous traits typical of racist German ultranationalism. But even if worst came to worst, and America did in fact become a fascist anti-Semitic country bent on exterminating Jews, then Israel would not afford a haven either. "If that was the prognosis, of a universal Sodom and Gomorrah, what then would be the chances of Israel in such a vortex, sweeping all mankind into an abyss of wickedness and evil." [56]

Rose Halprin vigorously joined the intellectual melee on the definition of *galut*: "We do not accept the concept that we are in exile. . . . Jews are in exile where they live in fear or in torture, or where they cannot leave their countries and emigrate freely to Israel. . . . Jews in the United States are part of the Diaspora where we live in freedom." [57]

With the basic principle implied in the Jerusalem Program—that a bona fide Zionist must view self-fulfillment as coming solely through emigration to Israel—adamantly opposed by the English-speaking delegates, led by the Hadassah contingent, the program had to be shelved. Instead, a less binding definition was adopted relating to the tasks—not the aim—of Zionism, which were defined as "the strengthening of the State of Israel, the ingathering of the exiles in Eretz Yisrael, and the fostering of the unity of the Jewish people." [58] This formula saved the congress from disintegrating into two irreconcilable camps.

The inevitable corollary to the acrimonious debate over the definition of Zionism was the equally heated discussion on *halutziut*. Eliahu Dobkin, the Jewish Agency Executive member in charge of immigration, who introduced the subject, warned the congress of an impending, and acute, manpower shortage facing Israel. Most of the immigrants from the Muslim countries would arrive within the next three years, he pointed out, and when that wave of immigration ended, "how shall we continue with the process of Ingathering of Exiles? Where will the next increase in immigration come from?" [59] The problem, Dobkin explained, was not just quantitative. The immigration of a large number of Jews from the culturally deprived Muslim countries might lower the qualitative edge of Israeli society. This danger could be averted only if the American Jewish community, the largest in the world, provided the major portion of five thousand pioneers annually—the minimum required for maintaining Israel's required rate of development. But American Zionist parents, he lambasted his audience, "were trembling with fear lest their children be infected by *aliyah.*" American Zionists, he charged, either did not believe in the possibility of *aliyah* from America, or rejected it outright, claiming that a pioneering movement could never arise in the conditions prevailing in America. Nevertheless, he had not yet completely despaired of the chances of fostering *halutziut* in America, and implored the congress to place it at the center of the American Zionist agenda.[60]

Beyond the debates on specific issues, the Zionist Congress illuminated with painful clarity what had been sensed since 1948: that, paradoxically, following the miracle of Israel's birth, the Zionist idea and its vehicle, the World Zionist Organization— including its erstwhile vibrant American branch— were in deep crisis. This crisis grew out of a feeling of despair at the recognition that the Zionist idea was unrealizable. It brought home to the Israelis that even after the emergence of the State of Israel there would still be a Diaspora, and no amount of exhortation by Israeli leaders or Zionist Congress resolutions would alter that fundamental situation. Nowhere was this unhappy realization more apparent than in the disputes over such terms as the ingathering of exiles, for beyond the bitter semantic debate on whether America was an exile or a dispersion was the reality that for America's Jews, as for the Jews in the rest of the Western Diaspora, their country of residence was indeed their home.

5

"I am sure that you have noted with consternation and a certain amount of horror the publicity that is coming out of Jerusalem on the Zionist Congress," Zvi Zinder, the press attaché at the Israel embassy in Washington, communicated to Abba Eban during the course of the congress. Israel could ill afford to alienate the American Jewish community "through partisan arguments and bitter personality fights regardless of who the personalities are," Zinder pointed out. "I think I know the American Jewish community well and I know what it will take. It is not prepared to take the type of message put out originally by Ben-Gurion [a reference to his address to the Ihud Olami] and by Dobkin of the Jewish Agency." While rejecting Rose Halprin's angry response to previous attacks on American Zionists and her threat that American Jewry would cut itself off from Israel, Zinder urged the Israeli ambassador to inform the prime minister and the government "in very firm terms" that if they "are to maintain any kind of amicable relations with the American Jewish community, [the prime minister] must be prepared to forego whatever pleasure he gets out of the fire-and-brimstone statements with regard to the American contribution to Israel."[61]

Moreover, the message emanating from the congress, Zinder warned, was providing ammunition to the "enemies of Israel such as Lessing J. Rosenwald, William Zuckerman [editor of the *Jewish Newsletter*, an anti-Israeli biweekly, affiliated with the American Council for Judaism] and others." It also jeopardized Israel's standing with major newspapers such as the *New York Times* and others "whose support of Israel is based principally on a recognition of Israel itself and not on any ties, links or connection imposed upon the American Jewish community." No less serious, he added, was the effect on the many non-Zionist groups that were being alienated by "our concentration on the purely Zionist bodies." Of course the Zionists were important, but this should not mean neglecting the "great non-Zionist groups wherein lie our most important strength in combating the fears, apprehensions and doubts of the American Jewish community," including the dual loyalty issue. Israel should neither disregard the significance of this concern nor "abuse those who are fearful of it. Israel has too much to offer morally and philosophically and in many other ways, to allow this valuable . . . contribution to American Jewish life to be vitiated by purely temporary victories and personality and partisan debates."

Referring to Israel's dire economic forecast for 1951 and 1952, Zinder observed: "By our actions in Israel we can either overcome this crisis in a healthy manner or continue to live simply by hanging on with our fingernails as we have done in the past three years." Because there was no way of ensuring a repetition of the miracles attending the birth of Israel, the young state must be prepared "for a long hard pull on our own." Finally, Zinder commented regretfully, "Nothing that is being done at the Zionist Congress today is contributing to the State or to the Jewish community in the United States."

This last comment was perhaps unfair to the Zionist Congress, for it overlooked the natural need of any democratic mass movement to indulge in inflated rhetoric from time to time in order to reinforce its members'—and its leaders'—enthusiasm for the cause. Yet Zinder's warning proved timely. Alarmed at the news releases coming from the Zionist Congress and distressed at the prime minister's continued failure to reply to his previous messages, Blaustein cabled Ben-Gurion once again, on the very day that Zinder alerted Eban (20 August 1951). Blaustein expressed anxiety about the special-status issue and also requested verification of a *New York Times* dispatch dated 18 August, which stated: "It appeared obvious this weekend that a majority could be mustered for adoption of the principles of liquidation of the Diaspora, the Jews living outside Palestine." This, he warned, was "both futile and harmful" for Jews living in free and democratic countries.

Reminding Ben-Gurion of their previous discussions, Blaustein repeated his suggestion that now was the time to "explore the possibility" of replacing the World Zionist Organization with a new kind of body, "Friends of Israel," to be composed of Jews "regardless of previous Zionist or non-Zionist affiliations." This new organization, he said, would have to be jointly created by both Zionists and non-Zionists, thereby avoiding the danger of one-sided control. It would be founded on the same basis as his understanding with Ben-Gurion, and would have no say in Israeli internal affairs.[62] A day later, replying to all of Blaustein's messages, Ben-Gurion asserted that his speech at the Ihud Olami conference could not be interpreted as a breach of their understanding. The *Jewish Telegraphic Agency* report of it was inaccurate, he claimed. What he had really said was that "Zionist organizations must agree to aid [the] Jewish state under all circumstances and conditions, even if they oppose [the] views or dislike [the] composition [of the] Government of Israel."[63]

But Blaustein would not accept this explanation. In a sharply worded response, he bluntly accused the Israeli leader of dodging the issue and contradicting the understanding between them. This evasiveness was obvious, he asserted, from Ben-Gurion's unfortunate statement on the obligation of every Zionist to assist Israel "whether the Government to which the Jews in question owe allegiance desire it or not," which, according to Blaustein, was "an unheard-of request for allegiance to a foreign power." Moreover, Ben-Gurion's use of the phrase "one Jewish nation," Blaustein expostulated, violated the legal and moral standing of American Jewry as U.S. citizens. Regarding the special-status issue, Blaustein found Ben-Gurion's assertion that the special status would apply only within Israel, and that it would have "no lesser status than that of the representative of any other power," dubious, inasmuch as "no other power has any status and authority that it exercises under Israel sovereignty, so why [the] WZO status should be 'no lesser' than any other is mystifying." In any event, because the Diaspora did not constitute a political entity, how could Ben-Gurion refer to it in terms of a "power" represented by the WZO? The only concession Blaustein was willing to make, he reiterated, would be to grant the WZO a special status "regarding resettlement and rehabilitation within Israel only." Lastly, the American Jewish leader accused Ben-Gurion once again of breaching the understanding between them by failing to acknowledge that Jews living in democratic countries like the United States were not in exile.[64] The committee's concern was underscored by a cable from Proskauer to Ben-Gurion exhorting him to acquiesce to Blaustein's request:

> As head of sovereignty make no alliance with group outside your state. . . . Deserve support all Jews not merely one faction. Your recognition officially of any faction will destroy support of thousands American Jews who will not countenance action based on concept of Jewish political internationalism. Believe me dear friend your country will face dire crisis if you proceed otherwise.[65]

A day later Blaustein cabled another plea to Ben-Gurion, specifically asking him to "discourage to the fullest WZO Congress resolutions which would violate our understanding, and that to the extent that you are unsuccessful in so doing you disassociate yourself therefrom." Ignoring the demands of the non-Zionists, Blaustein warned, might bring great harm to the cause of Israel in the United States.[66]

Contrary to Blaustein's impression, Ben-Gurion was far from indifferent to the non-Zionists' intense reactions, but he was forced to maneuver between conflicting personal, institutional, and ideological forces within the Zionist movement and the Israeli political system, including factions in his own party. Adroit and experienced politician that he was, he would, when necessary, do what all politicians do, namely, use fiery rhetoric to preach different gospels to different audiences, while away from the limelight pragmatically attempt to solve the problem at hand.

That was precisely the course of action he adopted as the Zionist Congress drew to a close. Alert to the non-Zionists' forebodings and to warnings by Eban, Kollek, and the Foreign Office of dangerous implications for Israeli-American Jewish relations, he dispatched his troubleshooter, Teddy Kollek, to America, while Eban urged Blaustein to keep the committee from taking any public action until a meeting between them could be arranged.[67]

Simultaneously, prodded by Eban and Sharett, Ben-Gurion formulated his ideas on the issues raised by Blaustein in a letter to him. Addressing the question of the special status, the prime minister reiterated his assurance to Blaustein "that the status to be granted, if at all, to the WZO [would] be limited to resettlement and rehabilitation of immigrants *inside* Israel [emphasis in original]." He and his colleagues also agreed with Blaustein's position that no exclusive representative status should be given to the WZO in the Diaspora. It was also perfectly clear from the text of his speech at the congress, he said, that there were no grounds for concern about dual loyalty, because he had stated unequivocally that the "the State of Israel has authority over its citizens only. It does not represent Jews living outside its boundaries and is not authorized to impose upon them any obligations whatsoever." But on the perennial question of Jewish peoplehood he remained firm. "As a Zionist," he declared, "I believe that there is one Jewish people in the world, and as a Zionist I reserve the right to express my Zionist convictions. A person who is not a Zionist may think otherwise, but in Israel, just as in the United States, there is freedom of opinion and freedom of speech and every Jew may express his convictions as he wishes."[68]

Fundamentally, the prime minister stated to Blaustein, he viewed the relationship between Israel and the Diaspora as resting on two pillars: partnership and equality. All Jews, Zionists and non-Zionists alike, were equal partners in the worldwide effort to aid *aliyah,* absorption, and economic independence.

Despite the conciliatory tone of Ben-Gurion's letter, however, Blaustein was neither able nor willing to consider the dispute settled. The reasons for this reluctance became apparent in light of resentment on the part of the non-Zionist leadership of the UJA of Greater New York regarding both the proceedings of the Zionist Congress and Ben-Gurion's controversial statements that preceded it. Samuel D. Leidesdorf, treasurer of the Greater New York UJA and a prominent New York accountant, expressed concern about the "antagonistic attitude [that] has been developed on the part of his associates in the UJA" in reaction to the appeals voiced at the Zionist Congress and endorsed by Ben-Gurion "for large scale immigration of American Jews to Israel which in turn will reflect on their position here." That stand, Leidesdorf warned, was likely to be "most harmful" to fund-raising activities.[69]

Another sharp critic of the news emanating from Jerusalem was Judge Samuel I. Rosenman, an influential member of the American Jewish Committee. Rosenman, who had served as special counsel, speech writer, and political advisor to Presidents Roosevelt and Truman, was upset by a *New York Times* report of a resolution adopted at the closing session of the Zionist Congress stating that "all activities relating to Israel have to be cleared and approved by the World Zionist Organization." Although the specific phrasing of the resolution as reported by the *Times* was inaccurate, it nevertheless reflected the intent of the supporters of the status law. Rosenman was emphatic that he would "never agree to help the State of Israel under such conditions." He could only assume that Ben-Gurion had been "under great pressure during the session of the congress to endorse such a policy." Nevertheless, he deplored the prime minister's "rather evasive" position in his exchange of cables with Blaustein. If no adequate clarification were provided on these controversial developments, Judge Rosenman warned, he would end his activity on behalf of Israel and was sure that all other so-called non-Zionist Jews would do the same. He predicted that the UJA and similar efforts would break up, and that the Zionist movement alone would not be able to achieve the same results.[70]

Leidesdorf's and Rosenman's warnings had a decisive impact on Blaustein's stand in his forthcoming meeting with Eban and Kollek, and played a role as well in subsequent developments surrounding Ben-Gurion's clarification of 30 September 1951.

6

Codifying Communal Relationships

1

THE ANTICIPATED MEETING between Blaustein, Eban, and Kollek, which was occasioned by objections to statements in Ben-Gurion's speech of 8 August to the Ihud Olami as well as to the resolutions of the Zionist Congress, was scheduled for 4 September 1951. Blaustein, a stickler for detail, asked Eban to provide full transcripts of the texts in question, a task that Eban assigned to Esther Herlitz, first secretary at the embassy in charge of liaison with American Jewish organizations. Anticipating the list of complaints by the non-Zionists, Herlitz also developed strongly worded rebuttals for Eban's and Kollek's use.

Inasmuch as the World Zionist Organization was a democratic movement, wrote Herlitz, and Ben-Gurion was not "its dictator, it is quite absurd to assume that he can prevent that organization from adopting resolutions that would not please Blaustein. In fact he can exert no more pressure or influence on them than Mr. Truman can on the US Congress. That is exactly what Blaustein has always claimed—[that] both the US and Israel are democracies." In any case, Herlitz thought, the Zionist Congress resolutions were harmless even from Blaustein's point of view, because they were only binding for the WZO. Furthermore, "whatever status will be accorded the Jewish Agency, will affect their activities in Israel only; the American Jewish Committee is not engaged in any activities in Israel."

Dealing with one of Ben-Gurion's most offensive statements, in the non-Zionists' statement made at the 8 August Ihud Olami conference, Herlitz maintained that it "was not really as bad as the *JTA* made it look." What the Israeli prime minister said, she explained, was

that Zionists who live in free and democratic countries—as against Russian Jews, for instance, who cannot help Israel at all, and Ben-Gurion does not

131

blame them for it—can and should assist Israel always. If the government of the country of which they are loyal citizens adopts a policy that is harmful to Israel, they should—and can, because they live in a country where people can express their opinions—make their views known to their government, as British Jews did during the [British] Mandate. That is exactly the sort of thing [that] Blaustein [himself] has been doing. Why and how, otherwise, does he explain his approaches to M. G. [George C. McGhee, assistant secretary of state for Near Eastern Affairs] on the subject of the Huleh, Suez, grant-in-aid, etc.? Because, being a loyal American citizen and a good Jew and pro-Israeli, he felt that he was doing the right thing as an American citizen and as a Jew. Hence, we can really claim that Ben-Gurion did not develop any theory now that is in violation of his "agreement" with Blaustein in Jerusalem last August.[1]

Herlitz informed Eban and Kollek that she had utilized this line of reasoning "quite successfully" with the B'nai B'rith membership.

Herlitz's counterattack might have been persuasive as far as American Zionists—and some non-Zionists such as members of B'nai B'rith—were concerned. Doubtless it would have merited points in a debating contest. But the American scene in the early 1950s was not an innocent debating match— it was more akin to a minefield strewn with cold war loyalty investigations and anti-Communist McCarthyist witch hunts. Significantly, Blaustein was to entitle his presidential address delivered to the committee in January 1952 "Freedom and Fear." In it he would refer to "the epidemic of loyalty oaths on university campuses and other nongovernmental, nondefense situations— where this new fever serves only to sacrifice honest thinking, honest speaking and honest teaching on the altar of hysteria." This hysteria had led to "growing fearful attitudes toward the freedoms to think, to speak, to be ourselves and in fact to be different."[2] American Jewry's anxieties were, in fact, understood by some Israeli representatives, such as press attaché Zvi Zinder, who had advised his government against old-style, and by then futile, Zionist polemics and recriminations. Presumably, Eban and Kollek too realized that Herlitz's arguments would not convince Blaustein and the non-Zionists.

Eban and Kollek traveled to Baltimore on 4 September for the meeting. Its results, Blaustein informed Eban, would "determine the future course of the American Jewish Committee with regard to Israel." The main topic of the conference, however, was Ben-Gurion's statements and the need to clear the air by means of a public explanation from him. Eban and Kollek complied with this demand and made an additional major concession to Blaustein: the American Jewish Committee—namely, Blaustein, Slawson, and Segal—would have the right to amend the text of the clarification to their satisfaction. These concessions stemmed from an awareness, Kollek explained after the meeting, that contrary to the prevailing misconception in Israel that the ZOA provided most of the assistance to Israel, 90 percent or more of the financial, political, and moral support for Israel came in fact "from other [segments] of the community [the non-Zionists] which are at present in revolt because of the privileges the Knesset might confer on the WZO." In consequence, Kollek warned, if the Knesset, "as is likely, endorses the recommendations of the [Zionist] Congress," the revolt of the non-Zionists would result in the breakup of the united American Jewish front aiding Israel.[3]

Abba Eban, preparing a masterful draft of the clarification, cabled it to the prime minister two days later for his personal attention, while submitting another copy to the committee. The text was designed to satisfy the non-Zionists' demands on four points: the special-status issue, Ben-Gurion's controversial speech of 8 August, the meaning of the term "ingathering of exiles," and Israel's continued cooperation with "a free and secure American Jewry." Apart from minor stylistic corrections, Blaustein, Slawson, and Segal focused on the condition that aid given by an American Jew to Israel "must be done within the framework of American interests and must in no way conflict with his obligation, duties and responsibilities as a citizen of his own country, the U.S.A." Textual reconciliation of the two outlooks turned out to be the easier part of the clarification process. Obtaining Ben-Gurion's imprimatur would prove to be an entirely different matter.

Ben-Gurion, annoyed with the American Jewish Committee's pressure for a clarification, was in fact caught up, more seriously, in a major government crisis. A political storm several months before the Zionist Congress had led to the dissolution of the government and new elections on 30 July 1951. It took Ben-Gurion the better part of two tense and exhausting months thereafter to form a new government, during which he had little time to devote to resolving the clarification matter.[4]

No one understood Ben-Gurion's predicament better than Teddy Kollek, who was involved with Blaustein's urgent demands for clarification firsthand in the United States. Kollek tried his best to get the prime minister to deal promptly with the matter of Blaustein's needs,[5] but this promptness proved impossible in the face of governmental pressures. "Postponement [in cabling the clarification] due entirely to terrific tension under which laboring at present," wired Ben-Gurion's aide, Ephraim Evron, to Kollek on 26 September.[6]

Meanwhile, Nahum Goldmann, who maintained that the clarification statement would be "very harmful" and dangerous to Zionist interests, volunteered to handle the matter himself. He suggested that the problem be resolved through a conference with the leadership of the UJA and the non-Zionists where "the issues and misunderstanding would be discussed in a friendly and frank atmosphere."[7] But Goldmann could not get past Eban and Kollek, as well as Sharett, who were convinced of the need to strengthen Blaustein's hand.[8]

On the American side, Judge Proskauer strongly supported Blaustein's demand for clarification. In a stern yet friendly letter drafted in a chastising tone, Proskauer depicted a "critical situation vis-à-vis Israel which has arisen in America and which I think calls on you to follow exactly the course Blaustein has asked you to do." Proskauer described the situation:

> Masses of people are utterly shocked by the chauvinistic utterances attributed to Dobkin [calling for *halutzim* from America], Goldmann [urging Zionists to strive for control of Jewish communities in America], and yourself [referring to the ingathering of exiles, thereby implying that America is exile]. They refuse any longer to accept the explanation of misquotation. Scores of people are using it as an excuse not to support [the] UJA. . . . More than this, we are confronted with the critical question as to whether we can any longer aid the state of Israel in non-financial ways.[9]

Indeed, the situation was so grave, the judge claimed, that "people like the [American] Council for Judaism have issued a pamphlet charging that men like myself have been made dupes of a Jewish internationalism [*sic!*] movement. I very much hope we have not been."

The immediate remedy, Proskauer stressed, entailed Ben-Gurion's publishing the desired clarification. "Mere statements are no longer enough," said the judge. "I hear on every hand: 'You get statements and then you get conduct completely at variance with those statements.' " In addition, he urged that diplomatic status not be granted to the WZO. "The Jewish Agency must keep its fingers off American life," a demand, he explained, that stemmed from reports he had received of projected Jewish Agency sponsorship of a program for teaching Hebrew to American Jewish children, to be paid for with

American philanthropic funds earmarked for Israel. What he objected to was not the teaching of Hebrew, but the sponsorship of the Jewish Agency, "which gives it a political color. Such a thing is unthinkable." Proskauer emphasized the importance of getting the clarification before 14 October, when the AJC executive committee was scheduled to meet. "I hope before that time you will enable your friends to say something for you."

Proskauer's letter arrived in Jerusalem after Ben-Gurion had finally decided to dispatch his clarification, cabling it to Abba Eban on 30 September for transmission to Blaustein and other American Jewish leaders, and later to the press. This final version was a composite of the text that had been amended by both the committee and the New York Jewish Agency Executive, and of rewritten segments prepared in the Prime Minister's Office in Jerusalem. The first part defined the nature of the relationship between Israel and the Diaspora by reaffirming the Blaustein-Ben-Gurion Understanding. In the second part Ben-Gurion retained Eban's draft with regard to the special-status issue, stating that the Knesset "may . . . be asked to confer a special status on the Jewish Agency inside Israel" to enable it to discharge its specific functions.

However, the prime minister omitted entire segments of the committee's amended version dealing with his 8 August speech to Ihud Olami, as well as the definition of the term "Jewish nation." As was his wont in all political matters, Ben-Gurion preserved his freedom of action, setting defined limits to his concessions both to the non-Zionists and to the Zionists.[10]

Fortified by Ben-Gurion's clarification, Blaustein succeeded in steering his organization's executive committee meeting in Chicago (13–14 October) along a course of continued support for Israel, although, he informed the prime minister, "we strenuously oppose any policy which would, in our opinion, affect adversely the position of American Jews."[11] Affirming its creed that "America is our home," in a resolution on Israel, the executive committee also categorically rejected any statements made at the Zionist Congress "that American Jews are in any sense 'exiles.' " The thrust of the resolution reiterated the committee's opposition to granting the JA-WZO (without mentioning these bodies explicitly) any kind of special status, whether diplomatic or political and whether within Israel or in the Diaspora. While the committee favored "liberal aid for Israel," it nevertheless objected strenuously to any educational activities initiated by Israel within the American Jewish community (a reference to the teaching of Hebrew) making use of funds earmarked for aid for Israel.[12]

The committee's resolution was received coolly by Ben-Gurion. It appeared to him "to be marked by a somewhat excessively apologetic spirit. Would Americans of English descent feel obliged to express themselves in the terms used in the first paragraph ['America is our home . . . we are integrated into its political, social and cultural life.']? Possibly, however I lack a full comprehension of the feelings of an American Jew." Regarding the committee's major concern—Israel's relationship with American Jewry, and particularly the issue of the special status—the prime minister kept his thoughts to himself, although he allowed himself to comment to Blaustein: "While there is not any serious difference of opinion between us on this point, were I an American Jew I would not have signed the resolution you have adopted, although I acknowledge fully your right to adopt such a resolution."[13]

Judge Proskauer, unlike many of the other committee leaders, considered it important that Ben-Gurion understand the psychology and sensitivities of the New World Jews in their encounter with the Jewish state. Appealing to Ben-Gurion's sense of himself as "a pragmatic idealist," and in view of his recent clarification, the judge implored Ben-Gurion to use

> greater care in making statements which are capable of being interpreted as inconsistent with this view [that the Jews of the United States consider themselves Americans]. I think there have been such statements, perhaps incautiously or inadvertently made. It is not enough to say that we do not regard ourselves in America as exiles. We do not want *you* [my emphasis] to say that you regard us as exiles.[14]

Such provocative statements by Israeli leaders, Proskauer pointed out, tended "to impair the integrity of the American Jewish position" and were likewise harmful to Israel's cause.

In Proskauer's opinion, the recent controversies could be "a useful thunderstorm" to help clear the air. In fact, both the past and the present presidents of the American Jewish Committee showed, in their correspondence with Ben-Gurion, a desire to turn over a new leaf in their relationship with the leader of the Jewish state. But given Ben-Gurion's basic attitude and policy concerning the Diaspora and the Zionists, along with the fact that the special-status issue was still unresolved in Israeli politics, the harmonious note achieved in the relationship between the American Jewish Committee and Israel was not destined to be sustained.

2

Nahum Goldmann in particular was not about to let the special—status issue
lie dormant. Just three months after the Zionist Congress ended, he resumed
his efforts to rally support for the idea among his colleagues in the Jewish
Agency Executive, within Israel's political parties, and from the prime minister. No amount of protests by the American Jewish Committee, he informed
his Jewish Agency Executive colleagues, would bury the special-status issue.
On the contrary, granting the status was vitally important, as it would enhance
"the prestige of Zionism." With most of the political parties in favor, enacting
a law on the issue depended on the government's initiative. As Goldmann understood it, Ben-Gurion also supported the idea, pending reviewing a draft of
the law being prepared by Minister of Justice Dov Joseph. Further delay, however, could ruin the chances of having the law passed, he sensed.

In fact, the Jewish Agency Executive was not of one mind regarding the
value of the special status. Yitzhak Raphael of the National Religious Party, for
example, felt that "the magic word 'status' has become obsolete." Although it
may have bestowed prestige in the past, he said, "the real 'status' [now] is reflected in our financial situation. If we go bankrupt, the 'status' will be of no
avail." [15] Still, Goldmann prevailed, and in early December 1951 he and the
other Jewish Agency Executive chairman, Berl Locker, submitted to Ben-
Gurion a unanimous official demand on behalf of the executive to retain the
statement in the draft of the special status law that the WZO "is the representative of the Jewish people in all matters relating to organized participation of
the Jews of the Diaspora in the development and upbuilding of the country
and the rapid absorption of the immigrants." Goldmann and Locker emphasized to Ben-Gurion that this sentence "represents the main foundation of the
law, without which the law will be meaningless." [16]

In the midst of this controversy, another remark of Ben-Gurion's sud-
denly made headlines in the United States. On 13 December the *New York
Times* carried a news item from Jerusalem under the headline: "Ben-Gurion
Scores U.S. Zionist Chiefs. Charges 'They Went Bankrupt' After Israel's
Founding—Says Few Came to Build." The report stated that the prime minister had attacked the American Zionist leaders during a 12 December Knesset
debate on the sharp decline in *aliyah,* saying: "They went bankrupt, and I told
that, a day or two ago, to one of the leaders who just came from there. There
were not even fifty leaders who got up to go to Israel when the State was es-

tablished. I don't maintain they would have been followed by masses, but they would have proved that Zionism was not void of meaning—at least in the eyes of its leaders." Perpetually haunted by the prospect of the end of mass immigration to Israel, Ben-Gurion asserted that *aliyah* to Israel never stemmed from ideological motivations but was induced by the [threat] "of a lash." The fact was that the Jewish communities in the free world (such as in America) were able but unwilling to immigrate to Israel, while persecuted communities (such as in the Soviet Union) were willing but unable to immigrate.

He repeated his conviction that *aliyah* from the free world would only be achieved if Israel were made attractive to *olim* with professional qualifications—if suitable conditions, especially proper housing, were provided for their absorption. Whatever happened, he thought such professionally trained immigrants would eventually come, for "economic forces in [America] might induce them. Since the United States work force had many professionals, and since the Jewish intelligentsia forms a much higher percentage than the total proportion of Jews in America, I don't know if Jewish firms are able to employ the entire Jewish intelligentsia." [17]

Soon thereafter Ben-Gurion grasped the extent of the furor his remarks aroused in America, and he tried to backtrack. Explaining himself to a veteran American Zionist leader, he said:

> I mentioned the leaders of American Zionists in my speech and expressed my disappointment that not even fifty of them had immigrated to Israel when the State was established. I did not, however, speak of 'the bankruptcy of American Zionism.' On the contrary, I spoke in its defense by stressing that Russian Zionists too did not immigrate until great distress, pogroms, Bolshevist revolution, persecution, etc., forced them to come.[18]

Ben-Gurion's latest indictment received wide publicity and was destined to plague him for years to come. American Jewish antagonism toward *aliyah,* combined with the sensitive psychological climate in the United States during the early 1950s, turned the statement into yet another Ben-Gurion bombshell.

Naturally enough, the American Zionists were furious. Initially, however, the executive of the Jewish Agency American section decided against making any individual statements, and instead accepted Nahum Goldmann's offer to act as spokesman. Even the suave and urbane Goldmann, an ally of Ben-Gurion's in the WZO, allowed himself to vent his dismay in a cable to Ben-Gurion:

Returned today found great excitement among Zionist and non-Zionist leaders about your statement in Knesset referring as papers report to bankruptcy [of] American Zionist leadership, discrimination against Jews in American economy, and other statements referring to emigration from here to Israel. Leaders [of] various Zionist organizations will make counterstatements these days. Myself must deal with your statement [in] my address UJA conference Atlantic City. On eve of this conference some of your utterances especially unfortunate and damaging. Generally don't think Knesset proper platform for criticism American Zionism or American Jewish policies and position [of] Jews [in] America. You must realize that we must counteract very damaging effect your statement which may have harmful consequences [for] UJA conference . . . [19]

But it was not only the Zionists who felt betrayed by Ben-Gurion's Knesset statement. Louis A. Novins, a former aide to Barney Balaban, the Hollywood mogul, working with the celebrated pro-Israel lobbyist I. L. Kenen to marshal support in the U.S. Congress for a bill authorizing a $100 million grant for Israel,[20] conveyed to Eban his "sense of utter helplessness and frustration. If the statement had been calculated to complicate our tasks, it could not have accomplished its objective more successfully." In fact, Novins told Eban, "the repercussions have already been dreadful. I have heard from some of the people who made critical contributions to this undertaking [the grant-in-aid program]. They are angry and will have nothing to do with any further efforts of this kind." The respected image and reputation won by Ben-Gurion through his outstanding achievements and leadership had become tarnished. "Let there be no doubt about it, the 'honeymoon' is over," Novins observed. "Mr. Ben-Gurion has now become a controversial figure in American Jewry."[21]

Two top leaders of the Anti-Defamation League (ADL) of B'nai B'rith sent Eban similar messages. "It is inconceivable to me," wrote National Chairman Meier Steinbrink, "that [Ben-Gurion] fails to see the danger implicit in such a statement as he is alleged to have made [urging American Jewish citizens to leave their native land and immigrate to Israel]. That can only form the basis for the continued charge made against us by our enemies that we of American birth and American citizenship are guilty of a dual loyalty." Equally distressing to American Jewry, ADL's National Director Benjamin R. Epstein bitterly complained to Eban, was Ben-Gurion's comment "on presumed bigoted economic and employment factors that will lead American

Jews to come to your country, coupled with his dismaying prediction 'I am sure they will come.' " The effect of this statement, the ADL leader pointed out, could create "the very deplorable situation that it inaccurately assumes as an existent fact." Further, Epstein charged, by making such a prognostication, Ben-Gurion appeared to be cherishing the hope that such a development "may serve the interests [of Israel] in terms of its needs for a trained, non-impoverished immigration." [22]

The reverberations of Ben-Gurion's unfortunate comments were not confined to American Jewry. Burton Y. Berry, deputy assistant secretary of state for Near Eastern affairs, in a meeting with Eban, expressed official criticism of the section in Ben-Gurion's statement, as quoted in the *Times,* dealing with the economic difficulties of the Jewish intelligentsia in the United States. The statement, Berry protested, "did not accurately reflect American reality nor the equal and solid status of America's Jewish citizens." After some persuasion Eban managed to convince Berry that the point Ben-Gurion intended to make was essentially the need for the immigration of professionals designed to help the upbuilding of Israel. Later he cabled Ben-Gurion and Sharett that despite the friendly atmosphere during his meeting with Berry, "its importance should not be underestimated. This was an explicit warning that the American government was not going to disregard matters relating to American Jewry, nor to relegate this question, under all circumstances, to an Israeli-American Jewish dialogue." [23] The financial effort for Israel was also affected. For example, a group of friends of Israel in Toronto reneged on a promise to lend Israel $150,000—a substantial sum in 1951.[24]

Eventually, this storm died down too. Still, considerable damage had been done to the fragile balance between the two Jewish centers—the small, struggling State of Israel dependent for its life on the economic aid and political goodwill of the affluent and influential American Jewish community. Ben-Gurion's puzzling behavior raises some questions about his underlying motives for these outbursts. What effect did the many exchanges with Teddy Kollek, Jacob Blaustein, and a large number of other individuals about the unique nature of American Jewry have on this enigmatic leader? They had warned him repeatedly that his statements were playing straight into the hands of the American Council for Judaism and other enemies of Israel, and at the same time damaging fund-raising efforts for Israel by supplying excuses to those UJA givers who in any case were ambivalent about contributing. Could these statements be attributed to a Machiavellian design to instill a constant feeling of guilt among America's Jews, thereby ensuring their continued and undiminished response to Israel's desperate needs? Or perhaps, as some American Jewish leaders suspected, there were no hidden motives.[25] Rather Ben-Gurion, after carrying a crushing burden for many years, and having led a life-and-death war for independence, was, at the age of sixty-five, weary.

3

Meanwhile, the Blaustein-Goldmann contest over the proposed special-status law continued unabated. Goldmann was furious to learn that, at Blaustein's request, Ben-Gurion was delaying submitting to the government the draft of the status law containing the first paragraph on the WZO as "the representative of the Jewish people," in anticipation of a forthcoming visit by Eban to Israel. Keeping up the pressure on Ben-Gurion, Goldmann alluded to widespread support for the law, insisting that it not be "overruled by a veto of Mr. Blaustein. . . . It is really becoming intolerable to have Mr. Blaustein act as a final arbiter in such matters." A major concession to Blaustein's sensitivities, he reminded the prime minister, had already been made at the Zionist Congress by denying the extension of the special status to the WZO in the Diaspora. With that accommodation, "and with the possibility of enlarging the Jewish Agency to include non-Zionists," he argued, "to give in now on the fundamental basis of the status would be a surrender which neither I personally nor, I think, any of my colleagues in the Executive could accept."[26]

Goldmann also foresaw that the political parties would not countenance a special-status law without the crucial first paragraph, and would introduce it themselves. He also correctly predicted that there would be a clear majority for such a law "based on the notion of a *representative* [my emphasis] of the Jewish people."

The crux of the matter was Goldmann's and the Zionist leadership's contest with the non-Zionists over fund-raising control in America. The acquisition of special status was perceived by Goldmann as a sine qua non on this issue. "The control of the fund-raising scene and the maintenance of the Jewish Agency's authority can be assured only if the Agency has a specific status,"[27] Goldmann told his Jewish Agency colleagues in New York. He needed this authority to deal with other Jewish organizations from a position of strength. "It is a matter of great importance to me and my colleagues," Goldmann advised Ben-Gurion, "and I ask you to regard it as such."[28] Attaining that authority from Israel, Goldmann apparently believed, would also enable him to overcome what he perceived as one of the most difficult problems in

America, namely, the chaotic nature of organizational life in the largest Jewish community in the world. In his view the basic question was: who spoke for the Jews, and in particular, who spoke for American Jewry vis-à-vis Israel? Yet with organizational life in America based on voluntarism and pluralism for Jews and non-Jews alike, attempts to create a central representative body of American Jewry had little chance of success. The American Jewish community had always been an undefined entity, so that Goldmann's goal for the Zionist movement, under his leadership, to become the community's single voice in relation to Israel was utopian. Inevitably, the American Jewish Committee, which maintained "that there can be no single voice speaking for the Jews," [29] spearheaded the offensive against including the first paragraph in the special-status law—the "representative of the Jewish people" stipulation—a struggle that was reminiscent, mutatis mutandis, of the committee's opposition to the founding of an umbrella organization, the American Jewish Conference, in 1943.

The Goldmann-Blaustein tug-of-war proved to be protracted. Abba Eban, on a home visit to Israel at the end of 1951, added his persuasive voice to the opposition to the controversial first paragraph. The Zionists' claim to represent the Jewish people, Eban pointed out to Ben-Gurion, was untenable on two counts. Firstly, "it is an untrue definition. Since Israel's creation the *Shekhinah* (Divine Presence) has left the Zionist movement. The Jewish people [now] view the State of Israel . . . as the organized embodiment of the instinct of the national revival." Devoid of its historic functions, the Zionist movement had become "a dry river." Strangely, the draft law disregarded this revolutionary development, Eban argued. Furthermore, "the Jewish people do not view the WZO as its representative—and lo, along comes the State of Israel and 'recognizes' something which is untrue, and which is unrecognized by the Jewish people." Secondly, the whole concept of "representative of the Jewish people" was in contradiction to the norms of international relations. For example, the "United States Government, as well as American Jewry, consider the 'representative' of the Jews of American citizenship to be Monnett B. Davis [the American ambassador to Israel then]—and not Berl Locker." Therefore, in order to prevent any confusion between the functions of the Jewish Agency and those of a diplomatic representative, Eban urged, the WZO should be described as "the official agency working *in Israel* for certain goals" [emphasis in original]. Even this amendment, he cautioned, might not be acceptable to Blaustein and the non-Zionists, "who are very active on our behalf," although he emphasized that his view was not influenced by their opposition but derived from the merits of the case.

Eban suggested two further modifications. Rather than granting a special status to the WZO, he said, this status should be granted to the Jewish Agency, "because the Jewish Agency is capable of expanding to include the entire Jewish people, whereas the WZO will always be narrowly confined within a single ideology." This being so, he also recommended omitting the phrase "in the name of the Jewish people." The whole matter, Eban concluded his trenchant criticism, "was quite painful. It would have been preferable if the WZO had accomplished great deeds in the Diaspora—and would have then insisted on recognition of these deeds." [30]

Teddy Kollek in Washington endorsed Eban's criticism, cabling to Ben-Gurion that he too believed that the problem could be solved by expanding the Jewish Agency, in fact even before the draft law was to be submitted to the Knesset.[31] Jacob Blaustein kept up his pressure on the prime minister and on Eban, urging them not to capitulate on the question of the first paragraph and requesting to "be afforded the opportunity to review in advance the pertinent portions of any proposed Knesset Act."

Ben-Gurion enigmatically cabled Blaustein on 31 December: "Please wait and see." [32] As usual, Ben-Gurion was not about to reveal any secrets about his delicate political balancing act between the elements involved. Yet in early 1952 it became apparent that Blaustein's objections, as well as his request to review the draft of the law, had been favorably received by the prime minister.[33]

The results of Ben-Gurion's attitude became tangible in March 1952 when the first paragraph of the draft status law, inferring that the WZO represents "the Jewish people," was eliminated and replaced by recognition of the WZO as the "authorized Agency operating in Israel on behalf of the Jewish people." Although pleased with this change, Blaustein still objected to the phrase "on behalf of the Jewish people." This phrase too was later dropped.[34]

The prime minister, submitting the law to the Knesset on 5 May, explained: "Two things that are in the Zionist Congress resolution cannot be in the law: (1) that the World Zionist Organization is the representative of the Jewish people; and (2) that the State of Israel will work in coordination with the WZO in regard to activities within Jewish communities in the Diaspora on behalf of the state." [35] This time Blaustein was satisfied that the government of Israel had given "great weight" to the views of the committee in this matter, and that he had had the opportunity to make his comments on the various drafts of the bill. The latest of those drafts, he reported to his colleagues, "while not entirely unexceptionable, meets our principal objections." [36]

He still had one reservation, however—the term "ingathering of exiles," which was used in describing "one of the major undertakings of the State of Israel." Contacting Eban about it, he found the ambassador to be adamant. The phrase "ingathering of exiles" had to stay, Eban said. Not only did it have "venerable roots" in Jewish history and literature, but in recent years it had become "the most popular and authentic description of the primary national purpose which unites the people of Israel. To ask us to avoid the use of this phrase would be equivalent to asking an American to put aside, as unworthy or obsolete, some of the most familiar concepts and formulations of the Declaration of Independence." Moreover, in view of Ben-Gurion's clarification, it was superfluous, he said, to reiterate that the phrase "exiles" applied to Jewish communities living under conditions of "insecurity and discrimination, and not to free Jewish communities such as those in the United States." [37]

Eban took the opportunity to review the list of concessions that Israel had made to the American Jewish Committee in response to the organization's sensitivities: the status law applied only to an organization operating within Israel and would have no jurisdiction outside Israel's borders; references to "the Jewish people as a whole are made only in relation to those functions which Israel and the Jewish people share together—the creation of conditions for the absorption of Israel's immigrants"; and the law did not cast any doubt on the status and well-being of American Jewry, nor did it favor the Zionists at the expense of the non-Zionists. "Surely, it must be conceded," Eban concluded, "that my government has shown patience, goodwill, and acute sensitivity to the opinion which you represent. May I hope that this responsiveness by my government merits appreciation on the part of the American Jewish Committee and its President, of whose constant and devoted support of Israel's cause we are gratefully conscious at all times." [38]

4

But Ben-Gurion's government faced two more hurdles before the arduous process of enacting the status law could be completed. Debated in both the Knesset and the Zionist General Council, the draft law came up against sharp criticism from the opposition parties both on the left and the right. The government, by putting a diluted version of the law before the Knesset, was accused of undermining the authority of the WZO and thereby contributing to its deterioration as a viable force in world Jewry.[39]

Ben-Gurion's attitude to the WZO was similarly attacked at the Zionist General Council, which was in session in Jerusalem during 7–15 May 1952. "In the opinion of the Government—insofar as Mr. Ben-Gurion reflects its outlook—the Zionist idea no longer exists," asserted Kurt Blumenfeld, a respected Zionist theoretician.[40] Ben-Gurion's concessions to the non-Zionists were equally unforgivable, according to his critics. Left-wing Mapam leader Ya'akov Hazan protested that it should not be Israeli diplomats who represent the Jewish state in relations with the Jewish people, but rather the WZO, which could "rally [the Jewish people] around the state." He also condemned Ben-Gurion's policy toward the non-Zionists, saying, "Those who speak about the Jewish masses and lower the prestige of the Zionist movement refer, in the final analysis, to Jewish notables who wield the power by virtue of their material riches. In the name of these Jewish 'masses' the status of the Zionist movement is being impaired."[41] Joseph Schechtman, speaking for the right-wing American Zionist Hatzohar-Herut Party at the other end of the political spectrum, went even further. Representing his party's fundamentalist Zionist stand, he called for a "difficult and bitter ideological conflict with the non-Zionists," even at the risk of losing their financial support. In any event, he contended, the whole issue of the special status was undignified. "We should cease pestering the government, asking for one status or another." Instead, the Zionist movement should concentrate on a Zionist revival, on "the strengthening of self-confidence . . . which will not suffer from any feeling of inferiority toward either Mr. Jacob Blaustein, the Israel government, or itself—in other words a Zionist movement that knows what it stood for in the past, what it represents today, and what its mission will be tomorrow."[42]

Nahum Goldmann was once again in the eye of the storm. Although he was the progenitor and champion of the special-status idea, he had become appreciative of Blaustein's and Ben-Gurion's constraints. True to his reputation as an inveterate compromiser,[43] he tried hard to coax the delegates at the Zionist General Council toward a position midway between the Zionist Congress resolutions and the Israeli government's desires. The Zionists, he cogently put it, faced a "paradoxical situation . . . forced to choose between our responsibility to the state and fulfillment of its most prosaic but sacred needs, and a far-reaching policy aimed at winning over the Jewish people to Zionism and taking over the leadership of local Jewish institutions." The solution to this dilemma, he suggested, lay in his idea of creating two bodies: the WZO, devoting itself to purely Zionist work, and an enlarged Jewish Agency, comprised of Zionists and non-Zionists, that would concentrate on political and financial aid for Israel.

> Once Messrs. Warburg and Blaustein and the Welfare Funds share responsibility with me for supplying Israel's material needs—and I of course do not mean thereby to forgo our influence on these matters—they will not be able to dismiss us at will. Then we shall have one foot free. With one foot we shall join forces with them, while with the [other] we shall be at liberty to follow the path we wish Zionism to take.[44]

In the same pragmatic spirit, Goldmann warned the delegates against putting forward maximalist suggestions "in the form of ultimatums which lead us to friction with the Knesset." Such a development, he told his fellow Zionists, might be disastrous for the relationship between Israel and the Zionist movement.[45]

Goldmann's warning was indeed timely. In August, when the law was submitted to the Knesset for its second reading, opposition members organized a parliamentary ambush, gained a small majority, and reintroduced the controversial phrase "representative of the Jewish people" to replace the government version: "authorized agent."[46] After almost two years of struggle over the special-status issue, it appeared that the entire matter had completely retrogressed. Blaustein was "shocked and distressed at press reports of the Knesset action."[47] But Ben-Gurion would not let the opposition get away with it, forcing the government to recall the law and threatening to resign if the original text were not reinstated.[48]

Blaustein's faith in Ben-Gurion's statesmanship was restored by the prime minister's "firm action [in] withdrawing the Bill. Had this Knesset action stood," he said, "it would have created a severe crisis in American Jewish life, causing serious, irreparable harm to Israel on all fronts, diplomatic and economic. [I] am glad [that] your statesmanship avoided this situation."[49]

Ben-Gurion's move in recalling the law received considerable attention in the American Yiddish press. The *Forward* lauded Ben-Gurion's statesmanship, commenting in an editorial that it did not oppose granting

> special recognition to the WZO as such. . . . But there is a great difference between granting it recognition and giving it a monopoly. We can say with

certainty that the Jewish labor movement in the United States will not apply to Rabbi Silver to approve [its] Jewishness, [its] friendship . . . to Israel. The American Jewish Committee will not ask Rabbi Silver or any other Zionist leader whether it should exert its influence in Washington on behalf of the State of Israel.

On the other hand, left-wing columnist B. Z. Goldberg, writing in *The Day*, strongly protested against exaggerating the importance of the American Jewish Committee at the expense of the Zionists, and censured Ben-Gurion, a "socialist Zionist," for negotiating with "oil industrialist, anti-Zionist" Jacob Blaustein.[50]

Yet another last-minute hitch developed as the special-status law neared its goal. Blaustein was surprised to learn in November 1952 that a change had been made in the draft at some point, so that the first paragraph, which had formerly read "The State of Israel, representing only its own inhabitants, regards itself as the work of the Jewish people and has opened the gates to every Jew who wishes to come," no longer contained the phrase "representing only its own inhabitants." To Blaustein this was a "fundamental" reversal that contradicted assurances received from Ben-Gurion that no changes would be made in the law when it was reintroduced in the Knesset. Blaustein asked Abba Eban to contact the prime minister immediately and "urge him to reinsert the phrase."[51]

But there was nothing to be done, Eban told him. In the final analysis the legislative power of the state rested with the Knesset and not the government, and the Knesset had acted within its rights in the matter of the change that was introduced. As for the deletion of the phrase, he pointed out:

The fact that the State of Israel represents only its own inhabitants is so axiomatic, that it should not be necessary to assert it. Indeed, the very need of assertion would seem prima facie to distinguish the character of Israel citizenship from the normal concepts of citizenship. I am certain that there are no documents in existence which specify that the United States or the United Kingdom command the allegiance of their own citizens alone.[52]

Ben-Gurion reiterated this view in a cable to Blaustein when the law was passed by the Knesset on 24 November 1952: "[The] State of Israel is like any other state, and has no need to define whom it represents."[53]

With the enactment of the law, the long and convoluted saga of the special-status issue came to an end. Formally entitled "Law of Status of the World Zionist Organization—Jewish Agency," it went a long way toward satisfying the non-Zionists' objections. The State of Israel recognized the WZO only as an "authorized agency." It also expressed hope for "the participation of all Jews and Jewish bodies in the upbuilding of the State and in assisting mass immigration thereto" and recognized "the need for uniting all Jewish communities to this end." Moreover, it raised the distinct possibility of recreating an enlarged Jewish Agency and indicated that such an enlarged agency be accorded the same status as granted to the WZO.[54]

In essence, the status law, together with the Blaustein-Ben-Gurion Understanding, codified new Jewish communal relationships that developed as a result of the emergence of the Jewish state. What was involved was a redefinition of the symbiotic relationship among an affluent and influential non-Zionist segment of American Jewry anxious to preserve its status and position, a declining Zionist movement searching for a new role, and the young sovereign State of Israel whose moral claim to centrality in Jewish life was inhibited by the actuality of its small population and meager financial and political resources.

PART
III

*Advocates of
Israel's Cause
in Washington*

7

The Second Truman Administration
and the Quest for an Arab-Israeli Peace,
1948–1952

1

THE IDEA OF RESTORING the Jewish state in Palestine had always aroused conflicting emotions and attitudes within the American public. One segment of the population that favored it consisted of Protestant millenarian groups who believed that "Jesus would return to earth to establish a kingdom that would last for a millennium, or 1,000 years, and that either before or after this Second Coming of Christ, the Jewish people would return to Zion and embrace Christianity." [1] Viewing the restoration of the Jews to Palestine as a step toward the Second Advent, the millenarians sympathized with and supported Zionist aspirations. One of the best-known Christian Zionists was William E. Blackstone, a Chicago merchant who in 1891 initiated a petition signed by many prominent Americans urging President Benjamin Harrison to impress upon European governments the need for an international conference "to consider the Israelite claim to Palestine as their ancient home, and to promote in all other just and proper ways the alleviation of their suffering condition." The Blackstone Petition, drawn up in reaction to the pogroms against Jews in Czarist Russia then, opened with the question: "What shall be done for the Russian Jews?" and went on:

> Why not give Palestine back to them [the Jews] again? According to God's distribution of nations it is their home—an inalienable possession from which they were expelled by force. . . . Let us now restore them to the land of which they were so cruelly despoiled by our Roman ancestors. [2]

From Blackstone to Billy Graham's film *His Land* some eighty years later, pro-Zionism and later strong support for the State of Israel have long been manifest among American evangelical groups.[3] But this sentiment was not confined to these groups alone. During the early 1930s, and in particular in the 1940s and 1950s, the pro-Zionist American Christian Palestine Committee, led by Dean Howard LeSourd of Boston University and Dr. Carl Herman Voss, enlisted the support of distinguished mainline Protestants such as Reinhold Niebuhr, S. Ralph Harlow, Henry A. Atkinson, Daniel A. Poling, and Paul Tillich. After the shock of the Holocaust, inspired by a conviction that "the destiny of the Jews is a matter of immediate concern to the Christian conscience, the amelioration of their lot a duty that rests upon all who profess Christian principles,"[4] members of this pro-Zionist group aided the Jewish political struggle aimed at restoring Jewish sovereignty in Palestine, and after 1948 at maintaining the secure existence of the young State of Israel.[5]

At the same time some influential liberal Protestant groups actively opposed Zionist aspirations. Their pro-Arab position stemmed from the locations of their educational and missionary institutions in the Middle East, as well as from financial contributions obtained from American oil companies. Sensitive to Arab opposition to Zionism, these groups and their spokesmen applied the Wilsonian idea of self-determination to the Arabs of Palestine, whom they considered victims of an unjustified alien Jewish encroachment. The hostility of these Protestant groups toward Zionism also led to an intimate association on their part with the anti-Israeli activities of the American Council for Judaism.[6]

Another formidable source of opposition to the Zionists from the 1940s onward was American oil companies once their commercial involvement in the Middle East increased dramatically. Oil had become more than simply a highly profitable commodity. With the cold war factor rapidly gaining supremacy in the formulation of American foreign policy and strategic planning during the post-World War II period, oil turned into a major strategic asset whose control had to be withheld from Soviet Russia at all costs. In the view of Washington's political and military planners, the small Jewish community in Palestine struggling with Great Britain—America's cold war ally—for a Jewish state was a nuisance and a dangerous burden that might jeopardize overall American strategic planning. Secretary of Defense James V. Forrestal explained to Senator Walter F. George [Democrat of Georgia] in March 1948 that those who favored American enforcement of the partition of Palestine "did not realize . . . that the deployable army troops left in this country [the

United States] total less than 30,000 . . . whereas the British had to employ 90,000 troops merely to police the Palestine area, without trying to impose any political partition."[7] Influenced by a mix of oil and cold war strategy, nearly the entire foreign policy and defense establishment under Forrestal's leadership strenuously opposed the establishment of Israel.[8]

This inhospitable atmosphere casts into relief the achievement attained by American Jewry in influencing President Truman to support the creation of the State of Israel on 14 May 1948. The secret of this success lay in the community's ability at the crucial moment to marshal pro-Zionist sentiment among members of Congress, the American labor movement, the Democratic Party, and important public-opinion molders as a powerful counterforce to establishment opposition. Nonetheless, this strength, however potent, was not enough in the longer-range Washington context, for none of these elements decided on policy, which was the prerogative of the White House. There, at President Truman's desk in the Oval Office, where "the buck stopped," major decisions—including the dramatic decision to recognize the young Jewish state eleven minutes after its establishment—were made.

Truman, although an avid student of history, reacted to issues not on an abstract intellectual level but in relation to his perception of the national interest and to his cherished values, as presented to him by a group of people whose judgment, advice, and political loyalty he felt were absolutely reliable. The views of this group of intimate advisors were largely responsible for Truman's overruling Forrestal's, General Marshall's and the State Department's opposition to an immediate recognition of the newly born Jewish state.[9]

Foremost among Truman's advisors in the White House inner circle on the Palestine question were Judge Samuel I. Rosenman of New York and his brilliant successor as special counsel to the president, the young Clark M. Clifford of Missouri;[10] Max Lowenthal, a Minneapolis-born lawyer whom the president held in high regard, described by Clifford as someone "who was never an official member of the White House staff at all, although he came and went as he pleased;"[11] and David Niles, the president's adviser on minority affairs, who had a well-known "passion for anonymity." Another close colleague, both politically and personally, was Oscar R. Ewing of Indiana, a former vice chairman of the Democratic National Committee and from 1947 the Federal Security Agency administrator.

Under concerted pressure by the American Jewish community, this circle of advisers and trusted friends influenced Truman to grant Israel immediate

de facto recognition on 14 May 1948. But it was precisely here that the limitations of American Jewish political power became evident, for Truman's immediate recognition was a one-time White House act. Once Israel was
established, the daily formulation and conduct of U.S. policy toward it passed
to the Office of Near Eastern Affairs of the State Department (NEA), whose
position on Israel's vital interests was viewed by Israeli leaders and American
supporters with apprehension.

To the surprise of the political pundits and the relief of Israel's supporters,
the man from Independence had routed Thomas E. Dewey, his Republican
adversary, in early November 1948. Still, Eliahu Elath, the first Israeli envoy
to Washington, conveyed a sense of deep concern in reporting the results of
Truman's upset victory. While Oscar L. Chapman, undersecretary of the inte-
rior, and Oscar Ewing were friendly to the Zionist cause, the situation was
bleak as far as the relationship of prominent Jews with the White House was
concerned, Elath cabled to Eban:

> No single Jew of importance [is] any close to [Truman] any more. [Bernard]
> Baruch and [Judge] Rosenman quarreled with him, [Henry] Morgenthau
> refused [Harold] Ickes proposal [to] publish statement supporting Truman.
> Silver [is] open enemy [of] Truman and personally non-grata with him.
> Proskauer and his friends favored Dewey. Only [Stephen] Wise and [Herbert
> H.] Lehman, remained faithful [to] Truman, but their effectiveness limited
> due lack of organizations behind them.[12]

Only a few prominent Jews were still close to Truman: Jacob Blaustein,
who was about to become the president of the American Jewish Committee;
Abe Feinberg, the Democratic fund-raiser; and two Jewish labor leaders—
Jacob Potofsky and David Dubinsky.[13] In light of this worrisome situation,
Elath informed Eban, he was concerned that

> Jewish and Zionist interests [in the] U.S.A. [are] bound [to] suffer seriously
> unless close and friendly relations established with White House. . . . This
> situation forces me [to] engage myself [in] constant contacts with White
> House, which may sooner or later [produce] undesirable complications [in
> terms of] my relations [with the] State Department, but I see no alternative
> [in the] nearest future.[14]

Access to the White House was of paramount importance to the struggling Jewish state still at war with its Arab neighbors. This problem, however, was just one aspect, albeit a major one, of significant changes taking place in American Jewish political activity on behalf of Israel. Apart from the precipitous decline in the membership of the ZOA, the entire Zionist political edifice was in a process of transformation. The American Zionist Emergency Council, under Rabbi Silver's leadership, deciding upon reorganization, in early 1949 became the American Zionist Council, under the direction of Louis Lipsky, a venerable American Zionist leader. This reconstructed body undertook to continue its pro-Israel political and public relations work, particularly its lobbying activities in Congress, appointing a veteran Zionist from Boston, Elihu D. Stone, as its lobbyist in Washington. Elihu Stone, and his successor in 1951, I. L. Kenen, would make significant contributions by marshaling support in Congress for economic aid to Israel. However, with the goal of establishing the Jewish state achieved, it soon became evident that the American Zionist Council, under the aging Lipsky, would not be able to duplicate the élan and zeal of the prestate era. Besides, the organization had to contend with the chaotic situation within the American Zionist movement—independent political initiatives in Washington by such leaders of the ZOA as Daniel Frisch and Benjamin G. Browdy, who were constituent members of the AZC, as well as uncoordinated, often conflicting political and diplomatic initiatives by Nahum Goldmann. Lacking an independent political power base within the American Jewish community, Goldmann aimed to turn the New York section of the Jewish Agency, under his leadership, into the center of pro-Israel diplomacy in Washington.

Goldmann's diplomatic ambitions inevitably elicited resentment by Israel's ambassadors. Ambassador Elath in Washington complained to Sharett after a meeting between Goldmann and Secretary of State Dean Acheson in early 1950: "With all my appreciation [of] Goldmann's political capacities and personal charm [I] would consider not only improper but also most damaging his becoming initiator [of] Israel's policies [at the State] Department."[15] However, Elath's and his successors' attempts to discipline Goldmann would be of no avail. Throughout his career Goldmann would remain a maverick soloist.

Two personal friends of President Truman, Edward (Eddie) Jacobson and Abraham (Abe) Feinberg, belonged to an entirely different category of Israel-supporters. Eddie Jacobson of Kansas City, Missouri, Truman's former haberdasher, business partner, and lifelong personal friend, interceded with his friend at the White House for immediate recognition of the newly born Jewish state and subsequently for economic aid on its behalf.[16] Abe Feinberg, a wealthy New York industrialist and a prominent Democratic fund-raiser, was credited with raising the money for the famous "Truman Special"—the sixteen-car train from which the incumbent underdog campaigned against Thomas E. Dewey in 1948.[17] Both these independent Israel-supporters, however, like Nahum Goldmann, had a basic deficiency that limited their usefulness: they did not represent a constituency with political clout. Accordingly, they alone could not affect Washington's policy decisions on Israel.

A vacuum thus existed with respect to pro-Israel advocacy at the White House as well as at the State and Defense Departments. This void was to be filled with the rise in importance of the American Jewish Committee under the leadership of Jacob Blaustein.

Blaustein was in a unique position to help build a bridge between the Truman administration and Ben-Gurion's government, endowed with several remarkable qualifications that were likely to earn him the president's confidence and trust. Apart from representing the most affluent segment of American Jewry, Blaustein, like Truman, came from humble origins, eventually becoming a highly successful oilman and industrialist and epitomizing the American success story. Moreover, in contrast to most wealthy Americans, Blaustein was a Democrat, had been a staunch backer of Truman's presidential campaign, and shared his progressive social vision. An active member of the Democratic Party National Finance Committee, he had contributed generously to the 1948 campaign and brought in contributions from others.[18] He was not seeking any job for himself, Blaustein explained to Truman in a meeting between them in December 1948, but wished to be helpful to the president, "to be in a position so that he can make suggestions to the President from time to time" on matters of his business expertise, and "perhaps be useful in getting across to the President from time to time the views of industry and of certain groups, like the Jewish group, and getting industry and these groups to see the President's point of view."[19]

Blaustein was offering Truman his services as an unofficial liaison between the president and the business community, as well as a "catalyst," as he put it, between the United States and Israel.[20] Truman's acceptance of this offer initiated Blaustein's self-motivated role as intermediary between Washington and Jerusalem with the aim of keeping U.S.-Israel relations cordial, a role he was to continue to fill even after his term as president of the Committee ended in 1954 and that would last until his death in 1970. Scrupulous in his dealings, Blaustein maintained highly discreet personal contact with every subsequent president, their secretaries of state, and principal aides, as well as with Israeli and world leaders, in particular UN Secretary-General Dag Hammarskjold. Blaustein pursued this mission intently, in addition to his demanding business career, while coping with several illnesses that he did not publicize, for over two decades.

Truman quickly discovered that Blaustein was not a single-issue advocate. In contrast to Rabbis Stephen Wise and Abba Hillel Silver, the past leaders of the American Zionist Emergency Council, whom Truman viewed as extremists on the issue of Zionism and Palestine, Blaustein projected the image of a more authentic all-American leader. His low-key style, and his involvement in a wide range of economic and political issues in which the president was greatly interested, were favorably received by Truman.[21]

While Truman's correspondence reveals little of his feelings about the Palestine problem, he did make a remarkable disclosure to Blaustein in early 1949, referring to how bruised he had felt by the pressure applied to him by Silver (although he did not mention the rabbi's name) and the American Zionist Emergency Council under his leadership: "I became thoroughly disgusted with some of the high pressure groups during the difficult times through which we had to go from 1946 to date, and it was in spite of the obstructive effort of some of them that the program was finally carried through. It is now up to the new State to make good on its own and I am of the opinion that it will."[22]

Truman's hope that Israel would "make good on its own" was not entirely realized, for the newborn state found itself in a perpetually precarious situation and looked to the United States to keep it going by providing economic, political, and military aid. To keep going required the continued goodwill of the White House, government offices, and Capitol Hill.

The list of items on Blaustein's agenda for his meetings with Truman was always long. He would usually begin with matters affecting America's business community and the oil industry. For example, Blaustein offered his advice in late 1948 on proposed legislation outlined in the president's State of the Union message to Congress; on the controversial issue of oil reserves under the Tidelands, which the president planned to place under the federal government's jurisdiction; on the Excess Profits Tax; and on proposed legislation regarding the Labor Act, which he found "equitable to both labor and industry."[23] Near the bottom of the list were issues concerning Israel and its

immediate needs from Washington that were awaiting the White House imprimatur. The most pressing of these issues in the second half of 1948 and
early 1949 were de jure recognition of the State of Israel by the United States
and the question of an immediate loan.

2

Achieving recognition of its status as a sovereign state was one of Israel's most
urgent needs in its struggle for international legitimacy. While the United
States, by Truman's dramatic gesture of 14 May 1948, had been the first
country to grant Israel immediate recognition, by withholding de jure recognition subsequently, the State Department, which was not favorable toward
Israel, gained a partial victory, putting Israel on probation. This anomaly was
reflected in the unusual title given by the U.S. government to Eliahu Elath,
the first Israeli envoy in Washington: "special representative of the provisional
government of Israel," and similarly the title "special representative of the
United States of America" given to James G. McDonald, the first American
envoy in Tel Aviv. Likewise, Israel's first representative to the United Nations,
Abba Eban, found himself in the insulting position of heading a delegation la-
beled "Jewish Agency for Palestine" on the identifying plaque. As a compromise, the U.S. secretary of state suggested, in late June 1948, that Eban, at the
Security Council deliberations on Palestine, be designated " 'representative of
Jewish authorities in Palestine' and he would still be free to style himself as
representative of the Provisional Government of Israel." [24]

Almost three months later, in September 1948, when the State of Israel
was an established fact, McDonald in Tel Aviv urged granting Israel full recognition. This act, McDonald explained "would accomplish four major US objectives": it would give a moral and political boost to the moderates in the
Israeli government who "want if humanly possible [to] avoid renewal [of]
warfare"; it would give a clear signal to Arab moderates, especially King Abdullah, to move toward a settlement with Israel; it would let Arab radicals
know that Israel was here to stay; and it would "encourage [the] British [to]
relax their non-recognition policy." [25]

The State Department, however, categorically rejected McDonald's advice. A prior apocalyptic vision of damaging consequences to American interests should the United States sponsor the establishment of Israel, held by
Director of the Office of Near Eastern Affairs Loy W. Henderson and Director of the Policy Planning Staff George F. Kennan, still held sway. [26] Granting

immediate recognition, the department warned, would not boost the moderates within the Israeli government, but rather would "sanction a regime before it had been established." [27] The Soviet specter was also raised in a highly exaggerated analysis of the potential of pro-Soviet leanings within small dissident organizations such as the right-wing Irgun and the even smaller Stern group. The State Department concluded that early recognition of Israel might, "unless we were satisfied as to its stability, place . . . [Washington] in the position of having relations with a government under Soviet influence." [28] Furthermore, it was feared, American relations with the Arab states and the Muslim world could be seriously damaged, which would endanger Count Bernadotte's UN mediation efforts, affect Western interests at the United Nations, and even tilt the cold war balance in the critical situation in Berlin.

The exchange between McDonald and the State Department paralleled a similar conflict between the White House and the State Department that took place in the spring of 1948. By June, Special Counsel Clark Clifford had come to the conclusion that the State Department's various excuses for nonrecognition were a smokescreen created by Loy Henderson that, he told the president, "some person [Henderson] or government [British] is trying to use, for the purpose of trading territory away from Israel" in exchange for de jure recognition. [29]

Clifford criticized the basic policy line formulated by Henderson, who, against the background of the deepening cold war, had won his superiors' approval for Anglo-American cooperation on the Palestine question. Although in contrast to the British Henderson and the State Department had reconciled themselves to Israel's existence, both the State Department diplomats and their Foreign Office counterparts in Whitehall shared the same views on almost all other aspects of a possible settlement of the Arab-Israeli conflict. They regarded continued British hegemony in the Middle East as an essential bulwark against Soviet encroachment as well as a means to maintain Arab goodwill. They also favored a suggestion by Robert M. McClintock of the State Department's Office of UN Affairs that Israel's physical area be drastically reduced "along the lines suggested by the [British] Peel Report [of 1937], in which the Jewish State would have occupied the coastal area from Tel Aviv to Haifa, with a considerable portion of Western Galilee . . . [and] the present areas in the Negeb now held by Israel should be given to the neighboring Arab countries, principally Trans-Jordan." [30] This view was expressed most clearly by Bernard Burrows, head of the Eastern Department at the Foreign Office in London:

Our political, strategic and commercial interests demand that the settlement should be one which is reasonably acceptable to the Arabs or which at least will not create such turmoil and hatred of the West in Arab countries as to ruin our position there. . . .

A Jewish state would be a spearhead of communism. On the other hand . . . the Palestinian Arabs . . . have shown themselves to be incapable of organization and entirely immature politically. . . . The Palestinian Arabs might very likely be under the extremist and inept leadership of the Mufti. . . .

Even if the Jewish state was strongly subject to communist influence this would have [a] good side since the Arabs would automatically dislike communism because it is associated with the Jews. . . .

The Negeb would clearly have to be Arab. There would have to be an Arab corridor up the coast from Gaza as far as Jaffa. There would have to be a large exchange of populations. . . . So that Western Galilee might become Jewish and Syria receive compensation. . . .

Jerusalem . . . should be a demilitarized city under United Nations control. . . .

The general conclusion of these thoughts . . . seems to be that the disadvantages of a separate Jewish state from our point of view and that of the Arabs, have been over-emphasized and that provided the boundaries could be very radically altered, it might be the least of many evils.[31]

Clifford's criticism of the State Department's basic Palestine policy and his advocacy of early de jure recognition, however, fell on deaf ears. Truman's reluctance to become closely involved in the Palestine question, and his overall tendency to allow the State Department wide latitude in formulating and executing foreign policy, enabled the State Department to prevail. On 30 August Truman approved the Department's two-pronged plan of delaying granting Israel full recognition until after the Knesset elections (initially planned for October 1948, later moved to 25 January 1949), and then recommending simultaneous recognition of both Israel and Trans-Jordan, thereby scoring points with the two major antagonists in the struggle over Palestine while also creating conducive conditions for the British to recognize Israel.[32]

Undaunted by Clifford's failure to persuade Truman on the issue of de jure recognition of Israel, Blaustein raised the issue in his two meetings with the president during that period (September and December 1948), emphasizing that immediate recognition "would aid materially in bringing about peace in the area." [33] Moreover, he explained to David Niles, with whom he maintained close contact, such an American act coming immediately prior to the Israeli elections would strengthen the hand of moderates such as Weizmann and Ben-Gurion. [34] Truman, however, true to the State Department line, would not budge, insisting that recognition would be made "as soon as the January [1949] Israeli elections are over." [35] Indeed, on the last day of January 1949, just six days after the elections in Israel, the White House announced the granting of de jure recognition "to the Government of Israel as of this date." [36] Henceforth, at least on the official level, the actual existence of the young Jewish state ceased to be a controversial issue.

Truman's de jure recognition of Israel was rightly termed by Eliahu Elath (whose title would be upgraded to ambassador of Israel) as marking an "historic hour." [37] However, from Israel's point of view, the country's economic situation was no less critical. As far back as December 1947, at the beginning of Israel's War of Independence, the Jewish Agency leadership realized that the projected goal of transporting and absorbing hundreds of thousands of destitute refugees would require huge funding, only a part of which could be obtained through contributions by world Jewry. U.S. government financial help was seen as essential.

Accordingly, a program had been submitted by Jewish Agency Treasurer Eliezer Kaplan to the State Department in December 1947, [38] which called for raising $1.25 billion ($750 million from private sources and the balance of $500 million from Washington) over a four-year period in order to resettle an anticipated 400,000 refugees from European and Muslim countries. Analyzing the program, Gordon P. Merriam, chief of the Division of Near Eastern Affairs, rejected the Jewish Agency's request. "It is inconceivable," he said, "that the Congress or the Export-Import Bank would provide funds for the purpose of setting up an economic and immigration regime on a shaky, indigent basis which would result only in further appeals for money and other forms of assistance, probably including arms and armed force, to carry forward an unsound investment." [39]

Six months later, in June 1948, the Provisional Government of Israel submitted another request to the Export-Import Bank, this time for a loan of $100 million "intended to facilitate productive absorption of large numbers of refugees in Israel and to promote [the] country's agricultural and industrial development," according to a cable sent by Sharett to Secretary of State Marshall. [40] Once again the State Department rejected the loan request, this time on the grounds that the Arab states might view it as violating "the present truce," and that it could endanger Count Bernadotte's mediation undertaking for the United Nations.[41] To Michael Comay, a senior Israeli diplomat, this rejection, and the delay in the de jure recognition, pointed to a wider pattern of State Department tactics vis-à-vis Israel. "Although no blatant hostility is shown," Comay wrote to Zvi Infeld, the general secretary of the South African Zionist Federation, "they work steadily to hold up certain concessions to us to which the President is committed, such as the loan and de jure recognition. One gets the feeling that while they regard such concessions as inevitable, they want to hang on to them as bargaining counters in a final settlement." In view of this situation, the White House, Comay explained, was the last resort. The great disadvantage of this state of affairs, however, was that it "makes periodic interventions as a result of local pressure, but these are spasmodic, and the President and his entourage are engrossed in their own affairs nearer home." Thus, Comay observed, Truman's favorable attitude and promises to Elath and to Eddie Jacobson did not seem to affect the State Department line.[42] The prospect of receiving a $100 million loan looked bleak in late August,[43] and Blaustein's services were called upon. It turned out, however, that Israel's concern was premature. In Blaustein's meetings with Truman at the White House, during which he urged the president to approve the granting of an early loan, he was impressed with the president's goodwill and assurance that an early favorable decision was near.[44] Indeed, in this matter too, as with the de jure recognition, Truman finally acted, moving at his own deliberate pace. In January 1949 the Export-Import Bank announced the granting of a $100 million loan to finance Israeli purchases in America and development projects in Israel.[45]

Obviously, the achievements of de jure recognition and the loan were not the outcome of Blaustein's efforts alone. They resulted from a combined effort in which Elath, Niles, Jacobson, Feinberg, and several other friends and supporters of the president also took part. Still, Blaustein's intervention, coming from the distinguished non-Zionist president of "the only Jewish organization with whom [Truman] felt he could really work,"[46] must have influenced the president's assessments, demonstrating to him the widespread support for Israel by the American Jewish community, which comprised an overwhelming majority of Democratic voters, and may have made it easier for him to take action not always in harmony with State Department recommendations.

Delighted at the outcome, Blaustein warmly thanked the president for keeping his word: "In the talks we had prior to, during and since your election, you assured me that the loan to Israel would be approved before the Israeli elections, and that the United States would grant de jure recognition to Israel forthwith after the elections there. Both of these objectives have now been fulfilled." Furthermore, Blaustein stated, obliquely referring to the cold war, these acts "not only benefited Israel but have given inspiration to the democratic forces of the world and made a great contribution to international order." [47]

Though pleased with Truman's important step, Blaustein also wanted the president to put two other pressing subjects on his agenda: "the restoration of peace in the Holy Land" and bringing American influence to bear on ensuring Israel's admission to the United Nations. [48] Taking into account a candid remark that Truman made to David Niles about his frustrated attempts to resolve the triangular Jewish-British-Arab conflict in the Holy Land—"I surely wish God Almighty would give the Children of Israel an Isaiah, the Christians a St. Paul and the Sons of Ishmael a peep [at] the Golden Rule" [49]—it is doubtful whether the president relished the idea of tackling Blaustein's first request.

3

Truman's pro-Israel moves notwithstanding, the basic fact was that Washington's foreign policy establishment still viewed Israel as a burden. As a CIA study put it in the summer of 1949:

> The existence of Israel poses certain problems for the US. Although Israel is linked more closely to the US than to any other foreign power, and territorially and otherwise might be of considerable strategic value in time of war, Israel's present policies and its embittered relationship with the Arabs and the British make it difficult to assume either that Israel would cooperate with the US in time of war or that its territory could be fully utilized even if such cooperation were extended. Meanwhile, the impact of Israel on the Near East has been a disruptive one, the effects of which are likely to persist. [50]

Fearful of the mounting possibility of a war with the Soviet Union, and sensitive to the strategic importance of the Near East in the cold war, the State Department sought to achieve Arab cooperation in the area of American strategic needs by working for a final settlement of all Arab-Israel disputes. The legal authority for such a settlement was provided in the UN General Assembly Resolution of 11 December 1948, which called for the establishment of the Palestine Conciliation Commission; reiterated the UN Resolution of November 1947 regarding the internationalization of Jerusalem; and urged that "[Arab] refugees wishing to return to their homes and live at peace with their neighbors should be permitted to do so . . . and that compensation should be paid for the property of those choosing not to return."[51]

These three components of the Palestine imbroglio—the Palestinian refugees, the status of Jerusalem, and Israel's final borders—were dealt with intensively by Mark F. Ethridge, the U.S. representative to the Palestine Conciliation Commission from early 1949.

The State Department astutely regarded the presence of hundreds of thousands of destitute Arab refugees huddled in miserable camps as an open sore in the Middle East. Their tragic situation aroused a great desire to solve the problem quickly by putting the onus on Israel to contribute its share. During deliberations by the Palestine Conciliation Commission in Lausanne in March 1949, however, Ethridge was told frankly by Arab diplomats that they recognized the "presence of 700,000 or 800,000 homeless idle people as a political weapon against the Jews. They feel they can summon world opinion even if some refugees die in the meantime." Still, complained Ethridge in a cable to Acheson, "since we gave Israel birth, we are blamed for her belligerence and her arrogance and for cold-bloodedness of her attitude toward refugees."[52] Prompt action was clearly needed, he advised, in order to defuse the explosive ramifications of the refugees' presence for the stability of Arab societies, and to arrest the concomitant decline of American prestige among the Arabs. Ethridge attempted to talk Israel into repatriating 200,000–250,000 Arab refugees, while the rest would be resettled elsewhere. Israel, however, fearing the return of vengeful and hostile refugees, adamantly refused to take them in.[53]

The struggle over the status of Jerusalem embodied the peculiar mix of power politics and religious interests that typified the history of the Holy Land. Essentially, the Vatican, with the support of some Protestant countries, was the driving force behind the November 1947 UN General Assembly Resolution calling for the internationalization of Jerusalem and its environs as a *corpus separatum*. This effort, which gained momentum in 1949, was led by the Catholic Near East Welfare Association headed by New York's Francis Cardinal Spellman and his emissary, Monsignor Thomas J. McMahon, the association's national secretary. The prime consideration behind this effort, McMahon candidly told Jacob Herzog, director of the Department for Christian Communities at the Israeli Ministry of Religious Affairs, was the

Catholics' "need to replace the tutelage over Christian communities through-out the Middle East, enforced in Turkish times through the capitulations sys-tem, by a center of refuge under direct Western control." [54] This need stemmed from the Church's deep anxiety over rising xenophobic Arab na-tionalism that could put an end to centuries of Catholic work and accomplish-ments in the Middle East. Furthermore, the Church was apprehensive at the prospect of a decline in prestige if Jerusalem were divided into a Jewish capital (of Israel) and a Muslim capital (of Jordan). Lastly, and no less serious in the Church's view, was Soviet religious penetration in the Middle East, which re-lated to the ancient struggle between the Greek Orthodox and Catholic churches. Thus threatened in the Holy Land, the Vatican, in partnership with American Catholics, carried on a relentless drive to bring about the speedy in-ternationalization of Jerusalem.

The U.S. government, responding to pressure by American Catholics and by some Protestant groups,[55] supported the *corpus separatum* clause of the November 1947 UN resolution and its reaffirmation in a resolution on 11 December 1948. Although Secretary of State Dean Acheson pointed out to Truman at the end of 1949 that it was "unrealistic" to expect that the plan for international control would be "implemented by the United Nations against the wishes of Israel and Jordan without the use of substantial force," [56] the United States chose to defer to the United Nations. As John Foster Dulles put it in July 1953, the United Nations had "a primary responsibility for deter-mining the future status of Jerusalem." [57] Washington maintained that the city should be considered an international city "rather than a purely national city," [58] and consistently refused to recognize Western Jerusalem (the Jewish part of the city) as the capital of Israel, locating the American embassy in Tel Aviv.[59]

The third issue—Israel's permanent borders—touched upon the essence of the perception of the Jewish state in the Arab mind. Both the U.S. State Department and the British Foreign Office, fearful of the Arab reaction to the creation of Israel, had envisioned the emergence in 1948 of a small, weak state at most. But as the fighting progressed, and after the armistice agreement with Jordan, Israel ended up with more territory than it would have had under the original UN partition plan. Arab resentment at Israel's establishment, there-fore, was exacerbated by the map of the new state that was created at the end of the War of Independence in 1949. In a long and frank talk held behind the scenes in the summer of 1949 between Abd al-Munim Mustafa, head of Egypt's delegation to the Lausanne conference, and Eliahu Sasson, the Israeli

Foreign Ministry's top Arabist, in order to explore the chances of a peaceful arrangement between the two countries, the senior Egyptian diplomat articulated the fundamental Egyptian—and Arab—attitude toward the Jewish state, as reported by Sasson to Sharett later on:

> Please understand, Egypt does not wish to have a common frontier with Israel. Egypt would have been delighted if Israel would not have been established. She made every effort to prevent its creation . . . an Israeli state, alien in all aspects to the Arabs, amidst the Arab ocean, must perforce serve as a cause for conflicts, complications and lack of stability in the [Middle] East. Perhaps, Egypt might be mistaken regarding Israel's intentions . . . but discussions would not be sufficient to do away with the mistaken Egyptian view.

All these facts, the Egyptian diplomat informed Sasson, had been explained to Ethridge and other American diplomats. The United States, he said,

> in order to regain the confidence of the Arab world—and thereby [ensure] durable stability in the Middle East—must see to it that Israel should not be large, neither strong nor containing a large Jewish population. Egypt . . . would not feel secure, so long as on its border, in the Negev, three to four million Jews dwell—all of them educated, motivated and imbued with a sense of self-sacrifice.[60]

This definition of the Egyptian position, which revealed that the Egyptians viewed control of the Negev by them as a sine qua non for any future reconciliation with the fact of Israel's existence, represented the moderate Arab position. At most it was willing to recognize a truncated and weak Israeli entity, in effect at the mercy of its stronger Arab neighbors.

Israel's adamant refusal to accede to Arab demands at the Lausanne conference—namely, to admit a large number of Arab refugees, as well as to give up territories (in particular the Negev)—led to a deadlock, which Ethridge and the State Department blamed on Israel's intransigence, urging the president to put pressure on Ben-Gurion. Truman complied, and in May 1949 a stern message was sent to the Israeli prime minister threatening a "revision" of American attitudes toward Israel unless it accepted "the principle of substantial repatriation" of Arab refugees while at the same time agreeing to "offer territorial compensation [to the Arab states] for territory which it [Israel] expects to acquire beyond the boundaries" of the UN resolution of 29 November 1947.[61]

Ben-Gurion, in an off-the-record response to Truman's threats delivered to James McDonald at the prime minister's home in Tel Aviv, challenged America's moral right to chastise Israel, pointing out that the UN resolution of 29 November 1947 was never implemented by either the United Nations, the United States, or the other Middle East states. "Had the Jews waited on United States or United Nations they would have been exterminated. Israel was established not on the basis [of] November 29 [resolution] but on that of successful war of defense," McDonald reported in a cable to the State Department. Truman's message, therefore, was "unjust and unrealistic for it ignores war and continued Arab threats which make November 29 boundaries impossible," Ben-Gurion asserted. Similarly, so long as the Arabs threaten to resume their war there can be no solution for the refugee problem, the prime minister said. The refugees "are potential enemies of Israel. If war were renewed could Israel appeal to [the] United States to send arms or troops for defense against refugees fighting on side of aggressors? Upon whom does the United States ask Israel to rely?" Ben-Gurion's final message to Truman was: "[The] United States is powerful and we are weak; we could be destroyed; but we do not intend to commit suicide by accepting the November 29 settlement in today's fundamentally changed conditions."[62]

Truman's pressure on Israel reflected motives for his administration's desire to solve the Palestine problem that went beyond the issues of the refugees or the borders. An American diplomat in Lausanne, meeting with an Israeli counterpart, explained that with the exacerbation of the cold war and the enhanced strategic importance of the Middle East in wartime, the United States had a "vital interest" in ensuring support by the Arab states for the West's security scheme. The State of Israel, he pointed out, was a "disturbing element in this scheme." To be sure, Washington "wishes no harm [to] Israel," but it "cannot go on pampering it."[63] The message was that in the interest of Western security, the Jewish state had no choice but to make concessions on the refugee and the Negev issues. Ben-Gurion, however, had made it clear that acceding to American desires would spell suicide for Israel. It seemed then, in the summer of 1949, that Washington and Jerusalem were moving toward an inexorable collision.

Trying to avert this collision, Israel's friends in America endeavored to defuse the situation, although in strikingly different ways. Daniel Frisch, the president of the ZOA, cabled Acheson requesting clarification of Washington's position regarding Arab refugees and Israel's borders. He also met with Assistant Secretary of State for Near Eastern Affairs George C. McGhee, who assured him of Washington's benign intentions on the issues in question, whereupon Frisch immediately publicized this information in the press.

Shocked at Frisch's uncoordinated move, which had bearing on vital issues affecting Israel, Ambassador Elath sharply rebuked the Zionist leader on two counts: for not informing him of his intention to see McGhee, and in particular for falling into the trap set for him by the State Department, which "in theory pretends to be an 'honest broker'—whereas in practice it undermines our position—and lo the president of the ZOA comes and exonerates it of any guilt."[64] Reporting to Sharett, Elath wrote: "Due to the general deterioration of Jewish and Zionist power, our situation is worse than ever. The Zionist parties are at an ebb, and as demonstrated by the Frisch affair there is nobody to elevate their moral and organizational standing."[65]

Frisch's self-instigated activity in Washington, which characterized certain other American Zionist leaders as well, including Frisch's successor as president of the ZOA, Benjamin G. Browdy, and most particularly Nahum Goldmann, contrasted completely with Blaustein's approach. Being a non-Zionist, Blaustein never viewed himself as a representative of Israeli interests in the United States. Rather, he saw his role as one of liaison and reconciliation, reflecting the American Jewish Committee's consistent desire "to understand the underlying policy of the United States in the Middle East, in order to avoid any conflict between our sympathetic support of Israel and our overriding duty to advocate nothing adverse to American national interests."[66]

Blaustein's modus operandi was lucidly described by Abba Eban a few years later in the context of an incident reminiscent of the Frisch affair, in which Benjamin Browdy, then president of the ZOA, publicized a statement advocating active UN mediation, with American encouragement, in the Arab-Israeli conflict. Alarmed at Browdy's uncoordinated statement, which conflicted with Israeli interests, Eban admonished him sharply:

> Your letter indicated that you regard yourself as nothing but an American citizen, head of an American organization, with a perfect right to suggest lines of action on Israel to your government while ignoring the wishes of mine. You thus openly repudiate traditional concepts of Zionist loyalty, which would require you to consult with Israel before taking steps involving Israel's most vital interests. . . . Even private American citizens and organizations,

with the exception of those hostile to us, do not as a rule make proposals affecting Israel's destiny without the courtesy of consulting us beforehand in order to determine if Israel's cause would be embarrassed or advanced. All Jewish organizations except the Zionist Organization of America take this course. The President of the American Jewish Committee, whom you mention, is especially scrupulous in this regard. He never visits the President in Israel's interests, or throws out any new unapproved program affecting Israel, without consulting me in detail in advance. . . . There is therefore no cause for any invidious reference to the heads of non-Zionists organizations; there is no lack of respect or courtesy from them towards the institutions of the Israel State. It is, of course, utterly untrue to say that I have accorded "honors" to these gentlemen or withheld them from yourself.[67]

Blaustein's first visit to Israel in early 1949 had evidently impressed upon him the limitations of a country the size of New Jersey or Massachusetts when it came to making concessions regarding borders, refugees, and the city of Jerusalem, and he adopted a double course of action on these issues. On the one hand, he refused to go along blindly with the State Department's request put to him, and through him to the American Jewish Committee, to pressure Israel into admitting 250,000 Arab refugees and giving up part of the southern Negev "to [an] unspecified Arab State," in return for American assistance [in] "every respect," including financial assistance for the repatriation of the Arab refugees.[68] On the other hand, he tried his best in his meetings with Truman, Secretary of Defense Louis A. Johnson, and George C. McGhee to search for a middle ground between the two opposing positions.

Blaustein was convinced of the absurdity of the internationalization concept for Jerusalem, which would entail severing modern Jewish western Jerusalem from the rest of Israel. He urged Truman, therefore, to accept "the validity of the demand that the New City be incorporated in Israel." In contrast to Proskauer's sensitivity to Catholic demands regarding Jerusalem, Blaustein advocated leaving the Old City in Arab hands and establishing "some form of international control" only for the holy places in Jerusalem and elsewhere in the country.[69] As for the Arab refugee question, he supported the idea of partial repatriation, but told the president that "it would be unrealistic to expect the young state to repatriate all of them, especially since it was Arab aggression that had put them into their present plight."[70]

Blaustein well understood that Israel, being so small, could hardly be regarded as a strategic asset to the United States. Still, affected by his first visit to Israel, where he saw its democracy at work, he tried to convince Truman "that Israel could become the bulwark of democracy in the Near East" and thereby be of aid in the steadily worsening cold war.[71]

Meetings at the White House with the harassed president, however, were too brief to permit thorough discussion (usually Truman's calendar allowed visitors a fifteen-minute meeting). Blaustein also met at length with top officials at the State Department, where policy was actually formulated and executed on a daily basis. In particular he developed a close rapport with George C. McGhee, a former geologist and oilman who was the new architect of American policy in the Middle East. Blaustein analyzed American and Israeli differences with McGhee and aired Israeli complaints, for example regarding Washington's efforts to impose a settlement on Israel and the State Department's evident support of the Arab position at Lausanne "to the extent that if Israel made an offer, the US would tell the Arabs not to accept, as the US would be able to help them to get something better." Blaustein also conveyed his impression that the United States was deliberately thwarting direct Arab-Israeli talks.

Categorically denying the validity of Israel's complaints, McGhee assured Blaustein that the State Department was only trying to be fair, "in no sense suggesting or urging that any of the parties should accept any definite plan for territorial settlement or any specific numbers with respect to refugees." McGhee did say, however, "that if peace is to be achieved, it seemed quite likely that Israel would have to offer something to the Arabs." When Blaustein articulated Israel's fundamental fears that in the event of a resurgence of Arab hostilities any agreement reached with the Arabs might be short-lived, McGhee termed the argument a "dangerous assumption to work on," because in the final analysis Israel's security lay "in her cooperation with the United Nations." Although Blaustein's response to McGhee's comment regarding the United Nations was not recorded, the comment must have seemed to him somewhat far-fetched, coming only a few months after the conclusion of Israel's War of Independence, which had demonstrated the utter ineffectiveness of the United Nations as a peace-keeping organization.[72]

4

American Jewry's concern about the Jewish state's precarious defense and economic condition continued unabated. One of Israel's major problems was ensuring the superiority of its defense forces. While Israeli soldiers were better educated and more highly motivated than the enemy forces, the Israeli army was at a clear disadvantage numerically and in terms of level of equipment, which consisted of a motley assortment of surplus World War II weapons that could hardly be considered a serious deterrent to a potentially fatal second round with the enemy.

Arab hatred of Israel proved real and palpable, with National Security Council officials at the White House concluding in October 1949 that although inter-Arab relations "are characterized by unproductive controversies and rivalries . . . their principal unity lies in their implacable animosity toward and common fear of Israel."[73] Increasingly, Arab politicians called for a second military round against Israel in speeches and in the Arab media.[74] Much more serious was the extensive effort mounted by Arab states to purchase modern offensive weapons for air, naval, and land attack. These weapons, according to a cable from Walter Eytan, director general of the Ministry of Foreign Affairs, to Elath in early 1950, were of "supreme quality never before possessed or used by [Arab] countries, nor needed for internal policing," and included "jet planes, war vessels, up to and including destroyer class, tanks and armor in large quantities, and guns of all caliber—including medium and heavy."[75] Egypt also signed contracts with various European companies to establish domestic armament and explosive industries. The main suppliers of this material were Britain, France, Sweden, Switzerland, and Belgium. An additional source was American war surplus in Europe.

Israel was put in a very tight position. Britain, selling arms to the Arab states, refused all Israeli arms-purchasing requests. "Israel was of little importance in the considerations of the Chiefs of Staff—merely an irritant in the Middle East—and they were compelled to base their strategic planning on Arab goodwill," a Foreign Office official candidly told an Israeli diplomat in London. "They were not interested in the Arabs as allies who could give military support in the event of another war, but as an element which must be kept quiet."[76]

The State Department, which traditionally viewed the British as having "primary responsibility" in the Middle East, fully supported British arms sales to Egypt and to the other Arab states, sales that fit into the Anglo-Arab cooperation scheme. "It should be recalled," Secretary of State Acheson explained to Congressman Jacob Javits, "that Egypt is an important and strategically located nation of 20,000,000 people."[77] Washington had maintained a total arms embargo against both Israel and its Arab neighbors until August 1949, when the UN Security Council lifted the embargo on the Palestine area. Afterwards, refusing to be drawn into an arms race in the Middle East, the State Department allowed Israel to purchase only limited quantities of spare parts and light weapons in the United States through regular commercial channels. It consistently refused Israel's requests to buy jets and heavy weapons until the mid-1960s, maintaining until then that arms shipments both to Israel and the Arab states should be limited to internal security needs and legitimate defensive requirements.[78]

This policy did not alleviate the American Jewish leaders' concern for Israel's security and ultimate survival. The issue of arms for Israel, Blaustein explained in April 1950 to the Committee's leadership, was not a parochial one—it had profound universal, in addition to Jewish, implications. As American citizens who were vitally interested in world peace, "and as Jews, we are concerned lest our brethren, having once found a haven in Israel, be slaughtered in another war. In addition, any military defeat of Israel would be serious not only for Israel and the Israelis, but for Jews everywhere."[79] Thus, in his meetings with President Truman, Secretary of Defense Louis Johnson, and State Department officials, Blaustein repeatedly rejected the argument put forward by the Department's Middle East experts that the Arab leaders did not really want another war with Israel and that their statements about a second round should be viewed as aimed for home consumption. "War talk for home consumption," Blaustein warned, "can readily get out of bounds."[80]

Ideally, Blaustein told Truman and Johnson, it would be best if no arms were sent to the Middle East at all. But knowing that to be unrealistic, the best deterrence to a second round of war, he advised, was for Israel to "promptly receive arms necessary for defense from the United States."[81] Truman, responding to Blaustein, wrote him a note in longhand: "Think I have the whole matter worked out," referring to allowing Israel to purchase small quantities of light weapons in 1950.[82] Blaustein's, Feinberg's, and Jacobson's intervention with the president, together with additional pressure by both Jewish and non-Jewish organizations, had been modestly successful. Both Ben-Gurion and Sharett gratefully acknowledged Blaustein's "valuable assistance . . . in our recent efforts to obtain defensive arms for Israel."[83] But the achievement left much to be desired, and Washington's basic arms-sale policy toward Israel would remain frozen for another twelve years until, in a significant breakthrough in 1962, the Kennedy administration approved the sale to Israel of several batteries of surface-to-air Hawk missiles.

Israel's chronic economic problems, a result of its mass immigration policy, peaked in the summer and fall of 1950 when the country's treasury had no currency left for purchasing vital foodstuffs and raw materials. "A drowning man grasps at a straw," observed Sharett,[84] as Israel decided to seek aid directly from President Truman.

In November Eddie Jacobson and Abe Feinberg gathered a group of twelve Jewish leaders, both Zionists and non-Zionists, and brought them to the White House, where they presented Truman with a confidential memorandum giving the background for Israel's urgent appeal for help. Nahum Goldmann, who was part of the group, was also actively involved in the preparations for this significant meeting. Astonishingly, no sooner was the meeting over than he released the memorandum to the press. Both Eban in Washington and Sharett in Jerusalem were aghast at this indiscretion. "Should I explain to an experienced . . . statesman like you," Sharett berated Goldmann, "that [the argument stated in the memorandum that Israel was weakening the Communist bloc and aiding the free world through the immigration of Jews from Eastern Europe to Israel] was intended . . . just for the ears of the highest echelons of the American government, and under no circumstances should it have been publicized?"[85]

Not only was Goldmann's reliability criticized by Sharett but his honesty was questioned as well. Goldmann had reported to Sharett that support by Senator Robert A. Taft of Ohio, the Republican leader in the Senate, in sponsoring a large appropriation for Israel, had been obtained without Rabbi Silver's help. Eban, however, had information precisely to the contrary and had reported to the foreign minister that the Cleveland rabbi had been in close contact with the highly influential Republican leader and that his effort was crucial in this regard.[86]

This incident highlighted the discord within the American Zionist movement and the absence of coordination with Israel's representatives, a situation that prompted Abba Eban to seek a practical remedy. Oddly, he consulted Goldmann himself in trying to devise a solution to these problems, despite perpetual doubts about Goldmann's integrity shared by Ben-Gurion, Sharett, and Eban over the years. Apparently they were impressed by his brilliant mind, his negotiating skills, and, most importantly, his valuable political services to Mapai, Ben-Gurion's party, for he had used his influence with the Progressive Party to persuade it to join Ben-Gurion's coalition governments. All of these attributes seemed to have made him an indispensable spokesman for American Zionism from the Israeli perspective.

Thus Eban related to Goldmann in May 1951: "I find it very difficult to derive much assistance from American Zionist bodies at times of emergency, because they are not in constant touch with our political affairs during times of normality." Eban therefore sought Goldmann's help in creating a small, "utterly private and unofficial" group of leaders, Zionists and non-Zionists, who would regularly meet with him "to hear confidential accounts of our political problems and take counsel on joint action." The list of leaders suggested by Eban included Nahum Goldmann, Louis Lipsky, Rose Halperin, Benjamin Browdy, Sam Rosenman, Jacob Blaustein, Abe Feinberg, and David Niles.[87] Although Eban's initiative was stillborn, probably owing to the consistent refusal of the non-Zionists to participate in joint activities with other organizations, especially with the Zionists, it contained the seeds of the "Presidents Club" eventually created by Nahum Goldmann in 1954 (without the participation of the American Jewish Committee), aimed at coordinating positions and activities relating to Israel by the major American Jewish organizations.

Even in Blaustein's own backyard there was no consensus over the role Israel should play in American Jewish life. John Slawson, the executive director of the Committee, was growing increasingly impatient about the amount of time Blaustein spent on Israel and its problems, and in October 1950 chastised the president of the Committee about his priorities. There was no denying that Blaustein was doing his fair share for the Committee, Slawson acknowledged, but he suggested bluntly:

> What you might be interested in doing some day is to compute the percentage of the total time you give to AJC that you utilize for Israel (contacts in Washington, contacts with Israeli officials, interpretation of Israeli matters to the public, etc.) and relate that to the need to give leadership to a communal enterprise . . . an enterprise that is characterized as American-centered and American-oriented.[88]

Blaustein dismissed the complaint out of hand, enumerating his many conferences with Truman, with State Department officials, and with foreign leaders on non-Israeli matters: alleged Communist sympathies of Jews, civil rights, American Jewish citizens denied visas by Arab countries, mistreatment of Jews in Iraq, German and Austrian restitution, a meeting with the Shah of Iran in New York to persuade him to cancel an expulsion order of Iraqi Jews from Iran. He admitted, however:

Of course, I have had a lot to do regarding Israel—and its relationship to our country in the event of a world conflict and its relationship to American Jewry—since I have been back [from Israel]. But I make no apology for staying with things until I accomplish my objective instead of jumping unduly from one undone thing to another. Incidentally, I would like to commend this procedure to staff. The important thing is not how many matters we start and drop, but how well we accomplish what we start.[89]

Paradoxically, Slawson's opposite numbers ideologically—the American Zionist leaders—also expressed "intense annoyance" at Blaustein's preoccupation with Israeli matters. In the highly competitive world of American Jewish organizational life, where a leader's standing was often determined by his access to the White House, Blaustein's conferences with Truman, and his "open door in high places in Washington,"[90] were viewed by the Zionist leaders not only as stealing a march on their representation in Washington, but as an invasion of their territory as custodians of Israel's cause in the United States. However, neither criticism within his own bailiwick nor invective from outside it would deter Blaustein from doggedly pursuing his two self-imposed tasks—advancing American-Israeli relations and achieving peace between Jews and Arabs—in his own individual way.[91]

5

No goal was closer to Blaustein's heart than achieving peace between Jews and Arabs. Aware of the fundamental denial of the legitimacy of Jewish sovereignty even in part of Palestine, and the Arabs' total refusal to negotiate directly with Israeli representatives, Blaustein at first thought that Washington held the key to bringing about a peaceful solution to the Arab-Israel conflict. As early as September 1948, while the first Arab-Israeli war still raged, Blaustein implored Truman to urge "the Arabs to negotiate peace directly with the Jews."[92]

Blaustein was privy to the Israeli leaders' assumption that King Abdullah of Jordan would be the first Arab leader to conclude a peace treaty with Israel, an assumption that appeared to be firmly based. Faced with a common archenemy—Haj Amin al-Husseini, the extremist Palestinian leader—Abdullah had maintained secret channels of communications with the Jewish Agency in Jerusalem since the 1930s. In late 1949 secret peace negotiations were initiated between the king and Israeli officials, and by February 1950 a break-through seemed to have been made. An agreement was initialed by representatives of the two governments that included provisions for a five-year nonaggression pact.[93] However, negotiations for implementing the agreement had reached an impasse. Blaustein, delegated by the Israeli government to try to obtain the American president's intervention, wrote to Truman in May: "I am advised that while Abdullah and Israel have agreed on terms of peace, he is hesitant about signing on account of the threats and implied sanctions of Egypt and other Arab countries." To offset the stalemate, Blaustein urged, if Washington and Whitehall "would make it *more* [emphasis in original] emphatically clear to Abdullah and Egypt particularly, and to the other Arab countries, that we and Britain really want them to make separate peace promptly with Israel, this would be done." Although Blaustein was aware of the president's willingness to encourage the Israel-Jordan peace process, he regretted, he told Truman, "that you are not at this time prepared personally to make your views to that effect more generally known. I think the Arab leaders may need just that, probably as a face-saver among themselves and with their populace, to enable them to proceed."[94]

Truman's reluctance to accede to Blaustein's suggestion and send a personal message of encouragement to the Jordanian king resulted from Secretary of State Dean Acheson's prior advice against such a move. "Abdullah's primary difficulty," Acheson informed the president, "was with his own Cabinet with which he had agreed not to press this matter until after the April elections."[95] But this explanation was only part of the story. The underlying cause for the State Department's reluctance to press King Abdullah and other Arab leaders was articulated by an American diplomat stationed in Tel Aviv who explained that the regional approach to the Middle East adopted by the United States, and its concern not to appear too pro-Israeli, mitigated against the prospect of American intervention, or pressure on the Arab states, for a peaceful resolution of the Arab-Israeli conflict.[96]

Thus, as Blaustein and many other peacemakers in the future were to learn, resolving the Arab-Israeli conflict would take more than American pressure. In the case of King Abdullah, the combination of Egyptian and Arab League threats, and the stiff opposition to the agreement by the Jordanian cabinet, led to the increasing isolation of the king. Moreover, faced with a restive and vengeful Palestinian majority in his own kingdom, and lacking effective American support, he had no means to win the battle for peace with Israel. Eventually, in July 1951, assassins in the service of Haj Amin al-Husseini murdered the king at the gate of the Al-Aksa mosque in Jerusalem, a clear warning of what lay in store for any Arab leader toying with the idea of concluding a peace agreement with Israel.[97]

Blaustein considered Egypt the next state most likely to make peace with Israel, an evaluation probably based on his talks with George McGhee and with Ben-Gurion. In May 1950 McGhee described, in a meeting with Elath, the Arab leaders as being in a defeatist mood and "now readier than ever [to] talk peace [with] Israel. This," said McGhee, was "especially true of Egypt."[98] Ben-Gurion considered a peace agreement with Egypt to be even more important than with Jordan from the Israeli point of view. "There are no natural obstacles to such an agreement," said Ben-Gurion in October 1950, "as we are conveniently separated by a desert and have no real claims upon each other. The main difficulty is with the *amour propre* of [King] Farouk. He was responsible for dragging his country into an inglorious military adventure in Palestine, and is thirsting to get his own back somehow."[99] However, both McGhee's and Ben-Gurion's estimates of Egypt's readiness for peace, Blaustein was to learn, were too sanguine, as the problem was much more complex than King Farouk's obsession with revenge for his military defeat by Israel.

Blaustein adopted a two-track approach in his initial attempts at mediating between Israel and Egypt. On the one hand, in his conferences and correspondence with Truman, he continued to urge the president to abandon the passive American approach to the Middle East conflict and exert more pressure on Egyptian leaders in a quest for peace.[100] Simultaneously, he tested the ground personally in meetings with Egyptian ministers and diplomats in Washington. As was his habit, each step was taken discreetly, preceded and followed by briefings and consultations with Simon Segal and John Slawson of the Committee, with the assistant secretary of state for Near Eastern affairs at the State Department, and with the Israeli ambassador to Washington.

Anticipating meeting Egyptian Foreign Minister Mohammed Salah-Adin in the autumn of 1950, Blaustein was briefed by Abba Eban, who gave him an illuminating introduction to the Byzantine nature of inter-Arab politics in the context of the possible achievement of peace between Israel and Egypt. The erudite ambassador, an Orientalist by training, pointed out that Salah-Adin

> has a pan-Arab rather than a purely Egyptian outlook. His arrival to power has considerably deferred the prospects of peace with Egypt. We have definite information that in the discussions which took place earlier this year be-

tween various leading personalities in Egypt on whether or not Egypt should make peace with Israel, the Foreign Minister took a strong negative line."[101]

Eban's information proved entirely accurate and was corroborated by American Ambassador to Cairo Jefferson Caffery, who, in a conversation with the Egyptian foreign minister in January 1950, was told by him that while Egypt would never attack Israel, neither would it make peace, recognize, or collaborate with Israel. Caffery had advised him that the time had come for Egypt to recognize that Israel was "an established fact and that Egypt should now balance its books concerning Israel" and concentrate on solving its major domestic and external problems. But the foreign minister "shook his head and said that any other policy on the part of Egypt would destroy the morale of all the Arab states that looked to Egypt for leadership. Any rapprochement with Israel by Egypt would further add to the morale of Israel." The only ray of hope in the gloomy report from Cairo could be found in the ambassador's comment that the foreign minister's "intransigent stand" was assumed to represent his personal attitude alone.[102]

Along with his concern with the Arab-Israeli conflict, Blaustein became immersed in a succession of crises that engulfed the Jews of Iraq during 1951. The rise of militant, violent Iraqi nationalism resulted in the exodus from Iraq to Israel of almost the entire Iraqi Jewish community, and Blaustein and the Committee were involved in all aspects of the uprooting and transfer of this 2,500-year-old Jewish community. In addition, the Israeli-Syrian dispute over the drainage of Lake Huleh in the Upper Galilee absorbed his attention, as did the annual struggle with the State Department over the amount of grant aid to be allotted to Israel. Nevertheless, he never lost sight of the supreme need for achieving an Israeli-Arab peace. "The Huleh controversy," Blaustein told McGhee during one of their frequent talks, "and the situation of the Iraqi Jews were all just symptoms of one fundamental malady, the lack of a final settlement of the Palestine problem."[103]

Firmly convinced that Egypt held the key to a peace settlement with Israel, Blaustein was certain that once Egypt agreed to peace with Israel, all the other Arab states would fall into line. McGhee tended to agree with this assessment, but cautioned him in May 1951 that during his recent visit to Egypt "he saw no signs that the Egyptians were ready to make peace unless substantial concessions were offered by Israel." Undaunted, Blaustein raised the possibility that his being a "non-Zionist American in no way associated with the Israel Government" might facilitate his playing a mediation role personally.

"If he or someone like him," Blaustein suggested, "could only talk with the Egyptians to ascertain their conditions for a peaceful settlement, it might be possible for him to persuade friends in Israel to make an offer along these lines." McGhee, although unsure of the value of such an experiment, agreed that "it was worth trying" [104] and accordingly arranged a meeting between Blaustein and Egyptian Ambassador Mohamed Kamil Abdul Rahim in Washington in June 1951.

The American Jewish leader opened the encounter by explaining to the ambassador that "he was a non-Zionist, but not an anti-Zionist. He was not a member of any Zionist organization nor a supporter of the more radical aspects of Zionism." He was motivated by a concern to achieve peace in the Middle East and by the hope that American economic aid within the framework of the Economic Cooperation Administration "could be extended to the area in order to fight Communism." Elaborating on what Egypt stood to gain from making peace with Israel, Blaustein told the ambassador that "nations were like individuals. There were times when you had to be realistic." Any hope Egypt entertained of waiting for Israel to collapse was unrealistic, he asserted, for "Israel was not going to collapse." The support Israel had in Congress for the grant-in-aid bill was conclusive proof that it was not only American Jewry but American public opinion as a whole that was firmly behind Israel.

The Egyptian ambassador agreed that "communism was a great menace," but would Israel, he wondered, "be willing to join an Arab bloc against communism?" Blaustein did not presume to know but thought it was "a good idea." Responding to Blaustein's observation that "there were basically no problems between Israel and Egypt," the ambassador stated that his country too desired peace. But he urged Blaustein to tell Abba Eban to "stop border incidents." [105]

Blaustein left the hour-and-one-half-long meeting with the Egyptian ambassador in an upbeat mood, writing to Slawson that he might have laid "the ground-work (thanks also to the splendid introduction Secretary McGhee had given me) for some fruitful results." [106] McGhee, however, was more skeptical. "We do not think any Egyptian government," he said, "would make peace at this time. The Arabs feel that they would not get anything from Israel, so they do not understand why they should make peace and give up their policy of noncooperation and no trade." But when Blaustein conveyed to McGhee, according to information he had received from Ben-Gurion, that Israel would be willing to undertake measures "to save face all around," McGhee became more enthusiastic, interpreting this as concessions to Egypt.

Blaustein had suggested to the Egyptian ambassador during their talk that they meet with Abba Eban at Blaustein's home in Baltimore, to which the Egyptian diplomat replied that he needed Cairo's permission for such a meeting. Blaustein also asked McGhee whether he would attend, but McGhee declined, arguing that his attendance would give the meeting an official status.[107]

Eban attempted to dampen Blaustein's enthusiasm as well. "Our immediate horizon with Egypt," he told Blaustein, "is filled with the Suez question [Egypt's continued blockade of Israeli shipping through the canal]. Egypt has not complied with the request of the United Nations Chief of Staff to cease warlike acts against Israel in violation of the purposes of the Armistice Agreement." Any progress toward peace with Egypt, Eban explained, would therefore require Cairo to "abandon a state of war and, at least, revert to the armistice relationship." Furthermore, he said, Israel had evidence of Egyptian plans for "taking measures against the property of Egyptian Jews." Under these circumstances, Eban advised Blaustein against any further contacts with the Egyptian ambassador for the time being.[108]

Nevertheless, Blaustein raised the subject again after a break of several months, in March 1952. Although the first meeting with the Egyptian ambassador "was quite inconclusive," he acknowledged to Eban, he was convinced that the success of diplomatic negotiations ultimately depended on give and take, and proposed that "Israel should hint at some concessions to Egypt to get [the] ball rolling." Eban, who seemed to have reservations about Blaustein's initiative, nevertheless asked Sharett to brief Blaustein on the parameters of possible Israeli inducements and concessions. Egyptian moderation toward Israel might create a favorable reaction in the American press, Eban pointed out to Sharett, and might also win American "support in pursuit of *Mataalib Wataniya*"—Egypt's demands calling for the immediate and complete withdrawal of the British army from Egypt, including from the Suez Canal area, as well as the unity of the Nile Valley, including Sudan, under Egyptian authority.[109] While Egypt's repeated demand for the ceding of the Negev would be rejected, Eban suggested proposing an "arrangement facilitating free passage from Egypt to [the] rest [of the] Arab world in time of peace within the framework of Israel sovereignty," thereby offering a solution to the Arab complaint that the establishment of Israel had created a wedge in their geographic continuity. Eban also proposed that Blaustein be briefed on Israel's thinking vis-à-vis the projected American-British regional security organization for the defense of the Middle East.[110]

Despite Blaustein's hopes and efforts, however, his peace initiative was abortive. Egypt's domestic situation deteriorated rapidly from 1951 onward with the eruption of anti-British terrorism, culminating in the infamous Black Sabbath of January 1952 when hundreds of British, and subsequently Jewish, homes and businesses in Cairo were burned to the ground. Concomitant with the breakdown of law and order, a succession of governments fell at short intervals. Although intermittent secret contacts between Israeli and Egyptian diplomats, politicians, and industrialists were made in Europe and the United States during this period, the internal Egyptian crisis rendered them unproductive.[111] With the overthrow of King Farouk by the Free Officers junta in July 1952, there was new uncertainty about future Egyptian policy.

Uncertainty also prevailed in Israel regarding the future course of the new Eisenhower administration in terms of Middle Eastern policy. "Is the direction in which the General [Eisenhower] is moving clear yet?" Ben-Gurion anxiously inquired of Nahum Goldmann at the end of 1952.[112] The answer to that crucial question would be actively sought by American Jewish leaders.

8

Attempts to Influence the Eisenhower-Dulles Policy Toward Israel, 1953–1957

1

WITH THE CHANGE OF ADMINISTRATION in Washington in 1952, Abba Eban, concerned that Israel's Democratic friends in the White House were no longer useful, went about locating Republican replacements. Two New York Republicans, Eban reported to the Foreign Office—industrialist David Sarnoff and Congressman Jacob K. Javits—as well as Cincinnati business executive Fred Lazarus Jr., had agreed to act as liaisons with Eisenhower. Despite Rabbi Silver's well-known Republican affiliation, Eban requested Sharett's and Ben-Gurion's concurrence—which was speedily obtained—that Silver not function in any liaison capacity, because this task "requires no publicity and [demands] complete cooperation with the Embassy with no collateral personal accounts." [1]

Eban's assumption that Blaustein, along with Israel's other Jewish liaisons with Truman, would no longer play a significant role was shared by the New York correspondent of the Israeli daily *Haaretz*, who commented that "in contrast to Abba Hillel Silver's position, the significant development is the political death of Jacob Blaustein, president of the American Jewish Committee." This assessment stemmed from the perception that Blaustein's primary value as a non-Zionist leader was his access to President Truman. Silver's star, on the other hand, seemed bound to rise, for the Republican rabbi from Cleveland was on good terms with Eisenhower and in addition had close ties with such major Republican figures as Senator Robert A. Taft of Ohio and Governor Thomas E. Dewey of New York. [2]

Eban's assumptions regarding both Blaustein's and Silver's anticipated roles, however, were premature, and illustrated as well that American Jewish leaders who had a strong power base and political contacts were not mere puppets to be operated by Israel. Both Blaustein and Silver had their own ideas about their field of activity vis-à-vis the Eisenhower administration and would continue to play a significant role in American-Israeli relations. Congressman Javits was also active in this area, as were, to a lesser extent, Fred Lazarus, Judge Proskauer, and Nahum Goldmann.

To be sure, Blaustein was a Democrat and a Truman supporter, and in addition had warm relations with Adlai Stevenson, Eisenhower's political opponent. Yet only two months after the elections he had obtained a conference with the president-elect to discuss the situation in the Middle East, in particular "the sending of arms to the Arab states which are still at a state of war with Israel."[3] This achievement was accomplished with the aid of John J. McCloy, Blaustein's former attorney and one of Washington's power brokers, who introduced Blaustein to Eisenhower. However, Blaustein's almost immediate success in establishing working relations with the new Republican administration stemmed essentially from Eisenhower's, and subsequently Dulles's, realization that in addition to being a man of wealth with experience in international affairs, Blaustein had a substantial constituency as one of the leading figures in the influential American Jewish Committee.

The Blaustein-Eisenhower meeting, which took place in January 1953, made front-page news in two leading Israeli papers. According to Simon Segal's analysis, this newsworthiness was not only because of the immediate concern about arms sales to the Arab states,

> but principally also because this is the first meeting between the President-elect and any official Jewish personality. The election of the Eisenhower administration had caught Israelis without sufficient contacts with the coming constellation. Indeed, there is some well-founded fear here that most of the Jewish and Israeli personalities presently in and around Washington will not be the most suitable contact men with the new men in the White House and the State Department.[4]

Under these circumstances, Segal observed, government circles in Israel were concerned that "*faute de mieux,* Rabbi Abba Hillel Silver would have to be called upon to act as go-between." Blaustein's meeting with Eisenhower put paid to that problem for the time being, although the General Zionists, Ben-Gurion's partners in his coalition government, would have preferred to have Rabbi Silver back "rather than the continued association with the American Jewish Committee." In fact, Segal also pointed out, any intensification of ties between the committee's leadership and the Eisenhower administration "will reinforce AJC's position vis-à-vis Israel in an unmeasurable degree."

The stir created in the American Jewish organizational community by the Blaustein-Eisenhower conference revived the competition for access to the White House and the perennial question of who spoke for the Jews. Soon the leadership of the American Jewish Congress, the committee's great rival, sought a meeting with the new president as well. In February 1953, Governor Theodore McKeldin of Maryland and Judge Simon Sobeloff, a prominent Baltimore citizen and a Jewish leader, met Eisenhower at the White House as a preliminary step to a meeting between American Jewish Congress President Rabbi Israel Goldstein and the president.

As they talked, it soon became clear that the president's knowledge of the American Jewish community was rudimentary at best. "He had no idea," Eisenhower told his two visitors, as reported by Simon Sobeloff in February 1953, "[of] there being different Jewish organizations, or that they represent different groups or hold different points of view—although [they] very frequently agree." Eisenhower's knowledge of Israel was similarly lacking. A year later he told an NSC meeting at the White House that he had been "astounded" to learn from an Israeli visitor that the "government in Israel was thoroughly unreligious and materialistic." He thought that "a good many of the Israeli government were religious fanatics." [5]

On the issue of Israel, Governor McKeldin conveyed to Eisenhower the prevailing anxiety among American Jewry that Israel might be " 'sold down the river' to placate [the] Arab world, [and that] there are people in the U.S. Government who would not regret such a development." Eisenhower assured them that there was no cause for anxiety: "Don't you worry about our selling the 'Israelites' down the river. The trouble is that people understand only words, [which explained why] Communists are . . . able to make a big impression. [The] U.S. may not be as effective in words but we stick by what we believe is right." As an illustration, he cited Korea, where 25,000 American lives were lost [and wounded] yearly because of America's adherence to the principle that it would be wrong to turn prisoners over to the Communists. "In our own way and time we will [do] what is right," Eisenhower solemnly promised. However, he said, the "Israelites" would have to go through "a tough time," as did the Americans during their formative years. "They can't expect the U.S. to bail them out." Their only chance for survival lay in their ability to industrialize, he advised. When Judge Sobeloff explained that nevertheless the Israelis needed help, Eisenhower countered: "They must sell to their neighbors, I told Sharett that." Lastly, the two visitors raised the question of rumors about Washington's plans to provide the Arabs with jet fighters. Could this deal, they asked, be conditional upon the Arabs' consent to arrive at a peaceful settlement with Israel? The president's reply was: "It's news to me. The Israelites are too disturbed. After all, the Egyptians only have 15,000 troops in Suez, while the British have 80,000." The State of Israel, Eisenhower concluded, "should 'woo' Arab goodwill." The impression gained by the two visitors during the conference was of the new president's "goodwill, high integrity—but general ignorance." [6]

Blaustein, for his part, saw in the Eisenhower team a double challenge. Gaining access to the new Republican administration and establishing working relations with Eisenhower, Dulles, and their aides was only the first stage. More substantively, Blaustein, as all of Israel's friends, had to cope with the fact that Eisenhower came to office not just "actively disliking Harry Truman," [7] but also determined to modify major elements of Truman's foreign policy, including Washington's attitude to Israel.

The Near East, according to Eisenhower's and Dulles's policy of active containment of Soviet encroachment worldwide, was perceived as a key area in the cold war. "The Near East is of great strategic, political and economic importance to the free world," declared a White House National Security Council policy statement at the beginning of Eisenhower's presidency.

> The area contains the greatest petroleum resources in the world; essential locations for strategic military bases in any world conflict against communism; the Suez Canal; and natural defensive barriers. It also contains the Holy Places of Christian, Jewish and Moslem worlds. . . . The security interests of the United States would be critically endangered if the Near East should fall under Soviet influence or control. [8]

A sine qua non of preventing Soviet penetration into the Near East was the creation of a Western-sponsored regional defense organization, according to this view a goal that could be achieved only by winning the confidence of the Arabs. However, two of the three great Western powers, France and Great Britain, were disliked and distrusted by the Arabs because of their colonial past. "Even more important," warned Washington's foreign policy experts, "the Arab nations are incensed by what they believe to be our pro-Israel policy." This Arab animosity aggravated the danger, together with the region's perennial political and economic instability; the Arab-Israeli conflict; British disputes with Egypt, Iran, and Saudi Arabia; North African resistance to French rule; and increasing Soviet penetration. "Unless these trends are reversed," the experts warned, "the Near East may well be lost to the West within the next few years."

Arab goodwill could be acquired largely by adopting a new policy toward Israel, dubbed impartiality, which in effect meant wooing Arab friendship at Israel's expense. Word of this policy was conveyed to the press shortly after the Eisenhower-Dulles team took office in a well-orchestrated series of leaks to the major wire services and metropolitan newspapers between mid-February and early March 1953. Joseph C. Harsch's column in the *Christian Science Monitor* on 25 February 1953 was typical: "The Truman administration's policy toward this area partially favored . . . Israel. In effect, Truman's policy treated Israel as equal in importance to the surrounding Arab states. . . . The Dulles policy is to withdraw any special consideration accorded Israel and regard it as deserving no more consideration than any other country in the area." Elucidating the underlying motives for this new look, Harsch pointed out that Dulles's bid to win the friendship of the Arabs did not derive from his appreciation of the

> potential military strength in the Arab states which could be mobilized, like the South Koreans, for greater service in holding back the Russian tide. However, the change does assume, perhaps naïvely, that backtracking on support of Israel will make possible arrangements with the Arab states which will strengthen their internal security and make military bases available to the West in [the] event of war.[9]

During a lengthy Middle East fact-finding tour in May 1953, the first ever undertaken by a secretary of state, Dulles defined the essence of the impartiality policy to the Lebanese minister of foreign affairs as a quest by President Eisenhower for a gradual, just, and equitable solution to the Arab-Israeli conflict. The State of Israel was an established fact, he emphasized, and "the past could not be undone." But a new set of attitudes toward the Arabs now prevailed in Washington, he asserted during the meeting in Beirut:

> There is a feeling that the past administration was dominated by Jewish influence . . . but that is not the case with this administration. . . . President

Eisenhower has a tremendous regard for the Arab peoples and the Arab states. That is primarily the reason for the Secretary's visit to the Near East. They came to visit the Arab states; Israel was included simply because it was in the area.[10]

A similar message was conveyed by President Eisenhower in a conversation with Egyptian Ambassador Ahmed Abboud Pasha in Washington in June. Egypt, Eisenhower told the ambassador, was "not only the most important country in the area, but really the only important country in the area." In his view the "Soviet danger which hangs over all of us" should serve as an impetus to peacefully resolve the two major disputes in the area—the Arab-Israeli conflict and the British-Egyptian dispute over the Suez base. Referring to the former as "the Arab-Israeli quarrel," the president emphasized that "it was essential that both sides stop quarreling and that they respect the existing frontiers." He enunciated the new impartiality policy, solemnly undertaking, according to the State Department record of the conversation, "to be fair to all the Near Eastern states and to show no favoritism. He knew it had been said that there were five or six million Jewish votes in the United States and very few Moslem votes, but he was not running for office. He had been dragged into office but he could not be made to do anything he did not believe was right."[11] In short, Eisenhower declared a new era in American-Arab relations.

Dulles's mission to the Middle East reinforced his prior view about the area's chronic instability, its vulnerability to Soviet penetration, and, most important, the perception of the centrality of the Arab-Israeli conflict as adversely affecting American-Arab relations. "United States position also not good," Dulles noted in a confidential report on his trip, "and the loss of respect for the United States varies almost directly with the nearness of the respective Arab states to Israel. The Israeli factor, and the association of the U.S. in the minds of the people of the area with French and British colonial and imperialistic policies, are millstones around our neck."[12]

Dulles, imbued with the American credo of anti-imperialism and anti-colonialism, had developed a simplistic doctrine divorced from the realities of the region. Although correctly recognizing the nationalistic and revolutionary tendencies in the area, he and his advisers failed to take into account the volatility and violence of Arab politics, the tradition of shifting alliances, and, most significantly, the pervasive hatred of the West generally. Thus the theory that Israel, as well as Great Britain and France, obstructed the Eisenhower-

Dulles security scheme for developing an Arab barrier against Soviet influence in the Middle East was fundamentally flawed, as it overlooked the fact that in the Arab mind the United States—the leader of the West—represented the ultimate threat. As Bernard Lewis cogently observed: "The impact of the West, with its railways and printing-presses, aeroplanes and cinemas, factories and universities, oil-prospectors and archaeologists, machine-guns and ideas, has shattered beyond repair" the traditional structure of Arab society.[13] It was these anti-Western feelings that accounted for the preference by many Arabs for the Axis camp during World War II, and for the Soviets in the cold war era.[14] Egypt's new leader, Gamal Abdul Nasser, would soon demonstrate that the Eisenhower-Dulles policy of disengagement from Israel, Great Britain, and France would neither buy Arab goodwill nor alter his ingrained anti-Western and anti-American stance.[15]

Dulles approached the idea of a peace settlement between Israel and the Arab states cautiously, first dealing with the fears of both sides. "We must seek every possible means to allay fear in the Arab world over future Israeli objectives," while trying to make the Arabs "realize that we accept the State of Israel as a fact and that any thought of turning back the pages of history is totally unrealistic." Returning home from his fact-finding tour, he determined that "[a]ny move on our part for immediate and total peace would be unrealistic." The preferred approach had to be gradual, moving forward on separate fronts: refugees, "reduction of friction along boundaries and realistic modification thereof [implying acceptance of Egypt's demand for Israel to surrender the Negev to Egypt], and the status of Jerusalem."[16]

The Eisenhower-Dulles impartiality policy was a source of great concern to Ambassador Eban as well as to Israel's friends. Eban soon came to the conclusion that there were no substitutes for Blaustein's and Silver's contacts with the Eisenhower administration (and for Silver's influence with Senator Robert A. Taft as well), and turned to them increasingly for help.[17] Blaustein, for his part, continued to devote himself to the possibility of achieving an early Egyptian-Israel peace. In April 1953 he tried to interest the president and Dulles in an imaginative proposal for an Egyptian-Israel peace conference. Because Egypt would not drop its demand for control of the Negev, claiming that the Negev in Israeli hands blocked Egyptian passage to the rest of the Arab countries, and because Israel was adamant in refusing to countenance the Egyptian demand, Blaustein suggested that Israel agree to some arrangement whereby communication between Egypt and Jordan could take place freely, and as a matter of right, by a new road or rail connection between those two countries. Thus the Egyptian's feelings about continuous communication would be satisfied without illegitimate demands upon Israel's territory. The arrangement . . . would not be free of complication and risk for Israel, but would be a price well worth paying if it were part of a peace settlement.[18]

The administration, however, was unresponsive.

Nevertheless, Blaustein and Silver played an important role in terms of their access to Eisenhower, Dulles, and other senior officials, enabling them to put forward pro-Israel positions. Conversely, Eisenhower and Dulles assumed that these leaders could be induced to influence Israeli policy in America's interests. Shortly after a meeting between Silver and the president on 8 July 1953, Dulles, unable to reach Silver on the phone, cabled the rabbi: "I had tried to reach you Saturday at the President's request to see if we could concert any measures to halt abrupt transfer . . . of Israel Foreign Office from Tel Aviv to Jerusalem and thus obviate unfortunate repercussions in [the] Middle East and elsewhere. Unfortunately could not reach you and action has been taken." In view of "outstanding UN Resolutions" on Jerusalem, he added, the United States did not intend to move its Embassy [from Tel Aviv] to Jerusalem.[19]

In September 1953 Blaustein met with Assistant Secretary of State for Near Eastern Affairs Henry A. Byroade, once again pursuing his theme of achieving a peace settlement between Israel and the Arab states. This goal, he emphasized, "ought to be conceived as the main objective" of American Middle East policy, and should be effected not in stages but in one step. While agreeing with Blaustein on the fundamental need for peace, Byroade argued that the "time was not ripe" because of two obstacles that had become clear during Dulles's Middle East visit: the British-Egyptian dispute, and the Arab refusal to make peace. Blaustein did not accept these arguments, contending that the Eisenhower administration should use its substantial leverage with the Arabs on a quid pro quo basis: arms and economic assistance for the Arabs in return for a peace settlement with Israel.

Blaustein also expressed his concern to Byroade over Washington's changed overall attitude toward Israel. "He could not agree with the defensive approach to the Arabs," noted a report on the meeting by Abe Harman.

"The Arabs were not proving cooperative, and now there was an impression that the Administration was leaning backwards in its approach to the Arabs. At the end of the Truman regime, he had hoped that a more correct understanding of [the] Arabs' psychology was evolving." Moreover, Blaustein pointed out, the Eisenhower administration had actually been at pains to publicize its differences with the Jewish state.

Equally worrisome was the question of arms. Sending "shooting arms" to the Arabs, Blaustein told Byroade, would be interpreted by the Arabs as "a reward for intransigence. Nor would it be fair to give less to Israel than to the Arabs. Byroade here interposed," according to the report, "that it would not be unfair because in any case the Arabs would not stick together. . . . Israel had nothing to fear." Blaustein argued, however, that "on the subject of Israel—if on no other subject—they could be expected to stick together." Byroade also claimed that his attitude on arms had been misunderstood. Sending arms to Iran, Iraq, and Syria was in the interests of American security, as it strengthened the Middle East against the Soviet danger. He assured Blaustein once again that the State Department was always concerned about Israel's "interest and welfare."[20] Clearly, Blaustein and Byroade were talking past each other. Blaustein's concern was Israel's increased vulnerability stemming from the Eisenhower-Dulles impartiality policy, while for Byroade, in light of the perceived assets of the Arabs in the cold war, Israel remained essentially a nuisance.

2

Israel's vulnerability was demonstrated by the ongoing undeclared war along its Egyptian and Jordanian borders. Immediately after the signing of the armistice agreements in 1949, Arab refugees had begun crossing the unmarked borders between the Jordanian part of Palestine and the Gaza Strip to collect possessions and harvest crops in their former fields. This infiltration was accompanied by systematic acts of theft and vandalism in the new Israeli agricultural villages established along the borders. The situation deteriorated markedly in 1953 when armed bands of infiltrators initiated a campaign of murder and terror, climaxing in October in an incident in Moshav Yahud when a mother and her two infants were murdered and another child injured.

Intent on forcing the Jordanian government to accept responsibility for preventing such terrorism initiated from its territory, Israel forces retaliated against the Arab village of Qibya, the suspected terrorist base across the border, destroying a large number of houses there. At least sixty-nine Arab villagers, including women and children, were killed during the attack, an unanticipated development that proved embarrassing to Ben-Gurion's government.[21]

The Qibya incident threatened to evoke a serious rift between Israel and American Jewry, which could not accept the fact that the Jewish state—like any state—might have to use violence, even against civilians, in reaction to extreme provocation. The image of Israel harbored by American Jewry as a utopian state—as a moral, idealistic pioneer commonwealth—had been tarnished.[22] The Qibya retaliation was universally condemned, with Israeli diplomats in Washington and New York reporting to Jerusalem that Jewish as well as non-Jewish friends of Israel were shocked and deeply troubled. In the same vein Jacob Blaustein told the leadership of his organization: "The Qibya incident was a tragic and clearly reprehensible affair . . . under no circumstances can it be condoned. The claim that this act was retaliatory, no matter how well substantiated, does not excuse it." Nevertheless, aware of the background to the Qibya attack, and having an intimate knowledge of Israel's vulnerable borders, Blaustein pointed out to his colleagues:

> Practically all of Israel is a border region . . . and this creates for it a security problem of unique difficulty. Particularly on its border with Jordan, incidents are constantly arising. The UN Truce Commission investigated 280 cases of disturbances in the year ending June, 1953. It was unable to fix responsibility for 97 of these, but of the remaining 183, Jordan was found responsible for 158 and Israel for 27.[23]

Blaustein's reaction to the Qibya incident, as well that of other American Jewish leaders, was so critical that Abe Harman, the Israeli consul general in New York, flew home and in a private meeting with Moshe Dayan, chief of operations of the Israel Defense Forces (soon to become chief of staff) warned the general that another such attack on civilians would destroy the American Jewish community's support for Israel. Apparently, Ben-Gurion and Dayan learned this lesson, for all Israeli retaliatory moves throughout the subsequent period of escalated border warfare were directed at military targets only.[24]

Blaustein, distressed about the Qibya incident and concerned as well about the Israeli-Syrian dispute over Israel's plan to construct a hydroelectric power project on the Jordan River at the Bnot Yaakov bridge, again focused on the urgent need to achieve peace. He pointed out, in conferences with State Department officials, that these incidents were "an outgrowth of the failure to convert an uneasy truce into a stable peace," and predicted that "they will recur unless something constructive is done about the underlying situation." Instead of useless American-inspired condemnations at the United Nations, he repeated, an American effort was needed to bring the two warring sides together "with a view of effectuating peace."[25]

Congressman Jacob Javits was also distressed at the deterioration of American-Israeli relations. Although he had previously defended Dulles's policies, he changed his mind as a result of State Department recommendations to withhold aid to Israel until it ceased work on the Jordan River project and until it stopped its retaliation policy.[26] Searching for ways to decrease State Department hostility toward Israel, Javits convened an intimate meeting of Jewish leaders in mid-December 1953. Edward M. M. Warburg, the highly respected general chairman of the UJA, reviewed the depressing picture: "It was clear to everybody that the Administration, even in its highest echelons, was pursuing [an] unfriendly policy toward Israel. All attempts to obtain a major official representative of the [Eisenhower Administration] to speak at the annual UJA convention ended in failure; consequently it had again to invite Mrs. Eleanor Roosevelt." People were worried, Warburg continued, and a few even stopped their contributions to the UJA, attributing it to the Qibya incident. Philip M. Klutznick, the president of B'nai B'rith, also sharply criticized the administration's practice of scoring points with the Arabs at the expense of Israel. This and similar meetings reflected the political helplessness of American Jewry. With two-thirds of the Jewish vote having gone to Adlai Stevenson during the 1952 presidential election, it was not surprising that the Eisenhower administration tended to disregard Jewish sensibilities and Israel's well-being.[27]

Javits, however, did not give up trying to improve relations between the American Jewish community and the Eisenhower administration. Alerting the American ambassador to the United Nations, Henry Cabot Lodge, with whom Javits maintained close contact, Javits argued that while he understood that oil was a "major consideration," Jewish resentment "is deeper than simply a matter of Jewish control of department store advertising in the New York press," and could have implications for the forthcoming 1954 election campaign.[28] However, it was becoming obvious that the weight of Jewish political resentment as against Arab oil did not favor the cause of Israel.

In late January 1954 Jacob Blaustein concluded his five-year tenure as president of the American Jewish Committee, transferring this responsibility to veteran New York lawyer Irving M. Engel. The prospect of Blaustein's ending his involvement in American-Israeli relations, and in particular his contacts with the White House and the State Department, was cause for concern to Abba Eban and other Israeli representatives. "I am frankly concerned," Eban told Blaustein, "by any prospect that you may be less available in the future to concentrate your government's attention on this aspect of its international policy, and I venture to express the hope that ways will be found of insuring that the American-Israel relationship does not lose the advantage of your own interpretation and advocacy." [29] Ben-Gurion, who had also just resigned his office and had settled in Kibbutz Sde Boker in the Negev desert, joined the well-wishers, cabling to Blaustein's friends in New York: "He acted bravely as American patriot and proud Jew. If after relinquishing [the] presidency he is willing to retire to the Negev the whole community of Sde-Boker will welcome him most heartily." [30] Moshe Sharett, the new prime minister, also expressed his "profound appreciation" for Blaustein's "unfailing interest in Israel . . . and effective support in our past emergencies." [31] While Blaustein entertained no ideas of settling in Sde Boker, he had put so much of himself into the effort to advance the cause of the struggling Jewish state that it had in fact become his life mission, and time was to show that nothing would deter him from continuing that advocacy.[32]

The year 1954 witnessed a further escalation of the Arab-Israeli conflict. Arab terrorism reached new heights on 17 March 1954, when a civilian bus traveling north from Eilat was ambushed at Scorpion's Pass in the Negev, with eleven passengers killed and two wounded.[33] Distressed both at the deterioration along Israel's borders and the nadir in American-Israeli relations, Blaustein arranged to confer again with Dulles and Eisenhower in two separate meetings held in May. On both occasions he outspokenly questioned the efficacy of the administration's "impartial" policy as reflected in Washington's determination to supply arms to Iraq in the context of the "northern tier concept"—the anti-Soviet defense alignment. He also conveyed his concern to Dulles about "the tenor of recent statements by the Administration," referring to two controversial speeches by Assistant Secretary of State Byroade, on 9 April and 1 May, the latter delivered at the tenth annual conference of the American Council for Judaism in Philadelphia. There, Byroade, who had a close relationship with Rabbi Elmer Berger, had called on the Jewish state "to see her own future in the context of a Middle Eastern state and not as a headquarters of worldwide groupings of peoples of a particular religious faith who must have special rights within and obligations to the Israeli State." [34] Such statements, Blaustein pointed out, "were giving rise to a cocksureness and intransigence among the Arab countries." Blaustein's awareness of the Arab hatred for Israel convinced him "that you could not afford to give them too much encouragement . . . it was more likely that these arms would be used against Israel, or even ultimately against the United States, than that they would be used in effective defense against a Soviet threat." Furthermore, he argued, this policy was likely to undermine the position of Israel's Prime Minister Moshe Sharett. "Sharett was a moderate," Blaustein stressed to Dulles, and the Eisenhower administration "needed 'to hold his hand.' "[35]

Attempting to allay Blaustein's fears about the allocation of weapons to Iraq, Dulles replied that Washington was not yet committed to supply Iraq with "specific weapons," and in any case this was only one element in his grand design for the defense of the Middle East known as the "northern tier." Subsequently better known as the Baghdad Pact, Dulles's defense concept, as developed upon his return home from the Middle East, envisaged the formation of an anti-Soviet security pact comprised of Turkey, Iraq, Syria, and Pakistan in the first stage.[36] Dulles was aware of Sharett's predicament, he told Blaustein, "because Washington could not furnish him the information required to enable him to make a satisfactory explanation of this concept to the Israeli people." Yet the "northern tier" plan for the defense of the region was beneficial for both Israeli and American interests, he pointed out, while not neglecting the need for "reducing tensions" between Israel and its Arab neighbors. This goal, he believed, might be achieved through the novel Trieste formula "of talking individually and secretly to both sides in order to find the base for some settlement."[37] Dulles, taking Blaustein into his confidence, thus revealed an element in his approach to a projected Arab-Israeli settlement—which was eventually incorporated in the top secret British-American Operation Alpha—details of which became known only during the last few years.[38]

Blaustein, however, was still worried. In his May meeting with President Eisenhower, and in a subsequent memorandum to the president summarizing his position, he objected to Washington's conclusion as to the impossibility of "the attainment of peace now or anytime in the foreseeable future. This attitude of defeatism is unfortunate and indeed dangerous, and should not prevail," he tried to convince Eisenhower. "I am of the firm conviction that peace is accomplishable, although I agree that the opportunity for it is further removed than some months ago. This, in the opinion of many, if I may say so, is in some large measures due to our government's 'impartial' attitude which in effect has been tending to lean backwards against Israel in a special effort to convince the Arabs that we are objective." What was needed, he advised Eisenhower, was a change in basic policy: an energetic American drive toward the attainment of peace between the Arab states and Israel, with no arms made available to Iraq or to any other Middle Eastern state—including Israel—until this goal is achieved. But if arms had to be supplied, then the logic of the impartiality policy dictated including Israel in the arms shipment program.[39]

Throughout their conferences with Blaustein, and during a similar meeting between Silver and the secretary of state, both Eisenhower and Dulles attempted to dispel the American Jewish community's agitation over the issue of arms shipments to Iraq. Israel was not going to be adversely affected, Eisenhower and Dulles solemnly assured the two Jewish leaders.[40] This assurance, however, was not translated into concrete steps, nor did it diminish Blaustein's sense of urgency regarding the need to try every possible endeavor for achieving an Arab-Israeli peace settlement.

3

In October 1954, responding to Blaustein's repeated pleas for an American initiative in bringing about an Arab-Israeli peace settlement, Henry Byroade finally took some action. Consulting with Ahmed Hussein, the Egyptian ambassador to Washington, he decided that the first step should be a meeting between Blaustein and General Mahmoud Riad, the Egyptian Foreign Ministry's director of Arab affairs and a member of the Egyptian delegation to the UN General Assembly. Riad had in the past been involved in Egyptian-Israeli armistice relations and was known as a confidant of Nasser. Byroade also informed Blaustein that "Nasser was willing to come to terms with Israel," and that although his position was still weak, "he would be more daring after the signing of the [Anglo-Egyptian] settlement."[41]

Meeting with Riad toward the end of October, Blaustein made it clear that a basic condition for support for Egypt by the American people and the American government was Egypt's recognition of the existence of Israel and the adoption of a policy leading to a settlement and peace. Riad responded that "Nasser's enemies in Egypt and throughout the Arab world were likely to exploit any moderate move [by him] toward . . . [Israel] to accuse him of treason." Important steps toward a settlement, therefore, could not be expected soon, he said. "But, since Egypt had to concentrate on its internal affairs, there was no fear of Egyptian aggression against Israel," he asserted. However, the Egyptian diplomat attacked Israel's reluctance to make concessions, claiming that all of Israel's recent "positive proposals" were merely a re-hash. "The burning question," said Riad, "was a solution to the refugee problem. It required compensation, more cooperation with the Johnston mission [intended mainly to secure agreement between Israel and its Arab neighbors on division and use of the Jordan River waters],[42] and principally Israel's ceding areas in the Negev for settling a quarter of a million [Arab] refugees."

Israel had already stated its readiness to discuss the matter of compensation for the refugees, Blaustein replied. He was not informed on the Johnston mission, he said, but the Negev was an altogether different story. It was inconceivable, he contended, that Israel would ever be willing to surrender the Negev. "Not just Israel, but any objective person would refuse to countenance the ceding of Israeli territory." He also categorically rejected an argument that Riad put forward as to the Negev being useless to Israel. His final point was an expression of his earnest belief in the importance of direct Egyptian-Israeli talks. Riad, however, thought that preliminary preparatory talks with Blaustein's participation would be more useful, and invited Blaustein to visit Cairo with a view to meeting Nasser and other Egyptian leaders in the near future.

Initially, the prospects of such a visit looked promising. Blaustein was told that the invitation to visit Cairo came from Nasser himself, which helped dispel skepticism shared by Eban and Reuben Shiloah, Eban's deputy at the Israeli embassy in Washington. Moreover, the State Department's Byroade served as godfather to the mission, hoping thereby, according to Shiloah's analysis, "to demonstrate to Blaustein and to other American Jewish leaders that there was a chance for an Egyptian-Israeli settlement and that Israel's fears were unfounded."[43] Eban and Shiloah, however, had another task in mind for Blaustein. Three months previously, in July 1954, a network of young Egyptian Jews operated by Aman (Israeli military intelligence) had been arrested by the Egyptian authorities on charges of spying for Israel. Aman, concerned about the danger Israel would be exposed to following the imminent departure of British forces from Egypt, had instructed the young Jewish volunteers to plant homemade fire bombs in movie theaters, post office buildings, and American and British libraries in Cairo and Alexandria to provoke popular unrest. This, the Aman planners hoped, would convince London and Washington that the Egyptian government was too weak and unreliable to be trusted with implementing the Anglo-Egyptian settlement, and London would therefore decide to continue to maintain its large Suez military base, which from Israel's point of view served as an invaluable buffer zone between Egypt and Israel. With the failure of this ill-starred operation, Eban and Shiloah decided to ask Blaustein to intervene in Cairo on behalf of the jailed young Egyptian Jews, who were facing the severest possible sentences.[44]

Meanwhile, Byroade cabled U.S. Ambassador Jefferson Caffery in Cairo, informing him of Blaustein's forthcoming trip to Europe and North Africa and describing the Blaustein-Riad conversation. Byroade related to Caffery that Riad had said

> he felt conversations of this nature were important to clear away "under-brush," prior to more direct governmental talks. His only concern seemed to be where Blaustein would stay in Cairo during his visit. Riad seemed [to] feel it mistake for any one as well known as Blaustein to stay in hotel at this juncture. According to Blaustein, Riad suggested it might be better if he stayed at [the] American Embassy.[45]

Requesting the ambassador to take care of accommodation and security problems, Byroade emphasized: "While [the State] Department has given encouragement to this type of conversation [with Nasser]," he still wished the ambassador to inform Washington "promptly" if he saw any objection to Blaustein's mission to Cairo.

Blaustein then left with an American Jewish Committee mission to Europe and North Africa in October 1954, assuming that his meeting in Cairo with Nasser was assured and awaiting notification of the exact date of the appointment, which he expected to receive on reaching Casablanca.[46] The American consul general in Tunis, Morris N. Hughes, meeting with Blaustein there, was impressed with his radiant optimism and high hopes for his mission in Cairo. The timing was auspicious, Blaustein told Hughes, because his trip to Europe and North Africa as a member of the American Jewish Committee delegation had provided a good cover, "thus avoiding the appearance of making a special journey to Egypt." In addition, "the breakup of the Muslim Brotherhood in Cairo, who were arch-enemies of Israel, creates a more favorable atmosphere in which to discuss peace between Egypt and Israel."

But most important, Blaustein told the American consul in Tunis, he had been "reliably informed that some months ago when Colonel Nasser was hard-pressed by opponents and feared for the life of his regime, he confided to friends that if he couldn't find help elsewhere he might be obliged to accept it from Russia, even though it would be highly unpalatable." Now, with Nasser's improved internal position, Blaustein felt the time was "opportune" to influence Nasser to apply for Western aid. He and his colleagues might be able to influence Nasser by assuring him "that they have sufficient influence to sway the Israeli Government toward peace with Egypt on terms Egypt could accept, when the time is right; and that Nasser might now successfully defy his foes in creating the right time and atmosphere for a rapprochement. Nasser could be assured . . . that if peace with Israel results, Egypt would be regarded more favorably by any United States agency that might be approached for aid."[47]

However, in early November, unbeknownst to Blaustein, uncertain cables from Cairo began arriving at the State Department. Caffery informed Byroade that he was not able to elicit any definite information from the Egyptians regarding Blaustein's interview with Nasser.[48] Finally, on 6 November, the Foreign Office in Cairo informed Caffery, with no explanation, that Nasser would not be able to see Blaustein, although, they said, the "Government of Egypt has no objection to Blaustein visiting Egypt as [a] tourist." Caffery interpreted the Egyptian volte-face as related to "current difficulties with Muslim Brotherhood which, although it is under heavy pressure, would be quick to use any contact between Nasser and Blaustein to [the] former's disadvantage."[49]

Blaustein landed in Paris on the day Byroade's final discouraging news arrived. "Deeply regret word from Cairo indicates trip [to] Egypt not profitable at present time," cabled Byroade. "Would not . . . advise you proceed."[50] Upon returning to the United States, Blaustein met General Riad, who apologized for the cancellation of the interview with Nasser but renewed his invitation to Blaustein to visit Cairo, promising to finalize a new date for a meeting with Nasser after Riad's return to Cairo in December during the General Assembly recess.[51] Prime Minister Sharett noted in his personal diary that the Blaustein mission to Cairo had been "ignominiously canceled."[52] Blaustein thus joined a long list of failed and frustrated prominent third-party mediators between Egypt and Israel during the Nasser era.[53]

The reason for the cancellation merits study, as it goes to the heart of the impasse in the Arab-Israeli conflict up until 1967. Mahmoud Riad was surely far too experienced a diplomat to deceive one of the most influential American Jewish leaders, whose mission had received the blessings of both Byroade and Eban. His invitation, then, was extended in good faith. But something had happened in Cairo between 22 October, when Riad extended the invitation, and 6 November, when Caffery informed Byroade and Blaustein that the meeting was off. The key lies in Caffery's reference to "current difficulties with Muslim Brotherhood." On 26 October, while Nasser was addressing a mass audience in Alexandria, an attempt was made on his life by a member of the Muslim Brotherhood who fired six shots at him. Nasser, unhurt, used the assassination attempt to break the power of the powerful Muslim Brotherhood by mass arrests, simultaneously removing his arch rival, the popular President General Muhammad Naguib, who was put under house arrest.[54] This internal political upheaval obviously preoccupied Nasser exclusively during the period in question.

More basically, however, in the Egyptian view there was no tangible benefit in making peace with Israel, a position that antedated Nasser and characterized Egyptian policy from 1948 onward. This outlook was noted by U.S. Ambassador Caffery in a cable to the State Department in early 1954: "Although Egyptian attitude to Israel is less intransigent than that of some Arab states, Egypt would probably be reluctant to abandon her pretensions to hegemony in Arab League by making a separate settlement with Israel."[55] Dulles, who was the first secretary of state to devote so much time and energy to finding a solution to the Arab-Israeli conflict, and who could hardly be described as pro-Israeli, reached a similar conclusion during the same period. Rejecting a recommendation by Byroade and his aides to deliver an ultimatum to Israel regarding its retaliation policy, Dulles made this surprising analysis:

> The basic fact of the matter is that the Arabs do not want peace and will not negotiate in any way for any sort of a settlement, even when obligated by the Armistice. The only argument which we have to make when we ask the Israelis to remain calm and peaceful is that in some way which has never been clear to me, we may in the course of a few years win sufficient confidence from the Arabs to persuade them to negotiate for peace. I can scarcely blame the Israelis for thinking this is wishful thinking.[56]

Realistically, then, a peace settlement was not foreseeable.

Still, Nasser artfully encouraged a succession of private mediators. He had led a junta that had seized power by force, relying on an elaborate secret police network, and coercion, for its survival. Outwardly, the legitimacy of his rule depended essentially on his charismatic leadership as the standard-bearer of Pan-Arabism—an ideology rooted in Arab grievances against Western influence in the Middle East—and on Egyptian aspirations for hegemony in the

Arab world. But as Nasser knew well, his hegemonic dreams rested on a flimsy base, for Egypt was a desperately poor country with a soaring rate of population growth. Aid to the ailing Egyptian economy was being proffered mainly by the West, but only, in Miles Copeland's description, if Egypt were perceived "as a factor to be contended with"—namely, as a potential troublemaker in the region whose good behavior had to be bought.[57]

Here Nasser revealed consummate political cunning. Realizing that American economic and military aid to Egypt (subject, of course, to congressional approval), hinged, inter alia, on his progress toward a peaceful settlement with Israel, he embarked on a two-tier policy: on the one hand, a combination of violent propaganda attacks against Israel, relentless economic sanctions, and border terrorism, and on the other, secret mediation efforts designed to gain favor with Washington. Invariably, when the mediation efforts reached the point where Nasser's representatives were asked "to prove their sincere goodwill," as Israeli Ambassador Gideon Rafael observed, "through an agreement for direct talks with Israeli representatives, and by way of cessation of hostile action—the talks would come to an end and the mediators would be rejected."[58] This skillfully executed policy enhanced Nasser's leadership position in the Arab world while achieving the enviable feat of eliciting sorely needed economic aid from Washington and arms from Moscow simultaneously.

Nasser's deviousness was also demonstrated in his handling of the trial of the young Egyptian Jews caught planting firebombs in Alexandria and Cairo. Sharett's government, anxious about their fate, mounted an intensive worldwide campaign of intercession on their behalf. Many intermediaries in Europe and in the United States appealed to Nasser for leniency. Blaustein, although prevented, in the course of events, from approaching Nasser directly, raised the matter with Mahmoud Riad in 1954 and was informed by him that the Egyptian government took a "broad-minded approach" toward the trial. Blaustein also received a message from Nasser through Caffery, in reply to a cable he had sent, assuring him that the trial in Cairo "was being properly conducted—as in the case of Egyptian citizens." Nasser similarly assured almost all the other intermediaries during late 1954 that the sentences would be moderate and that no death sentences were to be expected. The verdict, however, in late January 1955, was otherwise: two of the accused were sentenced to death, two to life imprisonment, two to fifteen years imprisonment, two to seven years imprisonment, and two were acquitted.[59]

4

By late 1954, "a new and unpleasant season [had] opened in relations between the United States and Israel . . . more dangerous—so Israel believes—
than any such season before," a *Commentary* article aptly observed.[60] The
Eisenhower administration, determined to implement its "northern tier" plan
in defense of the Middle East, committed itself to arming Iraq and influencing
the British to leave their base in Suez, to be followed by supplying arms to
Egypt. These moves, though undertaken in the context of America's global
policy of Soviet containment, could endanger Israel's very existence, its
friends in the United States feared. Abba Eban, in talks with Byroade in June
1954 and subsequently with Dulles, argued that "arms for the Arabs and assurances for Israel" hardly constituted a viable policy in relation to Israel's
acute security problem. He therefore proposed the idea of an American security guarantee for Israel, which would eventually lead to a security treaty.[61]

Dulles replied to Eban that he was "impressed by . . . Israel's sense of isolation and vulnerability; that in . . . [Israel's situation . . . he] would feel insecure and lonely." He was ready, therefore, to consider the possibility of
formulating a "Note to Israel," which would contain "something more than a
restatement of generalities." The four subjects to be included in the note, he
said, would be Washington's determination not to put Israel in "a disadvanta-
geous position"; to entitle Israel to military aid; to work for "a more specific
guarantee of Israel's security than that contained in the 1950 [Tripartite] Declaration"; and to make an energetic effort to bring the Egyptian blockade of
the Suez Canal to an end.[62] Israeli hopes of a breakthrough in American-
Israeli relations as a result of these discussions were dashed, however, when
Dulles's draft note was shown to Eban, for it made no reference to the points
he had promised and amounted, in effect, to a restatement of generalities.[63]

Distressed by Dulles's evasive tactics and by the mounting danger to Israel, Blaustein met the secretary of state in January 1955 and came straight to
the point. Why, he asked Dulles, despite all his declared concern for Israel's
predicament, were no concrete steps being taken? If the secretary of state had
changed his mind about Israel, Blaustein advised, he ought to say so publicly
because the present situation was "undignified." Blaustein then demanded
bluntly: "Do you intend to do something or not?"

Dulles emphatically denied any procrastination on his part, explaining
that the complexity of the problems involved necessitated the possibility of

months of study on the part of the State Department before the security guarantee was completed. He also denied that Arab considerations were involved. A debate was in progress within the State Department, he explained, over whether to "undertake a comprehensive action, namely to formulate a policy addressing all the issues raised by Israel—and consequently facing a long process; or better . . . to separately tackle each problem." Replying, Blaustein stressed again that further delay could damage the administration's credibility. Dulles inquired of Blaustein about the date of the forthcoming elections in Israel, and on learning that they were scheduled for the summer, promised once again not to delay, commenting that it was too bad "Israeli representatives did not sufficiently appreciate the benefits accruing to Israel from the success of the Northern Tier project" for which he was working during the past two years.[64]

Neither Eban nor Blaustein could have known that Dulles was disingenuously playing for time. His intimations of solicitude for Israel's predicament, and references to the dilemma of having to choose between "wholesale and retail action," were, in fact, efforts to deflect Israeli and American Jewish pressure so that he could have a free hand to develop and execute the ambitious British-American Alpha operation. The element of a territorial guarantee for Israel contained in this plan was, in Dulles's thinking, noted in his cable to Acting Secretary Herbert Hoover Jr., "[the] biggest carrot [for Israel] we had and it would be folly to give this away until we had a general settlement agreed between [the] Arabs and Israel."[65]

Meanwhile, a major personnel change took place at the State Department in January 1955 when Henry Byroade, long perceived by Israel's supporters as unfriendly to Israel, replaced Caffery in Cairo as ambassador, and George V. Allen, formerly ambassador to Yugoslavia and India, assumed Byroade's post as assistant secretary of state for Near Eastern affairs. Allen's views on the Middle East were as yet unknown. Two months after Allen's appointment, Blaustein took it upon himself to enlighten the new assistant secretary on American Jewry's anxiety about Israel's security. The situation, by then, had become acute.

In late February an Israeli cyclist was murdered by an Egyptian intelligence unit deep inside Israel territory. This murder had followed a series of other Egyptian raids, as well as the hanging of the two condemned young Egyptian Jews, which had profoundly shocked the Israeli government and the Israeli public. In retaliation, the Israelis mounted an attack on military targets in Gaza, killing thirty-seven Egyptian soldiers and injuring thirty, with eight

Israeli losses and eight injured. According to the American ambassador in Tel Aviv, the raid "was an explosion of pent-up feeling which has been mounting for some time" and which reached the boiling point with the cyclist's murder and "the conclusive evidence [that] Egyptian operations in Israel were being directed by [a] central organization of Egyptian Government."[66] Byroade reported from Cairo that the Egyptians considered this raid the "most serious incident since [the] signature [of the] armistice agreement," as "butchery," and as a "sneak attack." Salah Gohar, the senior Egyptian delegate to the Egyptian-Israeli Mixed Armistice Commission, claimed that the Egyptians had no explanation for the raid, that "things have been quiet recently along Demarcation Line, but Israelis were preparing for this."[67] Each side was keeping its own accounts in the syndrome of violence.

With the Gaza raid casting a shadow over Blaustein's meeting with George Allen in March 1955, the assistant secretary wondered aloud whether "Israel reprisal raids might result from a deliberate policy of the Israel Government," pointing out that "there had been major reprisal actions at almost regular intervals of six months since October 1953 [Qibya]. The latest [Gaza] raid almost led to the impression that the Israelis did not wish to see the Secretary's study [on the security guarantee] completed." For this reason, Blaustein was told, an additional State Department study was required—meaning another delay in the formulation of Washington's policy. Blaustein, however, rejected Allen's allegations completely, asserting that because "he knew as much about Israel as any American Jew," he was convinced of Israel's peaceful intentions. Israel's leaders, he added, were well aware that adopting an aggressive line could easily lose them the support of American Jewry. The last reprisal raid had unquestionably been sparked by the infiltration from Gaza. For his part, he said, "he wished the Israelis hadn't undertaken this raid; the timing was bad. On the other hand, he hoped that this raid would not interfere with the outcome of the Secretary's study. Frustration was increasing in Israel and while Ben-Gurion [who had rejoined the government as minister of defense under Sharett's premiership] could be restrained, he was more impetuous than Sharett." That Blaustein understood that the raid could be used as a pretext for delaying Dulles's study was revealed in his half-joking aside that he trusted "the Department hadn't yet reached any conclusion on its reappraisal."[68]

As in his previous talk with Dulles, Blaustein was impressed once again with the difficulty of bridging the gap between U.S. policy and Israel's needs. Allen, as Eisenhower and Dulles, viewed Israel exclusively within the context of American global and Middle Eastern interests, regarding Israel's reprisal policy as an irritant that delayed implementation of the Operation Alpha project—a subject that he touched on, swearing Blaustein to secrecy. While Blaustein was in substantial agreement with the overall goals of the Eisenhower-Dulles containment policy, he was gravely concerned that it did not address the problem of Israel's vulnerability.

There was no meeting of minds, then, on the substantive issue of an American security guarantee for Israel. Nevertheless, the State Department record of the interview shows that its policy-makers viewed the American Jewish Committee approach of behind-the-scenes intercession favorably. According to Allen, "anything the American Jewish Committee could do to keep issues relating to Israel out of U.S. domestic politics would be a most worthy effort indeed." [69] Moreover, two surprises resulted from the meeting. First, Allen broached the idea of arranging another interview with Nasser, although Blaustein was as yet unprepared to commit himself to this possibility. [70] Second, Blaustein was approached by Parker T. Hart, the director of the office of Near Eastern affairs, with a request from General Mahmoud Riad. Because Blaustein had previously intervened with the Egyptian government through Riad on behalf of the Egyptian Jewish detainees, Riad now asked for a comparable gesture by the Jewish leader on behalf of four Egyptian youths who had infiltrated into Israel and were captured at Kibbutz Zikim near the Gaza Strip. General Riad claimed that they were innocent, although they had been charged with espionage in Israel and sentenced to five years' imprisonment. Blaustein reacted indignantly, claiming that there was no comparison between the two cases. In the Cairo case the young Egyptian Jews had been sentenced and executed, whereas the Egyptian infiltrators had been given relatively light sentences in Israel. Nevertheless, at Hart's urging, Blaustein consented to receive the relevant material submitted by Riad and to transmit Riad's request to Jerusalem without his own opinion or recommendation. [71]

Blaustein's mooted visit to Cairo never materialized. Presumably because of developments connected with Operation Alpha, Parker Hart decided in May that a visit by Blaustein would be "inopportune in [the] near future," thereby ending the second attempt at a Blaustein-Nasser meeting. [72] Blaustein's intervention regarding the imprisoned Egyptian youths also proved unproductive. Responding to Blaustein's appeal, Sharett expressed his willingness to recommend commutation of the sentences to the president of Israel in return for a comparable commutation of the sentences of the Jewish youths imprisoned in Egypt, and in particular the release of Marcelle

Ninio, the only woman in the group. Presumably the Egyptians, however, were unresponsive.[73]

5

Although the Egyptian connection was disappointing, Blaustein was greatly buoyed at his appointment by the president as an alternate representative to the tenth session of the UN General Assembly in the summer of 1955. The appointment, surprisingly, was Dulles's idea. He had by then come to know and like Blaustein, placing him among a very small group of Jewish leaders whose advice on Jewish matters was valued and who consequently had free entree to the State Department. Blaustein's experience in foreign affairs, in particular his latest mission to North Africa, was relevant to the appointment. His Democratic affiliation was another contributing factor, because the administration's policy was to nominate Democrats for certain positions where majority-minority representation was required. The appointment, it was thought, might also boost Democratic support for Eisenhower and win Jewish votes. Furthermore, Blaustein's affluence may have also played a role in Dulles's calculations, for the IOU that was created might bring in tangible dividends for political campaigns in the future.[74]

Blaustein's designation demonstrated that the Eisenhower-Dulles team did not want to forego the Jewish vote and the political and financial weight of the American Jewish community, despite the cool relationship that existed until then. Nevertheless, the ability of the community's leadership to affect the Eisenhower administration's Middle Eastern policy was to remain limited.

These limitations were nowhere more apparent in 1955 than in Rabbi Silver's contacts with Assistant to the President Sherman Adams and with Dulles, as well as in Blaustein's ongoing talks with George Allen at the State Department. The fundamental difference of opinion over Israel's request for a security guarantee appeared unbridgeable.

Silver had met at the White House with Sherman Adams, whose responsibility included keeping a sharp eye on domestic politics. In a letter in May he emphasized to Adams that "a US-Israel Mutual Security Pact should be viewed on its own merits as an instrumentality for strengthening American interests, and for restoring the military balance which recent Western policy in the region has tilted in favor of the Arabs." Contrary to American demands, such a pact, Silver stressed, "should not be made dependent on prior concessions by Israel with respect to the unresolved issues of the Arab-Israel conflict."[75] Several months later, in a letter to Dulles, Silver returned to the issue of concessions: "I am very eager to be helpful in urging reasonableness and a spirit of give-and-take on the part of those who may be influenced by my voice in Israel. Of one thing, however, I am quite certain—prior to negotiations, Israel will not make concessions with respect to the unresolved issues."[76] However, Silver's reasoned arguments for the modification of the Eisenhower-Dulles Middle Eastern policy were of no avail. The policy remained as rigid as ever.

Blaustein's achievements in this area were no greater than Silver's. In Allen's view, as stated in a talk with Blaustein in August 1955, the issue boiled down to different perceptions of priorities.

> Israel felt that the U.S. should enter into a security arrangement with her immediately. The U.S., on the other hand, felt that our entering into a security arrangement with Israel while present tensions were so strong would be taken by the Arabs as proof that the U.S. would back Israel in any eventuality and that the effect on area stability would be negative rather than positive.[77]

Therefore, Allen explained to Blaustein, the State Department favored a line of "working with the Arabs in the hope of bringing about a real relaxation of tensions rather than to take a forceful line right at the present."

Blaustein, however, rejected the State Department's dogma that the goodwill of the Arabs had to be bought. In his view, as stated to Allen during their August meeting, "the Arabs could not be trusted to be allies of the West and that the only thing they understood was force," a position that aroused indignant opposition by Allen. Essentially, Allen saw no "real threat of an Arab attack on Israel under [the] present circumstances" and therefore questioned the "extreme urgency" in Israel's insistence on a security pact with the United States. This optimistic reading of the situation was unconvincing to Blaustein, who pointed to the success of the more militant right-wing Herut Party in the recent elections in Israel in July 1955 as symptomatic of a growing sense of insecurity within the Israeli electorate. A gesture by Washington to allay Israeli apprehensions, he recommended, would be helpful to David Ben-Gurion, who was trying to form a new government and struggling with extremist pressures.

Despite these ongoing dialogues with the State Department, neither Blaustein nor Silver could discern any change in the administration's understanding of Israel's sense of insecurity. The Alpha concept, according to which the onus of making concessions was on Israel, remained the guiding policy. When, during one of their meetings, Blaustein asked Allen what the Arab contribution toward reducing tension in the Middle East would be, Allen retorted that he was fed up with the insinuations and distortions describing America as hostile to Israel, asserting that in the final analysis it was the United States that supported Israel and felt responsibility for its fate. The Arabs, he claimed, were more afraid of the Israelis "than Israel was entitled to be afraid of the Arabs," and naturally they too were very interested in security pacts with America, he asserted.[78]

A month later, on 19 September 1955, the State Department's scenario for the Middle East fell apart when the American embassy in Cairo received word of the so-called Egyptian-Czech arms deal (actually an Egyptian-Soviet arms deal). A cable from the embassy informed Washington that an Egyptian military mission was already in Moscow, and that the "Soviet offer said to be almost embarrassing in size."[79] Although the Soviet arms deal actually dated back to March 1955,[80] the public announcement of it by Nasser in late September agitated Western and Israeli leaders, destroyed the fragile Egyptian-Israeli balance of power, and ultimately sowed the seeds of the Sinai-Suez War.

Reporting to the cabinet on the arms deal, Dulles pointed out that for the first time in the history of the Soviet-American global conflict, the Russians had made a "determined . . . effort to move into the Near East, an area which possesses two-thirds of the world's known oil reserves. The Russians . . . have massive amounts of obsolete armaments that can either be junked or used to make trouble." Moreover, Russia's "entrance into [the] Mid-East jeopardizes the near-settlement of affairs between Israel and the Arabs." During his recent meeting with Molotov in New York, the secretary of state reported, he had told the Russian foreign minister "how serious this affair could be, but Molotov just shrugged it off as a commercial move." Hence, in Dulles's analysis, apart from American "policies in relation to the Arabs [which] are handicapped by our relations with Israel," Russia's penetration into what was heretofore a Western preserve introduced a menacing element with serious implications "for all of Africa."[81]

The appearance of the red star on the Nile, initially through the so-called Czech arms deal, was indeed a turning point in the history of the Middle East. It heralded the end of Western political and economic hegemony there, and specifically the Western monopoly on arms supplies to the countries of the Middle East, with grave consequences for the course of the Arab-Israeli conflict. There was no doubt that the dimensions of the Soviet arms deal—two hundred jet aircraft, including medium jet bombers, hundreds of heavy and medium tanks, fixed and mobile artillery pieces, several submarines, destroyers and torpedo boats, as well as many other types of military equipment—would tip the military balance in Egypt's favor. Dulles's special assistant for intelligence, W. Park Armstrong Jr., reported to the secretary of state that "if the Egyptians could man and maintain [the Soviet arms, this would] give Egypt a numerical superiority in jet aircraft and heavy tanks over Israel . . . [which] is not known to have any medium jet bombers and to have only some 20 jet fighters, mainly French; Israel has no heavy tanks, but has about 300 medium and light tanks." [82]

No one was more agitated by this development than David Ben-Gurion, newly reelected as prime minister, especially as it followed British deliveries of Centurion tanks to Egypt and Britain's failure to honor prior commitments to deliver military equipment to Israel. In mid-November the prime minister warned American Ambassador to Israel Edward B. Lawson that the "threat to Israel's security becomes more dangerous every day; Nasser has boasted he will wipe out Israel in six months. . . . Israel cannot wait quietly to be struck down. Consciously or unconsciously [the] United Kingdom is giving Egypt [the] possibility of striking down Israel." [83] If Israel were pushed to the wall, Ben-Gurion stated explicitly, it would have no choice but to undertake a preemptive war against Egypt, a course that Washington was aware of all along.[84]

Nahum Goldmann also pursued his individual diplomatic efforts at the State Department, meeting with George Allen in early December 1955. According to a state department record of the meeting, Goldmann told Allen "that Israel's policy was becoming too rigid and that statements like 'we will not concede an inch of Israel territory' were unfortunate. . . . Dr. Goldmann stated that his influence with Mapai (and Ben-Gurion) was limited, but he did have influence with Achdut Avoda, the Progressives and the Mizrachi, and he intended to speak to members of these parties." [85]

Increasingly concerned, Blaustein met with Dulles in late January 1956, shortly after the end of his term with the American delegation to the United Nations. Referring to this experience, which had given him "an opportunity to study Soviet and Arab psychology," he hoped that "our Allies would not get the idea that we were softening toward the Russians. [The Russians] had to be played from strength." Dulles agreed that the Egyptian-Soviet bloc arms deal had created "a very dangerous situation," inasmuch as prior to this deal the West "had been able to keep the peace in the area through the maintenance of a rough balance of military power. This was no longer the case, and the theory that peace could be maintained on a basis of balance of power had had to be discarded." But though he could appreciate Israel's need for arms, "it was idle to assume that Israel with under two million people could match the absorptive capacity for arms of forty million Arabs." Moreover, Dulles argued, while delivery of American arms to Israel might provide security for a short time, it might lead to additional substantial Soviet arms shipments to the Arabs, putting Israel in a worse position.

In an effort to reassure Blaustein, Dulles reiterated the promise he had made to Eban that "the maintenance of Israel in all its essentials was U.S. policy," and informed him that at that very moment Washington was attempting "to get protection for Israel in other ways." The results of these efforts, said Dulles, were expected to be known within a short time. "We might have to end up by trimming down to a fighting basis in the area, but at this stage we were thinking of other things,"[86] according to the State Department's record of the meeting. Dulles was hinting at a top secret mediation mission to Nasser and Ben-Gurion initiated several days before the Blaustein-Dulles meeting by Robert B. Anderson, formerly deputy secretary of defense and a confidant of Eisenhower's.[87]

Blaustein was not reassured, and pointed out that with the Israelis feeling threatened, they might "be tempted to have a go at war while they could." Dulles replied emphatically that war would not be the answer, for "Israel might win a battle that could seal her doom." Blaustein complained: why was Washington so intimidated by the Arabs? "It seemed like the Arabs were shaping U.S. policy. The U.S. seemed to be afraid to take any step that might conceivably offend the Arabs in any way," Blaustein stated, according to the report. His dealings with them, he told Dulles, had convinced him that they were "untrustworthy and could be counted on to try to play the USSR against the U.S. [and that] they did not wish to make peace with Israel." Washington should play hardball with the Arabs, he advised, and warn the Arab states clearly of the price they were likely to pay "in terms of their own independence and sovereignty" for their cooperation with the Soviets.

If Israel undertook a preemptive war, Blaustein stated, he was sure that "the effect on U.S. Jews would not be pleasant. He had been asked [he did not indicate by whom] to go to Israel to try to restrain Ben-Gurion," according to the report, but in order to succeed in that mission he would need "something to show Ben-Gurion how Israel could be saved." Dulles once more expressed sympathy for Israel's predicament, stating that "he would not try to disguise the fact that Israel was in peril." But the solution to this state of affairs did not lie in providing Israel with American arms. Both he and the president, he declared, wished "to preserve Israel. The objective was to prevent World War III from breaking out in the Near East."[88]

Blaustein's arguments and pleas for tangible arms aid had failed to change Dulles's position. The secretary of state was locked into an apocalyptic scenario of the possible collapse of Washington's containment policy in the Middle East and the danger to the supply of Arab oil to the West should the Eisenhower administration restore the balance of power in the Middle East by supplying arms to Israel. Convinced that an understanding could be reached with Nasser even after the announcement of the Soviet arms deal, Dulles adamantly stuck to his policy of three No's: no arms for Israel; no funds to buy arms (although Washington "will not interpose objections to Israel's buying moderate amounts of arms with its own resources"); and no security guarantee for Israel's borders.[89]

Blaustein, however, did not mean to give up trying. A month later, in February 1956, he wrote to Dulles: "I continue gravely concerned about the situation in the Middle East—so much so that I am writing this to you while on an inspection trip of our company properties in the Southwest, in the hope it will reach you before you leave for abroad." Reminding Dulles of his promise during their latest conference that "if these other steps [the Anderson mission] did not show positive signs within a few weeks of developing satisfactorily, serious consideration would then promptly be given by you to letting Israel have the defensive arms. And I am now wondering, Mr. Secretary, if that time may not have arrived?" Appealing to Dulles to reconsider his position, Blaustein concluded his letter fervently: "As an American interested in peace, and as one to whom other Americans (both Jews and non-Jews) are looking for objective views on the subject, also one who has been urging Israel to exercise restraint, I do hope for a word of encouragement from you."[90]

But Dulles was already abroad when Blaustein's letter arrived, and it took two more months for Blaustein to arrange another meeting with him, in April 1956. Dulles was still as unyielding as ever on the question of Washington's arms embargo against Israel. When Blaustein asked whether Washington "could help the Israelis by training some jet pilots," the secretary replied that the question was under consideration, although "before training a pilot one had to know what kind of aircraft he would be flying." Blaustein, an experienced oilman and acutely aware of Dulles's susceptibility to Arab threats of withholding oil, then informed Dulles, according to a State Department report of the meeting, that after investigation of the oil question, "he came to the conclusion that the loss of this oil to Western Europe would be perhaps inconvenient and expensive but not disastrous. There was sufficient oil "locked in" in the Western Hemisphere to enable us to make up any losses to Western Europe very quickly. Also, since the Soviets couldn't use the oil, the Arabs would be faced with a choice of selling it to the West or not selling it at all."[91]

Dulles, conceding the logic of Blaustein's arguments, pointed out, however, that "in a tense situation" people's actions were not always guided by "purely economic motives." He also pointed out that the Arabs, by their control of the pipelines and the Suez Canal, possessed an additional potential to inflict damage on Western economic interests. He was, nevertheless, willing to study any figures that Blaustein might wish to provide in support of his thesis. Lastly, Blaustein expressed the hope that during the forthcoming NATO meeting a break in Washington's arms embargo might be indicated by the United States' agreeing to supply "a token quantity of arms to Israel."

The subject of the grave consequences of Washington's arms embargo against Israel was also raised by Rabbi Silver in a conversation with Eisenhower and Dulles at the White House on 26 April 1956, just after Silver had returned from a visit to Israel. Silver, according to an account written by Dulles, "made a very strong plea for arms to Israel along the conventional lines, picking up all of the arguments of Eban in answering the counterarguments which I had made to Eban." Dulles was apparently annoyed with Silver's presentation both because it "seemed obvious that Silver had been pretty well briefed by the Israelis" and because it reflected public pressure exerted by American Zionists. "I said that we did not want our policy to seem to be made by the Zionists and that I did not think that the mass meetings and public appeals helped the situation. Silver seemed somewhat resentful of this intimation." Referring to the approaching presidential elections, Eisenhower added that he was not going to be affected by "political considerations and that if doing what he thought right resulted in his not being elected, that would be quite agreeable to him. Silver, attempting to remove the domestic politics factor from the discussion, said: 'You can be reelected without a single Jewish vote.' "[92]

Back in Cleveland, Silver immediately wrote to Dulles to set him straight about the legitimacy of public pressure. "In a democracy, my dear Mr. Dulles, such pressures are unavoidable—at times desirable as an index of public opinion. It is the accepted way that any group which feels keenly about a subject close to its heart has of giving expression to its views and of defending its interests—whether it be a farm group, a labor group, a business group, or an oil group." [93] To be sure, Silver conceded, these pressures at times "become excessive and virulent." Still, officeholders continue to do what is right "without relation to them." However, this should not result, Silver stressed, in *"refraining* [emphasis in original] from an indicated action on the possibility that such action might be interpreted by some people as yielding to pressure. This is a negative and fatal form of pressure." Turning to the issue at hand, Silver argued that if the massive Soviet arms shipments to Egypt indeed upset the Arab-Israeli military balance, then Israel's "request [for arms] should be granted regardless of the pressures, at times unrestrained, which have been brought to bear upon you by those who feel very keenly that the thing *should* [emphasis in original] be done."

But, once more, both Blaustein's reasoned arguments and Silver's exhortations fell on deaf ears. Neither Eisenhower nor Dulles, focused as they were on the cold war, were about to reassess the wisdom of their embargo policy regarding the shipment of arms to Israel.

A dramatic development in the composition of the Israeli government during the summer of 1956 impelled Blaustein to make yet another attempt to alter U.S. policy. Prime Minister Ben-Gurion, long chafing at the restraint imposed on Israeli policy by Foreign Minister Moshe Sharett, forced Sharett's resignation. This cabinet reshuffle occurred amidst a marked deterioration along Israel's borders with Egypt at the Gaza Strip and with Jordan in the form of intensified raids by Fedayeen (trained armed infiltrators), as well as other kinds of organized assaults on Israeli civilians, which prompted full-scale Israeli reprisal raids. Alarmed at this situation, Blaustein warned Dulles that

> there is more and more frustration on the part of the Israelis (as I believe the change in the Israel Cabinet indicates) and arrogant cock-sureness among the Arabs. Under these circumstances, I fear war is inevitable as soon as the Arabs have learned how to use the Soviet arms—unless it gets to be a fact and is known that Israel will have arms to defend itself, adequate at least until other aid could be made available." [94]

Dulles was unperturbed. Israel, he told Blaustein, had lately been successful in increasing its "military strength." But, he remonstrated, Israel should not base its security on "her own military posture" only, advising that "Israel must seek her security primarily in the deterrents to aggression which the international community can bring to bear." [95] Where these deterrents could be found was not made clear.

Dulles reiterated his unchanged policy to Irving M. Engel, the American Jewish Committee president, at a meeting in early August 1956 shortly after the outbreak of the Suez crisis, when Engel too voiced his organization's concern about the winds of war blowing over Israel. Dulles granted that the Israelis were indeed "under the bombs of Nasser, and they had every reason to be worried, for, from a long-term standpoint their fears were certainly justified." However, he said, revealing his awareness of British-French war plans against Egypt, the outbreak of the Suez crisis had actually diminished Israel's present danger. "It would be incredibly stupid . . . for Nasser to attack Israel, now that England and France have their warships on their way to the Eastern Mediterranean and would like nothing better than a good excuse to intervene in the Middle East."[96] He therefore saw no need to provide Israel with "any further assurance that it was American policy to support her continued existence." Moreover, so far as arms were concerned, in particular Israel's urgent request for interceptor jets to counteract Soviet-made bombers, Dulles was skeptical of what good they would do. "If Nasser should decide to launch an air attack, he would send up bombers on what was ostensibly a training cruise, and then, at the last moment, send them over the Israeli borders . . . [so that they would] accomplish their mission in five minutes, with no chance for the interceptor planes to leave the ground." Apart from the flawed military reasoning (Dulles's argument disregarded the importance of Sinai as an ideal early warning zone and ignored the significant deterrent potential of modern radar and jet interceptors),[97] Engel got the clear impression that although Washington might deliver some military equipment to Israel, Dulles would not encourage Canada or France to sell interceptors to Israel—the type of weapon most vital for its survival.

The rigid Eisenhower-Dulles arms embargo policy had a decisive effect on Israel, Ben-Gurion revealed to a visiting delegation of the American Jewish Committee headed by Engel shortly after the Sinai Campaign (29 October–6 November) and the Suez War (31 October–6 November 1956). In a way, he said, Washington was responsible for the outbreak of the Sinai Campaign. In the wake of the Soviet arms deal, he told the delegation, "we applied [for arms] to the U.S. We met with great sympathy, but not with a single rifle, and you cannot fight Soviet MIG's and tanks with words of sympathy from the State Department. Then later [September 1956] the U.S. advised Canada to sell us some jet planes, and the latter, feeling in a way offended, refused. If America . . . had provided us in time with the necessary arms, the whole thing might not have [been] necessary."[98]

Ben-Gurion's testimony brings into focus the essential characteristic of the Sinai Campaign. It was an equalizing war, designed to restore the military balance destroyed by the Soviet-Egyptian arms deal. Had Eisenhower and Dulles been more responsive to Ben-Gurion's justified concern about Israel's vulnerability in the face of Nasser's arms buildup, they could have provided Israel with needed weapons, as well as diplomatic support, which would probably have averted the campaign.

Militarily, the Sinai Campaign was short and decisive: Israel occupied the Gaza Strip and the entire Sinai Peninsula in a few days. But the diplomatic and political struggle over the consequences of the war was prolonged, conducted thousands of miles away in Washington and at the United Nations. At the core of this struggle was the insistence by Eisenhower and Dulles, as well as by UN Secretary-General Dag Hammarskjold, that Israel withdraw from the Gaza Strip and the Sinai Peninsula immediately and completely.

One aspect of this struggle involved a curious reversal of roles that took place when Eisenhower twice attempted to influence Ben-Gurion's positions by appealing to American Jewish leaders to apply pressure on Israel. The first attempt occurred immediately after the outbreak of the Sinai Campaign when Eisenhower contacted Rabbi Silver through Sherman Adams on 30 and 31 October 1956. Eisenhower requested Silver to convey messages to Ben-Gurion urging the Israeli prime minister to have his army "voluntarily return immediately" to Israel's borders, and reminding him of Israel's vital dependence on American aid. In return for prompt compliance, Eisenhower promised Ben-Gurion to broadcast "a most friendly declaration toward Israel on a special television and radio program."[99]

Ben-Gurion, anxious to gain time for the Israeli army to complete the conquest of the Sinai Peninsula, did not respond to the messages. Oddly, the president, in choosing Silver as a conduit, seemed unaware that Ben-Gurion disliked Silver, thus making him an unacceptable mediator. Moreover, the approach to Silver reflected the administration's belief that American Jewry could exert influence on Israel. As shown in the case of the transfer of the Israeli Foreign Office to Jerusalem in 1953, however, the potential of the American Jewish community to influence Israeli leaders in matters deemed vital to Israel's national interest was negligible.[100]

The second attempt to utilize American Jewish leaders for this purpose occurred during the dramatic postwar diplomatic struggle when Ben-Gurion called for American guarantees for freedom of navigation in the Gulf of Aqaba (Eilat) and the Straits of Tiran, as well as a drastic change in the status of the

Gaza Strip (primarily the abolition of Egyptian rule in the Strip), as preconditions for complete withdrawal from these two areas. These conditions, vital to Israeli security, were irreconcilable with American commitments to satisfy Arab demands for an immediate and complete Israeli withdrawal leading Eisenhower to warn in early February 1957 that "[economic] sanctions against Israel might be considered if Israeli forces were not immediately withdrawn from Egypt." [101]

This threat evoked opposition both in the political realm and by the public. Attempting to convince the influential Republican Senate minority leader, William F. Knowland, as well as the Senate majority leader, Lyndon B. Johnson, both of whom opposed the sanctions move, Dulles stressed Washington's regional and global priorities: "We could not have any influence with the Arab countries if we could not get the Israelis out of Egypt. If we could not get the Israelis out the Russians would, and that [would] mean the loss of the Middle East and probable general war. We have tried everything else short of sanctions." [102]

In a telephone conversation with Henry Luce, who was also concerned about the sanctions, Dulles explained to the powerful Time-Life publisher about "how almost impossible it is in this country to carry out foreign policy not approved by the Jews. [George] Marshall and [James] Forrestal learned that. I am going to try to have one—that does not mean I am anti-Jewish, but I believe in what George Washington said in his Farewell Address that an emotional attachment to another country should not interfere." [103]

Searching for effective means to force Israel's hand, the president and the secretary of state decided to try to enlist the help of several non-Zionist Jewish leaders who might be able to put pressure on Ben-Gurion. This idea may have been evoked by a meeting Dulles had had with a delegation from the American Council for Judaism nearly a year previously. The council's president, Clarence Coleman, had conveyed the council's view to Dulles that

> the Secretary should be in a position to make decisions affecting vital U.S. interests in the Near East without pressure from any particular U.S. group. If the Council had done anything, it had destroyed the validity of the assumption that all U.S. Jews were united in demanding that the U.S. give special treatment to Israel.

The delegation had suggested that, in order to demonstrate to American Jews that the secretary of state was indeed working toward the advancement of America's best interests, Dulles "arrange a private meeting with U.S. Jewish leaders where the Secretary would discuss U.S. interests in the Near East and U.S. policies to advance those interests. Such a meeting would consist of Jews of stature who were uncommitted either to the Council or to the Zionist elements." [104]

With American-Israeli relations in crisis, Dulles and Eisenhower appeared to be taking the American Council for Judaism's advice literally. On February 15, Eisenhower, vacationing at his retreat at Thomasville, Georgia, Eisenhower called up two prominent Jews he knew—Barney Balaban of New York, president of Paramount Pictures, and Sidney J. Weinberg, a New York investment banker, asking them to help organize "some Jewish sentiment in support of what might be the President's final position." [105] On February 21, 1957, eight Jewish leaders in the "Balaban group" met with Dulles, along with Max Rabb, secretary to the cabinet, and Fraser Wilkins, a veteran Near Eastern expert at the State Department. Besides Balaban, the group included Sam Leidesdorf, treasurer of the UJA of Greater New York and a prominent member of the American Jewish Committee, Lou M. Novins, a public relations advisor of Balaban's, Jacob Blaustein, Irving M. Engel, William S. Rosenwald, general chairman of the UJA, Philip M. Klutznick, president of B'nai B'rith, and Mendel Silberberg, a leading member of the Jewish community in Los Angeles. [106]

Presenting his case to the group, Dulles, put forward an elaborate set of arguments touching on many bases. The fundamental question was, he said, who determined US national interest and whose responsibility it was to formulate national policy. In the case of policy disputes between "other groups" and the executive branch, he asserted, "the view of the elected leadership ought to prevail." Projecting an apocalyptic vision of the consequences of Israeli policy, he warned that

> it would be disastrous for Israel to remain in Gaza and Aqaba. Israel's best hope could be found in reliance on the members of the U.N., including the United States, to achieve tranquility in the area. If Israel were to remain in Gaza and Aqaba, there might be a breakdown of the cease-fire, a resumption of guerrilla activities in Israel by the Arab states, and continued blockade of the Suez Canal. There might also be closer relations between the Arab states and the Soviet Union.

In the final analysis, he emphasized, Israel's preservation was "a basic part of American foreign policy. If Israel now placed itself outside the law it would be difficult for the United States to move."

Barney Balaban replied by rejecting Dulles' insinuation that the group had a parochial interest, making the point that "none of them were present as 'professional Jews' but as Americans." As such, Balaban implied, he and the other participants felt free to probe the validity of Dulles' approach. Philip Klutznick, while accepting the proposition that the United States and Israel should work in tandem, pointed to a divergency emanating from "a feeling in the United States that the American proposals had been too tough and that Israel should be enabled to reach a decision without a 'gun at its temple.' "[107] Blaustein, one of the dominant participants in the discussion, underscored "Israel's desire for security"[108] and the necessity of bringing about a "fundamental change in the Middle East." This, he said, would entail providing Israel with a guarantee of its right of free passage in the Gulf of Aqaba and the Suez Canal, and insuring "that Israeli withdrawal should be preceded by assurances against attack, boycott and blockade on the part of Egypt."[109]

Dulles, however, was adamant. "The United States," he responded, "had gone as far as it could to create probability but it could not provide guarantees."[110] His maximum concession to Israel, he said, had been stated in a State Department aide memoire of February 11, 1957, in which the US had conveyed its readiness to declare "that it will use its influence, in concert with other members of the U.N., to the end that, following Israel's withdrawal," it would position the UN Emergency Force at the Gaza Strip border with Israel, and that "on behalf of vessels of US registry, is prepared to exercise the right of free and innocent passage, and to join with others to secure general recognition of this right."[111]

Although the meeting was unproductive, in retrospect it constituted a milestone. By standing their ground and refusing to sanction Dulles' position, and by turning down his bid for them to pressure Israel, the Jewish leaders were making a significant statement, namely that most American Jewry—Zionists and non-Zionists alike—not only expected America to aid Israel in its security needs, but perhaps more important, had come of age psychologically and politically. They had acquired sufficient self-confidence as American citizens to have their own concept of America's national interest.

Notes

Bibliography

Index

Notes

Abbreviations used for published and archival sources:

ACJA   American Council for Judaism Archives, State Historical Society of Wisconsin, Madison, Wisconsin
AHSA   Abba Hillel Silver Archives, Cleveland, Ohio
AJA   American Jewish Archives, Cincinnati, Ohio
AJCA   American Jewish Committee Archives, New York
AJHS   American Jewish Historical Society, Waltham, Massachusetts
AJYB *American Jewish Year Book*
AZECA   American Zionist Emergency Council Archives, New York
CZA   Central Zionist Archives, Jerusalem
DBGA   David Ben-Gurion Archives, Sde Boker
DDEL   Dwight D. Eisenhower Library, Abilene, Kansas
DFPI *Documents on the Foreign Policy of Israel,* Israel State Archives, Jerusalem
FRUS *Foreign Relations of the United States,* Department of State, Washington, D.C.
HSTL   Harry S. Truman Library, Independence, Missouri
IDFA   Israel Defense Forces Archives, Givatayim
ISA   Israel State Archives, Jerusalem
JA   Jewish Agency, Jerusalem and New York
JFDP   John Foster Dulles Papers, Princeton University
JTA   *Jewish Telegraphic Agency*
NAR   Department of State Records, National Archives, Washington, D.C.
NSC   National Security Council
PM   Prime Minister
PPF   President's Personal File
PSF   President's Secretary File
YIVO   Institute for Jewish Research, New York

Introduction

1. Gershom Scholem, *Explications and Implications: Writings on Jewish Heritage and Renaissance* [in Hebrew] (Tel-Aviv: Am Oved, 1989), 2:129.

2. Daniel Elazar, *Community and Polity* (Philadelphia: Jewish Publication Society of America, 1980), 74.

3. On the Biltmore program, see Ben Halpern, *The Idea of the Jewish State* (Cambridge, Mass.: Harvard Univ. Press, 1961), 39–42.

4. Samuel Halperin, *The Political World of American Zionism* (Detroit: Wayne State Univ. Press, 1961), 327.

5. British Zionist Federation, quoted in Mordecai M. Kaplan, "The Need for Diaspora Zionism," in *Mid-Century,* ed. Harold U. Ribalow (New York: Beechhurst Press, 1955), 445.

6. Ibid.

1. The Specter of Dual Loyalty

1. Louis Finkelstein, quoted in Morris D. Waldman, *Nor by Power* (New York: International Universities Press, 1953), 258–60.

2. American Jewish Committee, quoted in Charles Reznikoff, ed., *Louis Marshall: Champion of Liberty; Selected Papers and Addresses* (Philadelphia: Jewish Publication Society, 1957), 1:30.

3. American Reform Movement, quoted in Michael A. Meyer, *Response to Modernity* (New York: Oxford Univ. Press, 1988), 293.

4. Reznikoff, *Louis Marshall,* 2:704.

5. Naomi W. Cohen, *Not Free to Desist* (Philadelphia: Jewish Publication Society, 1972), 249–50; Menahem Kaufman, *Non-Zionists in America and the Struggle for Jewish Statehood, 1938–48* [in Hebrew] (Jerusalem: Hassifriya Haziyonit, 1984), 30.

6. Joseph M. Proskauer, *A Segment of My Times* (New York: Farrar, Straus and Co., 1950), 30, and see 12. See also Jerold S. Auerbach's excellent book *Rabbis and Lawyers: The Journey from Torah to Constitution* (Bloomington: Indiana Univ. Press, 1990), 151, 187–92.

7. Waldman, *Nor by Power* (New York: International Universities Press, 1953), 240.

8. Ibid.

9. "Background for the Palestine Discussion," appendix to Minutes, AJC Executive Committee meeting, 10–11 May 1947, Blaustein Library, AJCA.

10. Minutes, AJC Executive Committee meeting, 10–11 May 1947.

11. Ibid.

12. Correspondence among Proskauer, Moshe Shertok (later Sharett), and David Ben-Gurion, 27 Apr.–8 May 1948, 93.08/85/16, ISA. See also M. Kaufman, *Non-Zionists in America,* chaps. 7, 8.

13. Zvi Ganin, *Truman, American Jewry, and Israel, 1945–1948* (New York: Holmes and Meier, 1979), chap. 11.

14. Jacob Blaustein, untitled address given in Baltimore, Maryland, 15 Feb. 1948, Jacob Blaustein Papers, Baltimore.

15. Blaustein, untitled address, 15 Feb. 1948.

16. Ibid.

17. Ibid.

18. Ibid.

19. Ibid.

20. Minutes, AJC Executive Committee meeting, 16–17 Oct. 1948, AJCA.

21. Ibid.

22. *AJYB* 51 (1950): 562.

23. Blaustein, "At Dedication Ceremony. . . . The Blaustein Building," address given 28 May 1964, folder "Blaustein, Jacob," folder JSX 64, AJCA.

24. John Slawson, address given at memorial service for Jacob Blaustein, 1971, 5–6, Blaustein Library, AJCA.

25. Selma Hirsh, interview by the author, Sept. 1990, New York.

26. Ibid.

27. Blaustein, "1948, The Year in Retrospect," address given on 23 Jan. 1948, AJC Papers, Blaustein's addresses, YIVO.

28. The activities of the American Council for Judaism are fully documented at the ACJA, located at the State Historical Society in Madison, Wisconsin. See also Thomas A. Kolsky, *Jews Against Zionism: The American Council for Judaism, 1942–1948* (Philadelphia: Temple Univ. Press, 1990).

29. *Reader's Digest*, Sept. 1949, 49–54.

30. Ibid.

31. Elmer Berger, *Memoirs of an Anti-Zionist Jew* (Beirut: Institute for Palestine Studies, 1978), 2.

32. On Rabbi Elmer Berger's connection with Kermit Roosevelt, see folder "Roosevelt, Kermit, 1949–1953," box 106; folder "Fayez Sayegh–1955," box 7, ACJA. On American Friends of the Middle East, see Hertzl Fishman, *American Protestantism and a Jewish State* (Detroit: Wayne State Univ. Press, 1973), 101–7.

33. Minutes, ACJ Executive Committee meeting, 18 May 1948, box 10, ACJA.

34. Lessing J. Rosenwald to Robert A. Lovett, 29 Dec. 1948; 13 Jan. 1949, and attachments, 867N.01/1–1349, NAR.

35. Ibid.

36. Ibid.

37. Ben Halpern, "The Anti-Zionist Phobia: Legal Style," in *The Arab-Israeli Conflict*, ed. John N. Moore (Princeton, N.J.: Princeton Univ. Press, 1974), 190.

38. Tate to Rosenwald, 1 Feb. 1949, 867N.01/1–1349; Berger to Satterthwaite, 8 Feb. 1949, 867N.01/2–849, NAR.

39. Berger to Satterthwaite, 8 Feb. 1949, 867N.O1/2–849, NAR.

40. Berger to Kermit Roosevelt, 8 Feb. 1949, box 106, ACJA.

41. William Zukerman to Berger, 16 Jan. 1954, box 5, ACJA.

42. Minutes, American Zionist Emergency Council meeting, 11 Dec. 1947, Sharett Archives, Tel-Aviv Zionist Archives, New York.

43. Ibid.

44. Edmund I. Kaufmann to David K. Niles, 26 May 1948, OF 502, HSTL.

45. Ibid.

46. Reuven Dafni to Zvi Borenstein, 10 Feb. 1949, 130.20/2463/16, ISA.

47. Minutes, Jewish Agency Executive meeting, 18–19 Aug. 1948, CZA.

48. Minutes, Jewish Agency Executive meeting, 19 Aug. 1948, CZA.

49. Ibid.

50. Israel Goldstein, *My World as a Jew: The Memoirs of Israel Goldstein* (New York: Herzl Press, 1984), 1:241.

51. Chaim Weizmann, *Trial and Error* (New York: Harper and Brothers, 1949), 314.

52. Jacob Robinson, "The Relationship of the WZO and the State of Israel," memo, 25 July 1948, 93.03/125/18, ISA.

53. Minutes, Jewish Agency Executive meeting, 19 Aug. 1948, CZA.

54. Daniel Frisch, "The ZOA at the Crossroad," *The New Palestine,* 13 Jan. 1949.

55. Arthur Hertzberg, "American Zionism at an Impasse," *Commentary,* Oct. 1949.

56. Frisch, "The ZOA at the Crossroad."

57. Ibid.

58. See chapter 3.

59. "The Rifkind Report of the Commission on the Future Program . . . of the WZO," 1949, A364/1600, Israel Goldstein Papers, CZA.

60. Ibid., 14.

61. Minutes, American Zionist Emergency Council meeting, 7 Mar. 1949, AZECA, Zionist Archives, New York.

62. Minutes, American Zionist Emergency Council meeting, 29 Apr. 1949, AZECA, Tel-Aviv Zionist Archives.

2. Skirmishes Between the American Jewish Committee and Ben-Gurion

1. Blaustein to Eliahu Elath, 2 Mar. 1949, 130.20/2464/A, ISA.

2. Ibid; Chaim Weizmann, *Ha-Olam* [in Hebrew] (complete text of speech), 17 Feb. 1949; Weizmann, *Ha-Olam* (abridged English translation), JTA, 15 Feb. 1949.

3. See Bernard Joseph, *British Rule in Eretz Yisrael* [in Hebrew] (Jerusalem: Mosad Bialik, 1948), 44. Milton Himmelfarb, interview by the author, Sept. 1990, White Plains, N.Y.; Irving M. Engel to Slawson, 13 Feb. 1951, box 55, AJC Papers, FAD-1, YIVO.

4. Blaustein to Elath, 2 Mar. 1949, 130.20/2464/A, ISA.

5. Ibid. On earlier semantic concerns of the AJC, see Ben-Gurion, Minutes, Jewish Agency Executive meeting, 4 Oct. 1942, S100/36b, CZA; M. Kaufman, *Non-Zionists in America,* 55.

6. Blaustein to Elath, 14 Mar. 1949, 93.08/85/16, ISA.

7. Elath to Blaustein, 10 Mar. 1949, 130.20/2464/A, ISA.

8. Ibid.

9. Ibid.

10. Arthur Lourie to Simon Segal, 11 Mar. 1949, 93.08/85/16, ISA.

11. AJC press release, 24 Mar. 1949, 93.08/85/16, ISA.

12. Blaustein, NBC radio address, 4 May 1949, Blaustein's addresses, AJC Papers, YIVO. On Blaustein's sacroiliac condition, see Slawson, address given at memorial service for Jacob Blaustein, 3 Feb. 1971, AJCA, 10–11.

13. Blaustein, NBC radio address, 4 May 1949, Blaustein's addresses, AJC Papers, YIVO.

14. Ibid.

15. Ibid.

16. Minutes, AJC Executive Committee meeting, 7–8 May 1949, AJCA.

17. Ben-Gurion, diary, entries for 17 Apr. 1949, 29 Jan. 1951, DBGA.

18. Minutes, AJC Executive Committee meeting, 7–8 May 1949, AJCA.

19. Ibid.

20. Ibid.

21. Ibid.

22. Ibid.

23. Ibid. See also Ben-Gurion, diary, enry for 6 Apr. 1949, DBGA.

24. Minutes, AJC Executive Committee meeting, 7–8 May 1949, AJCA.

25. Ibid.

26. Ibid.

27. Ibid.

28. Proskauer to Ben-Gurion, 28 Apr. 1949, Prime Minister's Papers, 5563/29, ISA.

29. *DFPI* 4, May-Dec. 1949 *(1986), 19–23.*

30. *JTA,* 1 Sept. 1949; *Daily News Bulletin,* 1 Sept. 1949.

31. Rosenwald to Dean Acheson, 8 Sept. 1949, 867N/01/9–849, NAR.

32. Blaustein to Ben-Gurion, 19 Sept. 1949, 93.08/366/18, ISA.

33. Ibid.

34. Arthur S. Rosichan to Elath, 21 Sept. 1949, 93.08/366/18, ISA.

35. Ibid.

36. Leopold Lerner to Reuven Dafni, 27 Sept. 1949, 93.08/366/18, ISA.

37. Ibid. See also also the letter in a similar vein by a veteran Zionist, George Gersony, to Elath, 27 Sept. 1949, 93.08/366/18, ISA.

38. Moshe Sharett to Si Kenen, 2 Oct. 1949, 93.08/366/18, ISA.

39. Minutes, AJC Administrative Committee, 4 Oct. 1949, AJCA.

40. Proskauer to Ben-Gurion, 5 Oct. 1949, 93.08/377/25, ISA.

41. Memo, Michael S. Comay to Arthur Lourie, 7 Oct. 1949, 93.08/366/18, ISA.

42. Ibid.

43. Ben-Gurion, statement of 19 Oct. 1949, 93.08/366/18, ISA.

44. Elath to Blaustein, 20 Oct. 1949, 93.08/366/18, ISA.

45. Ibid.

46. Minutes, AJC Executive Committee meeting, 22–23 Oct. 1949, AJCA. All subsequent quotations, unless otherwise attributed, are taken from this document.

47. Ibid.

48. Ibid.

49. *The New Palestine* 40, no. 2 (30 Aug. 1949).

50. Frisch, quoted at length in Minutes, AJC Executive Committee meeting, 22–23 Oct. 1949, AJCA.

51. Ibid.

52. Ibid.

53. Ibid.

54. Ben-Gurion to Proskauer, 1 Nov. 1949, 93.08/366/18, ISA.

55. Ibid.

56. Ibid.

57. Ibid.

58. Proskauer to Ben-Gurion, 8 Dec. 1949, 93.08/366/17, ISA.

59. Ibid. See also Proskauer to Elath, 8 Dec. 1949, 93.08/366/18, ISA.

60. Blaustein to Slawson, 17 Dec. 1949, AJC Papers, record group 347.7/56, YIVO, copy at DBGA.

3. The American Jewish Community Viewed from Israel

1. *DFPI* 3, Dec. 1948-July 1949 (1983), appendixes F, G, H, J.

2. Sasson to Sharett, 27 Sept. 1949, *DFPI* 4, 497–99.

3. Ibid., 498.

4. Six years later, in 1955, after visiting the Arab Middle East, Berger reached a similar conclusion, although he detected "an open or hidden fear of Israeli expansion so long as the [Israeli] Law of Return was in effect." Memo of conversation, Shimshon Arad with Berger, 7 June 1955, 130.20/2465/5, ISA.

5. CIA study, "Israel," SR 61, 24 July 1950, 43, PSF, HSTL.

6. Teddy Kollek, *One Jerusalem* [in Hebrew] (Tel-Aviv: Maariv, 1979), 155.

7. There is voluminous biographical material on Ben-Gurion. The best works are: Shabtai Teveth, *Ben-Gurion: The Burning Ground* (Boston: Houghton Mifflin Co., 1987); and Michael Bar-Zohar, *Ben-Gurion* [in Hebrew], 3 vols. (Tel-Aviv: Am Oved, 1977).

8. David Ben-Gurion, *Yihud Veyeud* [in Hebrew] (Tel-Aviv: Ministry of Defense, 1972), 55.

9. Ibid., 56.

10. David Ben-Gurion, *The Restored State of Israel* [in Hebrew] (Tel-Aviv: Am Oved, 1969), 349.

11. Emanuel Neumann, *In the Arena* (New York: Herzl Press, 1976), 21.

12. For biographical material on Abba Hillel Silver, see Daniel J. Silver, ed., *In the Time of Harvest* (New York: Macmillan Co., 1963); Ganin, *Truman, American Jewry, and Israel*; Noah Orian, "The Leadership of Abba Hillel Silver, 1938–1949," Ph.D. diss., Tel-Aviv Univ., 1982; and Marc L. Raphael, *Abba Hillel Silver* (New York: Holmes and Meier, 1989).

13. Minutes, Jewish Agency Executive meeting, 24 Oct. 1948, CZA.

14. Report, David Goitein to Ministry for Foreign Affairs, June [?] 1952, 130.20/2460/8, ISA.

15. Murray I. Gurfein, quoted in Marc L. Raphael, *A History of the UJA, 1939–82* (Providence, R.I.: Brown Univ. Scholars Press, 1982), 35; Henry Montor, oral history, 14 Oct. 1975, Institute of Contemporary Jewry, Hebrew Univ. of Jerusalem.

16. *Davar*, 4 Mar. 1949.

17. *The Reconstructionist* 14 (4 Feb. 1949): 17–23; *AJYB* 51 (1950): 168. See also Ernest Stock, *Partners and Pursestrings: A History of the United Israel Appeal* (Lanham, Md.: University Press of America, 1987), chap. 27.

18. *Haaretz*, 21 Jan. 1949; *Jerusalem Post*, 21 Feb. 1949.

19. *Yiddish News Digest*, 16 Dec. 1948, Blaustein Library, AJCA.

20. *Davar*, 17 Feb. 1949; *Haaretz*, 21 Feb. 1949; *Jerusalem Post*, 21 Feb. 1949.

21. David Niv, *Battle for Freedom: The Irgun Zvai Leumi* [in Hebrew], part 1 (Tel-Aviv: Klausner Institute, 1975), 205–6; Neumann, *In the Arena*, 137–38.

22. Ben-Gurion, diary, entries for 13 Apr. 1950, 15, 21 Aug. 1951, DBGA. See also Allon

Gal, *David Ben-Gurion and the American Alignment for a Jewish State* (Bloomington: Indiana Univ. Press, 1991), 36, 185, 211.

23. Ganin, *Truman, American Jewry, and Israel,* chap. 8.

24. Allon Gal, *David Ben-Gurion and the American Alignment for a Jewish State* (Bloomington: Indiana Univ. Press, 1991), 125.

25. David Ben-Gurion, *The Restored State of Israel,* 65–68; Leonard Slater, *The Pledge* (New York: Simon and Schuster, 1970), chap. 11; Doron Almog, *Weapons Acquisitions in the US, 1945–49* [in Hebrew] (Tel-Aviv: Ministry of Defense, 1987); telephone interview with General (ret.) Shlomo Shamir, Tel-Aviv, Dec. 1992.

26. David Niv, *The Irgun Zvai Leumi,* part 6, 184; Menahem Begin, *Ha-Mered* [in Hebrew] (Jerusalem: Achiasaf, 1950), 392–93, quoting Abba Hillel Silver: "The Irgun will go down in history as a factor without which the State of Israel would not have come into being."

27. David Ben-Gurion, *The War of Independence Diary* [in Hebrew](Tel-Aviv: Ministry of Defense, 1982), 963. For earlier references to Abba Hillel Silver and Neumann, see 41, 192, 266, 572, 657, 770–72, 909. See also minutes of Mapai, Political Committee, 5 Aug. 1951, 21, in which Ben-Gurion called Silver and Neumann and their supporters in the ZOA "a gang which is not Zionist at all." Mapai Archives, Beit Berl College, Israel.

28. Richard Ford to State Department, 18 May 1949, 867N.01\5–1849, NAR.

29. Jacques Torczyner, interview with author, New York, Sept. 1990; Zvi Herman, interview with author, Haifa, Israel, Nov. 1992.

30. Ganin, *Truman, American Jewry, and Israel,* 115–18; Zvi Ganin, "Activism versus Moderation: The Conflict Between Silver and Wise," *Studies in Zionism* 5, no. 1 (Spring 1984): 71–95.

31. Ben Halpern, *A Clash of Heroes: Brandeis, Weizmann, and American Zionism* (New York: Oxford Univ. Press, 1987).

32. Weizmann, *Trial and Error,* 244.

33. A summary of Israeli ambassadors' meeting, 17–23 July 1950, 130.02/2408/9, 3, ISA.

34. Ibid., 64.

35. Ibid.

36. Ibid., 1.

37. Moshe Sharett, quoted in Michael Brecher, *The Foreign Policy System of Israel* (London: Oxford Univ. Press, 1972), 248.

38. Ibid., 65.

39. Meron Medzini, *Israel's Foreign Relations: Selected Documents, 1947–1974* (Jerusalem: Ministry for Foreign Affairs, 1976), 119–20.

40. Moshe Sharett, address, *Divrei Ha-Knesset,* 15 June 1949, 718.

41. A summary of Israeli ambassadors' meeting, 17–23 July 1950, 66.

42. Ibid.

43. Eliezer Livneh to Ben-Gurion, 28 Feb. 1950, Eliezer Livneh Papers, box 9, Yad Tabenkin, Ephal. The discussion that follows is based on this document. Ephraim Evron, Sharett's private secretary (Ben-Gurion's secretary from Sept. 1951), claimed that the mission might have been initiated by Livneh.

44. Ibid.

45. Ibid.

46. Ibid.

47. Daniel J. Silver, *In the Time of Harvest*, 78.

48. Abba Hillel Silver, "The Case for Zionism," *Reader's Digest*, Sept. 1949, 57.

49. Cable, Ben-Gurion to Livneh, 18 Jan. 1950, DBGA.

50. Zvi Zinder's report, Mar. 1950, attached to memo, Kollek to Sharett et al., 26 Mar. 1950, 130.20/2463/16, ISA. All subsequent quotations taken from this document.

51. Ibid.

52. Ibid.

53. Minutes, meeting in the Ministry for Foreign Affairs, 8 May 1949, *DFPI* 4, 1986, 44–48, ISA.

54. Minutes, "Our Approach Toward American Jewry," meeting at Ben-Gurion's office, 25 July 1950, folder 230/72/656, IDFA. All subsequent quotations taken from this document.

55. Ibid.

56. Ben-Gurion to Abe Feinberg, 30 Dec. 1948, 130.02/2389/2, ISA.

57. Minutes, "Our Approach Toward American Jewry," 31 July 1950. All subsequent quotations taken from this document.

58. Ibid.

59. Minutes, meetings at Ben-Gurion's office, 31 July, 1, 2 Aug. 1950, folder 5563, PM Office, ISA. All subsequent quotations taken from this document.

60. On the internal debate over foreign policy orientation, see *DFPI* 4, May–Dec. 1949, 96–98, 452–55, 471. See also Uri Bialer, *Between East and West: Israel's Foreign Policy Orientation, 1948–56* (Cambridge, UK: Cambridge Univ. Press, 1990).

61. Minutes, conference with American Jewish leaders, 5 Sept. 1950, 130.02/2420/12, ISA; *Haaretz*, 31 Aug. 1950.

62. Minutes, conference with American Jewish leaders.

63. Eliezer Kaplan, report to Hadassah National Board Meeting, 16 Nov. 1950, Hadassah Archives, New York.

64. David Horowitz, report to Hadassah National Board Meeting, 12 Apr. 1951, Hadassah Archives, New York.

4. The Blaustein–Ben-Gurion Understanding of 1950

1. *New York Herald Tribune*, 7 Nov. 1949; *Davar*, 7 Nov. 1949; *JTA*, 8 Nov. 1949.

2. Jerome K. Crossman to Blaustein, 14 Nov. 1949, AJC Papers, record group 347.7/56, YIVO, copy at DBGA.

3. Blaustein to Jerome K. Crossman, 5 Dec. 1949, AJC Papers, record group 347.7/56, YIVO, copy at DBGA.

4. *Jewish Morning Journal*, 21 Dec. 1949; memo, Moshe Keren to Esther Herlitz, 12 Jan. 1950, 130.20/2463/16, ISA.

5. *Jewish Morning Journal*, 21 Dec. 1949.

6. Moshe Keren to Michael Comay, 18 Nov. 1949, 93.08/377/25, ISA.

7. Ibid.

8. Minutes, AJC Executive Committee meeting, 21 Jan. 1950, AJCA.

9. Ibid.

10. NCRAC condemnation, 18 Jan. 1950, 130.20/2463/16, ISA.

11. Blaustein, "The Voice of Reason," address to AJC Executive Committee, 29 Apr. 1950, box 24, AJC Papers, YIVO.

12. *New York Times,* 23, 24 Apr. 1950, reports on the sixth annual conference of the ACJ in Cincinnati.

13. Blaustein, "The Voice of Reason."

14. Blaustein, letter to AJC members, 10 Mar. 1950, box 66, ACJ Papers.

15. Minutes, AJC Executive Committee meeting, 29–30 Apr. 1950, AJCA.

16. Henry J. Kaufman to Blaustein, 14 June 1950, box 56, AJC Papers, FAD-1, YIVO.

17. Elath to Blaustein, 24 Apr. 1950, 93.08/377/25, ISA.

18. Elath to Blaustein, 19 June 1950; cable, Elath to Blaustein, 29 June 1950, box 76, AJC Papers, FAD-1, YIVO.

19. Cable, Ben-Gurion to Blaustein, 28 July 1950, 93.08/2388/23, ISA.

20. Cable, Elath to Blaustein, 28 July 1950, box 76, AJC Papers, FAD-1, YIVO.

21. Minutes, AJC Executive Committee meeting, 14–15 Oct. 1950, AJCA.

22. Ibid.

23. Ibid.

24. Blaustein, report of trip to Israel (copy), 9 Sept. 1950, DBGA.

25. Ibid.

26. Segal's notes on Blaustein's meetings with Ben-Gurion and Israeli leaders, 13–26 Aug. 1950, box 26, AJC Papers, FAD-1, YIVO. All subsequent quotations taken from notes of 13 Aug. 1950.

27. Cable, Ben-Gurion to Shertok, 6 June 1942, S25/1458, CZA; Samuel Halperin, *The Political World of American Zionism,* 121–26.

28. Official version of the understanding, Israel Office of Information, 23 Aug. 1950, 93.03/85/16, ISA. Subsequently, Blaustein insisted on obtaining reaffirmations of the understanding from Ben-Gurion (1956, 1961), in DGBA; from Levi Eshkol (1963, 1965), and from Golda Meir (1969, 1970), in AJCA, folder "Blaustein-Ben-Gurion Agreement Reaffirmation," AJCA.

29. Official version of the understanding, Israel Office of Information, 23 Aug. 1950, 93.03/85/16, ISA; Ben-Gurion (1956, 1961), in DGBA; Levi Eshkol (1963, 1965); and Golda Meir (1969, 1970), in AJCA, folder "Blaustein-Ben-Gurion Agreement Reaffirmation," AJCA.

30. Simon Segal to Slawson, 23 Aug. 1950, box 56, AJC Papers, FAD-1, YIVO.

31. Arthur Hertzberg, *The Zionist Idea* (New York: Atheneum, 1969), 609.

32. Minutes, AJC Executive Committee meeting, 14–15 Oct. 1950; Ben-Gurion, diary, entry for 23 Aug. 1950, DBGA.

33. Segal's notes, 13 Aug. 1950. See also cable, Elath to American Division, Ministry of Foreign Affairs, 5 May 1950, 93.01/2207/8, ISA.

34. Segal's notes, 13 Aug. 1950.

35. Michael Brecher, *Decisions in Israel's Foreign Policy* (London: Oxford Univ. Press, 1974), 130–31.

36. Editorial note, *DFPI* 5, 1950, 457; Keren to Sharett, 28 July 1950, *DFPI* 5, 1950, 449–50.

37. Editorial note, *DFPI* 5, 1950, 457.

38. Segal's notes, meeting of 13 Aug. 1950.

39. This account is based on Segal's notes, meeting of 26 Aug. 1950; Ben-Gurion, diary, entry for 26 Aug. 1950, DBGA.

40. Segal's notes, meeting of 26 Aug.; Ben-Gurion, diary, entry for 4 Sept. 1950, DBGA.

41. Segal's notes, meeting of 26 Aug.

42. See S. Z. Abramov's excellent study, *Perpetual Dilemma: Jewish Religion in the Jewish State* (Rutherford, N.J.: Fairleigh Dickinson Univ. Press, 1979).

43. Segal's notes, meeting of 26 Aug. 1950.

44. Ibid.

45. *Jerusalem Post,* 24 Aug. 1950.

46. *Davar,* 24 Aug. 1950.

47. Nathan Alterman, "An Unfounded Assumption" [in Hebrew], in *The Seventh Column* (Tel-Aviv: Davar, 1954), 71–73.

48. *Haboker,* 24 Aug. 1950.

49. *Hatzofe,* 3 Sept. 1950.

50. *Haaretz,* 25, 30 Aug. 1950.

51. Abba Eban, memo to U.S. Ministry for Foreign Affairs, 31 Aug. 1950, 93.08/377/25, ISA.

52. *Jewish Morning Journal,* 15 Sept. 1950; *Yiddish News Digest,* Blaustein Library, AJCA.

53. *The Day,* 27 Aug. 1950; *Yiddish News Digest,* Blaustein Library, AJCA.

54. *Congress Weekly* 17, no. 23 (11 Sept. 1950): 4–5.

55. M. J. Blumenfeld to Blaustein, 24 Nov. 1950, box 56, AJC Papers, FAD-1, YIVO.

56. *AJYB* 52 (1951): 62–63.

57. Ira M. Younker to Blaustein, 15 Oct. 1950, box 56, AJC Papers, FAD-1, YIVO.

58. L. H. Grunebaum to Blaustein, 20 Nov. 1950, box 56, AJC Papers, FAD-1, YIVO.

59. Salo W. Baron to Blaustein, 20 Nov. 1950, ibid. See also Baron, *A Social and Religious History of the Jews* (New York: Columbia Univ. Press, 1952), 1:212–21; Melvin I. Urofsky, *We Are One* (Garden City, N.Y.: Doubleday, 1978), 193–95; Charles S. Liebman, *Pressure Without Sanctions* (Rutherford, N.J.: Fairleigh Dickenson Univ. Press, 1977), 118–31.

5. The Struggle Between the American Jewish Committee and the Zionist Movement, 1951

1. On the AJC and the Zionists, see Halperin, *The Political World of American Zionism,* chap. 5; M. Kaufman, *Non-Zionists in America;* Halpern, *A Clash of Heroes,* 109–12; and Yigal Elam's excellent new book *The Jewish Agency* [in Hebrew] (Jerusalem: Hassifriya Haziyonit, 1990).

2. Nahum Goldmann, *Autobiography* (New York: Holt, Reinhart and Winston, 1969), 1.

3. Ibid., 138.

4. Goldmann, *Le Paradoxe Juif* [in Hebrew] (Ramat-Gan: Massada, 1978), 53. I wish to thank Jacques Torczyner, Natan Lerner, and Zvi Herman for sharing their detailed knowledge of Nahum Goldmann's career with me.

5. See, for example, cable, Rusk to Marshall and Lovett, 6 May 1948, 501.BB Palestine/5–648, NAR.

6. A. Leon Kubowitzki, *Unity in Dispersion: A History of the World Jewish Congress* (New York: Institute of Jewish Affairs, 1948), 33.

7. Waldman, *Nor by Power* (New York: International Universities Press, 1953), chap. 19.

8. Blaustein to Berl Locker, 20 Mar. 1951, Goldmann Papers, Z6/508, CZA. For text of the agreement, n.d. [Nov. 1950], ibid.

9. Identical letters, Blaustein and Edward M. M. Warburg to Berl Locker, 14 Mar. 1951, box 22, AJC Papers, YIVO.

10. Ibid.

11. Ibid.

12. Minutes, AJC Executive Committee meeting, 5–6 May 1951, AJCA.

13. Blaustein to Slawson, 30 Mar. 1951, box 22, AJC Papers, YIVO.

14. Ben-Gurion left Israel on 2 May and returned on 7 June 1951. Blaustein, letters to Ben-Gurion, Abba Eban, 24 May 1951, 93.08/345/38, ISA.

15. Goldmann to Locker, 4 June 1951, Z6/508, CZA.

16. Goldmann to Locker, 15 June 1951, Z6/452, CZA

17. Blaustein to Goldmann, 23 July 1951, Z6/508, CZA.

18. Goldmann to Blaustein, 14 Sept. 1951, Z6/508, CZA.

19. Goldmann to Berl Locker, 14 Sept. 1951, Z6/508, CZA.

20. Blaustein to Locker, 23 July 1951, Z6/508, CZA. See also a similar historic controversy over "commingling of funds" in Halpern, *A Clash of Heroes,* 221–22.

21. Emanuel Neumann, "Towards the World Zionist Congress," *Zionist Quarterly,* June 1951, 5–15.

22. Ibid.

23. Ibid.

24. Ibid.

25. Session of the Zionist General Council, 19–28 Apr. 1950, English version 20, CZA.

26. Ibid., 26.

27. On the status controversy, see Liebman, *Pressure Without Sanctions,* (131–47; Ernest Stock, *Chosen Instrument* (New York: Herzl Press, 1988), chap. 4; Yosef Gorny, *The Quest for Collective Identity* (Tel-Aviv: Am Oved, 1990), 59–78.

28. Eban to Blaustein, 3 May 1951, box 22, AJC Papers, YIVO.

29. Minutes, JA, American section, 11 May 1951, Z6/453, CZA.

30. *The Reconstructionist* 17, no. 7 (18 May 1951).

31. David Ben-Gurion, *The Restored State of Israel* [in Hebrew] (Tel-Aviv: Am Oved, 1969), 421.

32. Neumann, *In the Arena,* 280.

33. Ibid., 280–81.

34. *New York Times,* 17 June 1951. Full text of Ben-Gurion's message, memo, Eban to Blaustein, 22 June 1951, 93.08/345/38, ISA.

35. *New York Times,* 17 June 1951.

36. Blaustein to Eban, 18 June 1951, 93.08/345/38, ISA.

37. Eban to Foreign Ministry, 16 July 1951, 93.08/345/37, ISA.

38. Harman to Kollek, 16 Apr. 1951, 93.03/109/23, ISA.

39. Comay to Elath, 29 July 1951, 130.20/2463/16, ISA.

40. Blaustein to Eban, 2 Aug. 1951, 93.08/345/38, ISA.

41. Eban to Blaustein, 3 Aug. 1951, 130.02/2388/23/a, ISA.

42. *JTA*, 9 Aug. 1951.

43. Complete Hebrew text, 8 Aug. 1951, 93.08/345/345, ISA.

44. Ibid.

45. Cables, Warburg and Schwartz to Goldmann, 10 Aug. 1951, Goldmann Papers, Z6/466, CZA; Blaustein to Ben-Gurion, 10 Aug. 1951, 130.20/2464/a, ISA.

46. Cable, Ben-Gurion to Blaustein, 12 Aug. 1951, 130.20/2464/a, ISA.

47. Cable, Elkanah Galli to Warburg and Schwartz, 13 Aug. 1951, Z6/466, CZA.

48. Ben-Gurion, excerpts from speech given 8 Aug. 1951, DBGA.

49. Cable, Eban to Blaustein, 13 Aug. 1951, 93.08/345/38, ISA.

50. *AJYB* 53 (1952): 135–41.

51. Blaustein to Ben-Gurion, 15 Aug. 1951, 93.08/2388/23, ISA. This letter expanded on Blaustein's cable to Ben-Gurion of 14 Aug. 1951, 93.08/2388/23, ISA.

52. "Stenographic Report" [in Hebrew], Twenty-third Zionist Congress (Jerusalem: Zionist Executive, 1951), 165.

53. Ibid., 583.

54. Ibid., 497.

55. Ibid., 152.

56. Ibid., 154.

57. Ibid., 149.

58. *Stenographic Report*, 583; minutes, Hadassah National Board, 13 Sept. 1951, Hadassah Archives.

59. *Stenographic Report*, 133.

60. Ibid., 138.

61. Memo, Harry (Zvi) Zinder to Abba Eban, 20 Aug. 1951, 93.08/345/38, ISA.

62. Cable, Blaustein to Ben-Gurion, 20 Aug. 1951, 93.08/2388/23, ISA.

63. Cable, Ben-Gurion to Blaustein, 21 Aug. 1951, 93.08/2388/23, ISA.

64. Cable, Blaustein to Ben-Gurion, 22 Aug. 1951, 93.08/2388/23, ISA.

65. Cable, Proskauer to Ben-Gurion, 22 Aug. 1951, 93.08/2388/23, ISA.

66. Cable, Blaustein to Ben-Gurion, 23 Aug. 1951, 93.08/2388/23, ISA.

67. Cable, Eban to Blaustein, 23 Aug. 1951, 93.08/345/38, ISA.

68. Ben-Gurion to Blaustein, 29 Aug. 1951, 93.08/345/38, ISA.

69. Memo of conversation, Josef Cohn with Sam Leidesdorf and Judge Rosenman, 30 Aug. 1951, box 31, David K. Niles Papers, HSTL. On Sam Rosenman, see Eliahu Elath, "Samuel I. Rosenman's Role in Israel's Creation" [in Hebrew], *Molad*, 37–38 (1976): 448—54; Clark Clifford, *Counsel to the President* (New York: Random House, 1991), 53–56, 60–61, 75, 90–91, 213–15.

70. Memo of conversation, Josef Cohn with Sam Leidesdorf and Judge Rosenman, 30 Aug. 1951.

6. Codifying Communal Relationships

1. Memo, Herlitz to Eban, 31 Aug. 1951, 93.08/345/37, ISA.

2. Blaustein, "Freedom and Fear," 26 Jan. 1952, AJC Papers, Blaustein addresses, YIVO.

3. Kollek to Gershon Agron, 6 Sept. 1951, 93.03/109/23, ISA.

4. For Eban's text, see cable, Eban to Ben-Gurion, 6 Sept. 1951, 93.03/73/10. For the Committee's amended text, see cable, Kollek to Ben-Gurion, 11 Sept. 1951, PM Office, 5563/29. See also cables, Ben-Gurion to Kollek, 12 Sept. 1951, PM Office, 5563/29; Ben-Gurion to Eban, 10 Sept. 1951, 93.08/345/38, ISA.

5. On the Israeli domestic scene, see David Shaham, *Israel—Forty Years* [in Hebrew] (Tel-Aviv: Am Oved, 1991), chap. 2; cable, Teddy Kollek to Ben-Gurion, 20 Sept. 1951, PM Office, 5563/2, ISA.

6. Cable, Ephraim Evron to Arthur Lourie, 26 Sept. 1951, PM Office, 5563/29, ISA.

7. Minutes, JA American section, 28 Sept. 1951, Z6/453, CZA.

8. Minutes, JA American section, 5 Oct. 1951, Z6/453, CZA.

9. Proskauer to Ben-Gurion, 28 Sept. 1951, PM Office, 5563/760/71, ISA.

10. Text of clarification message, cable, Ben-Gurion to Abba Eban, 30 Sept. 1951, 93/08/345/38, ISA.

11. Blaustein to Ben-Gurion, 30 Oct. 1951, 93.08/345/38, ISA.

12. Text of AJC resolution, 14 Oct. 1951, 93/08/345/38, ISA.

13. Ben-Gurion to Blaustein, 14 Nov. 1951, DBGA. The resolution elicited much sharper criticism from the veteran American Zionist leader Louis Lipsky: "The American Jewish Committee in Retreat," n.d. [Nov. 1951?], Z6/511, CZA.

14. Proskauer to Ben-Gurion, 21 Nov. 1951, PM Office, 5563/29, ISA. See also Ben-Gurion to Proskauer, 29 Oct. 1951, 230/72/656, IDFA.

15. Minutes, Jewish Agency Executive meeting, Jerusalem, 25 Nov. 1951, Z6/448, CZA.

16. Goldmann and Locker to Ben-Gurion, 4 Dec. 1951, Z6/466, CZA.

17. *Divrei Ha-Knesset* 10 (12 Dec. 1951): 634–37; *New York Times,* 13 Dec. 1951.

18. Ben-Gurion to Bernard Rosenblatt, 24 Dec. 1951, 230/72/656, IDFA.

19. Cable, Goldmann to Ben-Gurion, 14 Dec. 1951, Z6/659, CZA.

20. I. L. Kenen, *Israel's Defense Line* (Buffalo, N.Y.: Prometheus Books, 1981), 69.

21. Louis A. Novins to Eban, 14 Dec. 1951, 93.08/345/38, ISA.

22. Meier Steinbrink to Eban, 17 Dec. 1951, 93.08/345/38, ISA; Benjamin R. Epstein to Eban, 20 Dec. 1951, 93.08/345/38, ISA.

23. Cable, Eban to Ben-Gurion and Sharett, 18 Dec. 1951, *DFPI* 6, 1951, 869.

24. Memo, Meir Shalit to Ministry of Foreign Affairs, 20 Dec. 1951, 93.08/345/37, ISA.

25. Confidential source.

26. Goldmann to Ben-Gurion, 18 Dec. 1951, Z6/659, CZA.

27. Minutes, JA American section, 1 Feb. 1952, Z6/641, CZA.

28. Goldmann to Ben-Gurion, 18 Dec. 1951, Z6/659, CZA.

29. Bertram H. Gold, "Who Speaks for the Jews," AJCA, 1972, 16; and see Will Maslow, *The Structure and Functioning of the American Jewish Community* (New York: American Jewish Congress, 1974); Elazar, *Community and Polity,* chap. 5; Goldmann, *Autobiography,* chap. 24.

30. Eban to Ben-Gurion, 21 Dec. 1951, DBGA.

31. Cable, Kollek to Eban (in Israel), 23 Dec. 1951, 130.20/2464, ISA.

32. Cables, Blaustein to Ben-Gurion and to Eban, 29 Dec. 1951, PM Office, 5563/29; 130.20/2464/a, ISA; Ben-Gurion's response, cable to Blaustein, 31 Dec. 1951, DBGA.

33. See Liebman, *Pressure Without Sanctions,* 140–41. See also cable, Blaustein to Ben-Gurion, 3 Mar. 1952, DBGA.

34. Liebman, *Pressure Without Sanctions,* 141; minutes, JA American section, 28 Mar. 1952, Z6/641, CZA.

35. *Divrei Ha-Knesset* 11 (6 May 1952): 1924; Stock, *Chosen Instrument,* 65.

36. Minutes, AJC Executive Committee meeting, 10–11 May 1952.

37. Eban to Blaustein, 14 May 1952, 130.20/2464, ISA.

38. Ibid.

39. *Divrei Ha-Knesset* 11 (5–6 May 1952): 1886 ff., 1919 ff.

40. Session of the Zionist General Council, 7–15 May 1952, 57, CZA.

41. Ibid., 52–53.

42. Ibid., 64–66.

43. B. Z. Goldberg, *The Day,* 19, 20 Aug., in AJCA; Yiddish *News Digest,* 20 Aug. 1952, and in 130.20/2464/a, ISA.

44. Session of the Zionist General Council, 7–15 May 1952, 23.

45. Ibid., 180–81.

46. Liebman, *Pressure Without Sanctions,* 144; Stock, *Chosen Instrument,* 69.

47. Cable, Blaustein to Ben-Gurion, 14 Aug. 1952, PM Office, 5563/29, ISA.

48. *Haaretz,* 13 Aug. 1952.

49. Cable, Blaustein to Ben-Gurion, 14 Aug. 1952, PM Office, 5563/29, ISA.

50. AJC, *Yiddish News Digest,* 20 Aug. 1952, and in 130.20/2464/a, ISA.

51. Blaustein to Eban, 6 Nov. 1952, 130.20/2464; cables, Blaustein to Ben-Gurion and to Kollek, 8 Nov. 1952, PM Office, 5563/29, ISA.

52. Eban to Blaustein, 8 Nov. 1952, 130.20/2464, ISA.

53. Cable, Ben-Gurion to Blaustein, 24 Nov. 1952, DBGA.

54. *AJYB* 55 (1954): 116. On Blaustein's and the AJC's satisfaction with the results, see Blaustein to AJC members, 18 Nov. 1952, box 66, ACJ Papers; *AJYB* 55 (1954): 117.

7. The Second Truman Administration and the Quest for an Arab-Israeli Peace, 1948–1952

1. Raphael Patai, ed., *Encyclopedia of Zionism and Israel* (New York: McGraw-Hill, 1971), 2:948–51.

2. Reuben Fink, *America and Palestine* (New York: American Zionist Emergency Council, 1944), 20–23.

3. Carl Herman Voss, "Christian Friends of the New Israel," *Congress Weekly* 17, no. 24 (9 Oct. 1950): 6–8; Moshe Davis, ed., *With Eyes Toward Zion,* vol. 2 (New York: Praeger, 1986), 323–32.

4. Patai, *Encyclopedia of Zionism and Israel,* 34.

5. Neumann, *In the Arena,* 114–15, 150–56, 170–73.

6. Karl Baehr, executive secretary of the American Christian Palestine Committee, to Morris Fine, 8 Apr. 1949, folder, "Arabs in the US—propaganda," Blaustein Library, AJCA.

7. Walter Millis, ed., *The Forrestal Diaries* (New York: Viking Press, 1951), 386.

8. Ganin, *Truman, American Jewry, and Israel*, xiv, 23–24.

9. Ibid., chap. 11.

10. Clifford, *Counsel to the President*, chap. 1.

11. Ibid., 7, 183. See also Michael J. Cohen, *Truman and Israel* (Berkeley: Univ. of California Press, 1990), passim.

12. Cable, Elath to Eban, 5 Nov. 1948, *DFPI* 2, Oct. 1948-Apr. 1949, 146–47.

13. Elath to Sharett, 25 Dec. 1948, 130.02/2382/22a, ISA.

14. Cable, Elath to Eban, 5 Nov. 1948, *DFPI* 2, 146–47.

15. Memo and cable, Elath to Sharett, 26 Apr. 1950, 130.02/2389/6/b, ISA.

16. On Eddie Jacobson, see Frank J. Adler, *Roots in a Moving Stream: The Centennial History of Congregation B'nai Jehudah of Kansas City, 1870–1970* (Kansas City: The Temple, 1972), chap. 9; Ganin, *Truman, American Jewry, and Israel*, 20, 74, 146, 167–69, 177–79.

17. On Abe Feinberg, see I. L. Kenen's interview with Feinberg, 6 Feb. 1973, Kenen private papers, Washington, D.C.

18. On Blaustein's financial support for Truman's campaign, see Truman to Blaustein, 1 Apr. 1949, PPF, box 4650, HSTL.

19. Memo of conversation, Blaustein with Truman, 20 Dec. 1948, Jacob Blaustein Papers, Baltimore.

20. Address, Blaustein to AJC Executive Committee meeting, 2 May 1953, 27, box 24, AJC Papers, YIVO; memo of conversation, Blaustein with G. Lewis Jones of the State Department, 17 Dec. 1959, 611.84a/12–1759, NAR. Blaustein, in this conversation, described his past role "as an intermediary on a number of questions involving U.S.-Israel relations."

21. One of the best examples can be found in the Blaustein-Truman correspondence, Blaustein to Truman, 19 May, and Truman's response, 23 May 1951, PSF, box 113, HSTL.

22. Truman to Blaustein, 12 Feb. 1949, PSF, box 113, HSTL.

23. Blaustein to Truman, 10 Jan. 1949, PPF, box 4650, HSTL.

24. Cable, Marshall to Jessup, 30 June 1948, *FRUS*, 1948, 5:1160; Abba Eban, *An Autobiography* (London: Futura Publications, 1977), 127–28.

25. Cable, McDonald to Truman, 12 Sept. 1948, *FRUS*, 1948, 5:1392–94.

26. Ganin, *Truman, American Jewry, and Israel*, chap. 10.

27. Cable, Marshall to McDonald, 17 Sept. 1948, *FRUS*, 1948, 5:1408–9.

28. Memo of conversation, Lovett with McDonald, 21 July 1948, *FRUS*, 1948, 5:1232–34.

29. Memo, Clark M. Clifford, 17 June 1948, *FRUS*, 1948, 5:1117–19.

30. Memo, Robert M. McClintock, 23 June 1948, *FRUS*, 1948, 5:1134–37, and see also 5:1148–49.

31. Minute by Bernard Burrows, 9 June 1948, FO 371/68566, quoted in William Roger Louis, *The British Empire in the Middle East, 1945–1951* (Oxford, UK: Clarendon Press, 1984), 539–40. Permission to quote granted.

32. Memo, Marshall to Truman, 30 Aug. 1948, *FRUS*, 1948, 5:1359–60.

33. Memo of conversation, Blaustein with Truman, 17 Sept. 1948, Jacob Blaustein Papers, Baltimore.

34. Memo, phone conversation, Blaustein with Niles, 6 Jan. 1949, Jacob Blaustein Papers, Baltimore.

35. Memo of conversation, Blaustein with Truman, 20 Dec. 1948, Jacob Blaustein Papers, Baltimore.

36. Cable, Elath to Sharett, 31 Jan. 1949, *DFPI* 2, 402–3.

37. Ibid.

38. Eliezer Kaplan to Willard L. Thorp, 22 Dec. 1947, *Political and Diplomatic Documents, December 1947-May 1948*, 92–94, ISA, 1979.

39. Editorial Note, *FRUS*, 1947, 5:1317.

40. Cable, Sharett to Marshall, 8 June 1948, *DFPI* 1, May-Sept. 1948, 141. See also cable, Epstein and Gass to Eliezer Kaplan, 2 June 1948, *DFPI* 1, May-Sept. 1948, 114–15.

41. Memo, Satterthwaite to Lovett, 30 July 1948, *FRUS*, 1948, 5:1261–62.

42. Comay to Infeld, 17 Aug. 1948, *DFPI* 1, May-Sept. 1948, 526–30.

43. Cable, Heydt et al. to Epstein, 31 Aug. 1948, *DFPI* 1, May-Sept. 1948, 566.

44. Memo of phone conversation, Blaustein with Niles, 6 Jan. 1949, Jacob Blaustein Papers, Baltimore.

45. Editorial Note, *FRUS*, 1949, 6:681.

46. Memo of conversation, Blaustein with Truman, 20 Dec. 1948, Jacob Blaustein Papers, Baltimore.

47. Blaustein to Truman, 2 Feb. 1949, JB-JSX, 65, AJCA.

48. Ibid.

49. Memo, Truman to Niles, 13 May 1947, in Eliahu Elath, *The Struggle for Statehood* [in Hebrew] (Tel-Aviv: Am Oved, 1982), 594.

50. "The Current Situation in Israel," ORE 68–49, 18 July 1949, 1, box 256, PSF, HSTL.

51. Text of UN Resolution, 11 Dec. 1948, *DFPI* 2, 639–41.

52. Cable, Ethridge to Acheson, 28 Mar. 1949, *FRUS*, 1949, 6:876–78.

53. Cable, Eytan to Eban, 13 June 1949, *DFPI* 4, 128–30.

54. Jacob Herzog to Eban, 29 Sept. 1949, *DFPI* 4, 511–16.

55. Elath, *The Struggle for Statehood*, 2:381–86; cable, Burdett to the Secretary of State, 20 Apr. 1949, *FRUS*, 1949, 6:928–30.

56. Memo, Acheson to Truman, 20 Dec. 1949, *FRUS*, 1949, 6:1551–55.

57. Department of State Press Release, 28 July 1953, *FRUS*, 1952–54, 9:1263–64.

58. Ibid.

59. For a good summary of this subject, see Yossi Feintuch, *U.S. Policy on Jerusalem* (New York: Greenwood Press, 1987).

60. Sasson to Sharett, 21 Aug. 1949, *DFPI* 4, 380–82.

61. Cable, Webb to McDonald, 28 May 1949, *FRUS*, 1949, 6:1072–74. For previous pressure by Truman on Israel, see *FRUS*, 1948, 5:1704.

62. Cable, McDonald to Secretary of State, 29 May 1949, *FRUS*, 1949, 6:1074–75.

63. Cable, Shiloah to Sharett, 14 Aug. 1949, *DFPI* 4, 333–34.

64. Elath to Frisch, 22 Aug. 1949, 130.02/2389/1, ISA.

65. Elath to Sharett, 30 Aug. 1949, *DFPI* 4, 408–10.

66. Minutes, AJC Executive Committee meeting, 22–23 Oct. 1949.

67. Eban to Browdy, 28 Mar. 1952, Goldmann Papers, Z6/665, CZA.

68. Cable, Elath to Sharett, 26 July 1949, *DFPI* 4, 250.

69. Minutes, AJC Executive Committee meeting, 7–8 May 1949. On Proskauer's position, see Proskauer to Sharett and Eban, 13 Apr. 1949, 93.03/85/16, ISA.

70. Minutes, AJC Administrative Committee, 7 June 1949, AJCA.

71. Blaustein to members of the AJC, 21 Sept. 1949, attached to memo, Comay to Sharett, 18 Oct. 1949, 130.20/2464/a, ISA.

72. Memo of conversation, Blaustein with McGhee, 15 Sept. 1949, 867N.01/9–1549, NAR.

73. National Security Council, 47/2, 17 Oct. 1949, *FRUS*, 1949, 6:1430–40.

74. Cables, Ministry for Foreign Affairs, U.S. Division, to Elath, 30 Jan.; Sharett to Elath, 30 Mar. 1950, *DFPI* 5, 76–77, 221.

75. Cable, Eytan to Elath, 15/16 Jan. 1950, *DFPI* 5, 33–34.

76. Report of meeting between Kidron and Sheringham, 12 Jan. 1950, *DFPI* 5, 26–28.

77. Acheson to Javits, 12 Jan. 1950, *FRUS*, 1950, 5:684–85.

78. On American arms shipment policy to the Middle East, see extensive documentation in *FRUS*, 1950, in particular 5:134–38, 5:186 ff., 5:712–15, 5:1150.

79. Blaustein, "The Voice of Reason."

80. Blaustein to Slawson, 26 Feb. 1950, box 22, AJC Papers, YIVO.

81. Blaustein to Louis A. Johnson, 8 May 1950; Blaustein to Truman, 10 May 1950, Jacob Blaustein Papers, Baltimore.

82. Truman to Blaustein, 17 May 1950, Jacob Blaustein Papers, Baltimore.

83. Elath to Blaustein, 26 May 1950, box 4, Herbert B. Ehrmann Papers, AJHS. See also cable, Elath to U.S. Division, Ministry for Foreign Affairs, 5 May 1950, *DFPI* 4, 315–16; Keren to U.S. Division, 3 July 1950, *DFPI* 4, 421–22. See also Mordecai Gazit, "Israeli Military Procurement from the U.S.," in *Dynamics of Dependence: U.S.-Israeli Relations,* ed. Gabriel Sheffer (Boulder, Colo.: Westview Press, 1987), 83–123.

84. Sharett to Israeli Minister in Prague, 23 Aug. 1950, 130.02/2414/26/b, ISA.

85. Memo, Niles to Connelly, 10 Nov. 1950, box 31, Niles Papers, HSTL; memos, Eban to Goldmann, 15 Nov. 1950, Goldmann Papers, Z6/342, CZA; Sharett to Goldmann, 17 Nov. 1950, 130.02/2389/1, ISA. On the State Department's view of Israel's request, see *FRUS*, 1951, 5:594–98.

86. Memo, Sharett to Goldmann, 25 Apr. 1951, Goldmann Papers, Z6/466, CZA.

87. Eban to Goldmann, 22 May 1951, Goldmann Papers, Z6/469, CZA.

88. Slawson to Blaustein, 18 Oct. 1950, box 22, AJC Papers, YIVO.

89. Blaustein to Slawson, 21 Oct. 1950, box 22, AJC Papers, YIVO.

90. *National Jewish Post,* 27 Oct. 1950.

91. Invited to attend a Jewish Agency "working committee" on aid to Israel, Blaustein explained to Segal that he thought he could be "more effective in this direction if I continue to serve as an individual." Blaustein to Segal, 29 Dec. 1950, box 22, AJC Papers, YIVO.

92. Memo, Blaustein to Truman, 17 Sept. 1948, Jacob Blaustein Papers.

93. Text of agreement, 24 Feb. 1950, *DFPI* 5, 140; cable, McDonald to the Secretary of State, 26 Feb. 1950, *FRUS*, 1950, 5:757–58.

94. Memo, Blaustein to Truman, 10 May 1950, Jacob Blaustein Papers; Blaustein, "The Voice of Reason."

95. Memo of conversation, Acheson with Truman, 9 Mar. 1950. See also memo, Hare to Acheson, 8 Mar. 1950, *FRUS*, 1950, 5:787–89.

96. Cable, Elath to U.S. Division, 19 Apr. 1950, *DFPI* 5, 279 and in particular n. 1.

97. See Abraham Selah, *From Contacts to Negotiations: The Jewish Agency and Israel's Relationship with King Abdullah, 1946–1950* (Tel-Aviv: Tel-Aviv Univ., 1985); M. Sasson to E. Sasson, 17 Apr. 1950, *DFPI* 5, 272–74; cable, Sharett to Elath, 18 Apr. 1950, *DFPI* 5, 275; cable, Acheson to Legation in Jordan, 8 Apr. 1950, *FRUS*, 1950, 5:850.

98. Cable, Elath to U.S. Division, 12 May 1950, *DFPI* 5, 326.

99. Report of meeting btween Ben-Gurion and A. Henderson, British secretary of state for air, 1 Oct. 1950, *DFPI* 5, 562–65; and see Ben-Gurion, diary, entry for 1 May 1950, DBGA.

100. Memos, Blaustein to Truman, 27 Sept., 7 Oct. 1950, box 113, PSF, HSTL.

101. Eban to Blaustein, 5 Oct. 1950, 93.08/347/26, ISA.

102. Cable, Caffery to the Secretary of State, 25 Jan. 1950, *FRUS*, 1950, 5:702.

103. Memo of conversation, McGhee-Barrow with Blaustein, 7 May 1951, *FRUS*, 1951, 5:663–67.

104. Ibid.

105. Memo of conversation, McGhee with Blaustein, 11 June 1951, *FRUS*, 1951, 5:707–10.

106. Blaustein to Slawson, 13 June 1951, box 22, AJC Papers, YIVO.

107. Ibid.

108. All quotations from Eban to Blaustein, 24 July 1951, 130.20/2464/a. See also Eban to Ministry for Foreign Affairs, U.S. Division, 16 July 1951, 93.08/345/37, ISA.

109. Yaacov Shimoni, *The Arab States* [in Hebrew] (Tel-Aviv: Am Oved, 1988), 392–94.

110. Cable, Eban to Sharett, 19 Mar. 1952, 130.02/2453/12, ISA.

111. Michael B. Oren, "Secret Egypt-Israel Peace Initiatives Prior to the Suez Campaign," *Middle Eastern Studies* 26, no. 3 (July 1990): 351–70.

112. Ben-Gurion to Goldmann, 29 Dec. 1952, Goldmann Papers, Z6/721, CZA.

8. Attempts to Influence the Eisenhower-Dulles Policy Toward Israel, 1953–1957

1. Cables, Eban to U.S. Division, Ministry for Foreign Affairs, 5 Nov. 1952, *DFPI* 7, 606–8; Eban to Sharett and Ben-Gurion, 8 Nov. 1952, 93.01/2208/15, ISA.

2. *Haaretz*, 6 Nov. 1952.

3. *Haaretz*, 11 Jan. 1953; *Davar*, 11 Jan. 1953; Blaustein to Eisenhower, 26 Jan. 1953, box 565, PPF, 20-B, DDEL; 7 Mar. 1953, box 786, PPF 47, DDEL.

4. Memo, Segal to Blaustein, 9 Feb. 1953, box 22, AJC Papers, YIVO.

5. On Eisenhower's meeting with Governor McKelding and Judge Sobeloff, see memo of phone conversation, Simon Sobeloff with Shad Polier, 20 Feb. 1953, Israel Goldstein Papers, A364/1204, CZA. On the president's comments at a NSC meeting, see Discussion at the 207th Meeting, NSC, 22 July 1954, box 5, Ann Whitman File, DDEL. On Eisenhower's contacts with Jews, see Judah Nadich, *Eisenhower and the Jews* (New York: Twayne Publishers, 1953); Eli Ginzberg, *My Brother's Keeper* (New Brunswick, N.J.: Transaction Publishers, 1989), 77–81.

6. Memo of phone conversation, Simon Sobeloff with Shad Polier, 20 Feb. 1953, Israel Goldstein Papers, A364/1204, CZA. See also Goldstein, *My World as a Jew*, 1:293.

7. Stephen E. Ambrose, *Eisenhower, The President* (New York: Simon and Schuster, 1984), 2:13.

8. NSC, 155/1, 14 July 1953, *FRUS*, 1952–54, 9:399–404; Robert A. Divine, *Eisenhower and the Cold War* (Oxford, UK: Oxford Univ. Press, 1981), chap. 3.

9. Joseph C. Harsch, *Christian Science Monitor*, 25 Feb. 1953. Copies of this piece and of similar news items and articles from *Associated Press*, 18 Feb., 3 Mar.; *Baltimore Sun*, 2 Mar.; *Washington Post*, 2 Mar.; *New York Times, New York Herald Tribune*, 3 Mar. 1953, all in Israeli Washington Embassy to U.S. Division, 5 Mar. 1953, 130.20/2479, ISA.

10. Memo of conversation, Dulles with George Bey Hakim, 16 May 1953, *FRUS*, 1952–54, 9:72–75.

11. Memo of conversation, Eisenhower with Abboud Pasha, 1 June 1953, *FRUS*, 1952–54, 9:377–79.

12. Dulles, "Important Points of Trip," 1953, box 73, Dulles Papers, Princeton Univ. Library,

13. Bernard Lewis, *The Arabs in History* (New York: Harper and Row, 1966), 177–78.

14. Bernard Lewis, "At Stake in the Gulf," *New York Review of Books*, 20 Dec. 1990, 44–46; Bernard Lewis, "The Middle East Crisis in Historical Perspective," *The American Scholar* (Winter 1992): 33–46.

15. See Steven L. Spiegel, *The Other Arab-Israeli Conflict: Making America's Middle East Policy, from Truman to Reagan* (Chicago: Univ. of Chicago Press, 1985), chap. 3, for an excellent discussion of the Eisenhower era; Herman F. Eilts, "Reflections on the Suez Crisis: Security in the Middle East," in *Suez 1956*, ed. William Roger Louis and Roger Owen (Oxford, UK: Clarendon Press, 1989), 347–61.

16. "Important Points of Trip", 1953, box 73, Dulles Papers, Princeton Univ. Library.

17. The "Abba Eban" folder at the AHSA provides ample evidence for Eban's frequent solicitation of Silver's help, both regarding Senator Robert A. Taft of Ohio and Eisenhower and Dulles.

18. Blaustein to Eisenhower and Dulles, 20 Apr., box 22, AJC Papers, YIVO. See also Blaustein to Dulles, 7 May 1953, box 67, Dulles Papers, Princeton Univ. Library.

19. Cable, Dulles to Abba Hillel Silver, 13 July 1953, box 71, Dulles Papers, Princeton Univ. Library. See also *FRUS*, 1952–54, 9:1256.

20. Memo, Harman to Eban, 4 Sept. 1953, 93.03/107/4, ISA.

21. Shabtai Teveth, *Moshe Dayan* [in Hebrew] (Jerusalem-Tel-Aviv: Schocken, 1971), 392–96. See also Jonathan Shimshoni, *Israel and Conventional Deterrence* (Ithaca, N.Y.: Cornell Univ. Press, 1988), 46–49. Official misleading version of statement, 19 Oct. 1953, 93.08/395/5, ISA.

22. On Zionism and the use of force, see Anita Shapira, *Land and Power* (Tel-Aviv: Am Oved, 1992).

23. Minutes, AJC Executive Committee meeting, 24–25 Oct. 1953, Blaustein Library, AJCA.

24. Moshe Dayan, *The Story of My Life* [in Hebrew] (Jerusalem: Edanim Publishers, 1976), 115. For American Jewish reaction, see Herlitz to U.S. Division, 23 Oct. 1953, 93.08/395/5;

Harman to Mahav, 26 Oct. 1953, 130.20/2463/17; Edward M. M. Warburg to Kollek, 13 Nov. 1953, PM Office, 5523/5720/71; Shalit to Mahav, 16 Nov. 1953, 93.08/395/7; and Eban's sharply worded letter to Sharett and Dayan, 26 Nov. 1953, 130.02/2440/1, ISA, asserting that the Qibya affair "was the first act since our establishment [as a state] with which world Jewry refused to identify, viewing it as depreciating the prestige of the Jewish people."

25. Minutes, AJC Executive Committee meeting, 24–25 Oct. 1953.

26. Memo, Walter B. Smith, acting secretary of state, to Eisenhower, 21 Oct. 1953, *FRUS, 1952–54*, 9:1371–72.

27. Memo, Evron to U.S. Division, 14 Dec. 1953, 130.20/2463/17, ISA. See also Stephen D. Isaacs, *Jews and American Politics* (Garden City, N.Y.: Doubleday, 1974), 157.

28. Memo of phone conversation, Ambassador Henry C. Lodge with Robert D. Murphy, deputy undersecretary of state, 22 Jan. 1954, 648A.86/1–2254, NAR.

29. Eban to Blaustein, 12 Jan. 1954, 93.08/351/10, ISA.

30. Cable, Ben-Gurion to Blaustein, 21 Jan. 1954, box 22, AJC Papers, YIVO.

31. Eban to Blaustein, 5 Feb. 1954, 93.08/351/10, ISA.

32. Blaustein to Slawson, 1 Apr. 1954; Engel to Blaustein, 2 Apr. 1954; Blaustein to Engel, 5 Apr. 1954, box 22, AJC Papers, YIVO.

33. Shimshoni, *Israel and Conventional Deterrence*, 50.

34. For the quote from Byroade's speech of 1 May, see *Department of State Bulletin* 30, no. 776 (10 May 1954).

35. All quotations from Blaustein's criticism of the administration policy taken from memo of conversation, Dulles with Blaustein, 12 May 1954, *FRUS, 1952–54*, 9:1555–56.

36. On the "northern tier" concept, see memo of discussion of the NSC, 1 June 1953, *FRUS, 1952–54*, 9:384; John C. Campbell, *Defense of the Middle East* (New York: Harper and Brothers, 1960), chap. 5.

37. Memo of conversation, Dulles with Blaustein, 12 May 1954, *FRUS, 1952–54*, 9:1555–56.

38. On Alpha, see *FRUS, 1952–54*, 9:1683 ff.; *FRUS, 1955*, 14:1–401; Oren, "Secret Egypt-Israel Peace Initiatives," 351–70; Evelyn Shuckburgh, *Descent to Suez: Diaries, 1951–1956* (New York: W. W. Norton, 1986), 205–356; Shimon Shamir, "The Collapse of Project Alpha," in *Suez 1956*, ed. William Roger Louis and Roger Owen (Oxford, UK: Clarendon Press, 1989), 73–100.

39. Memos, Blaustein to Thomas E. Stephens, 14 May, White House Central Files, box 331; Blaustein to Eisenhower, 11 June 1954, White House Central Files, box 589, DDEL.

40. Cable, Reuven Shiloah to Sharett, 14 May 1954, 130.02/2455/2, ISA.

41. Cable, Shiloah to Jacob Herzog, n.d. [Oct. 1954], Shiloah Papers, 4374/20, ISA.

42. On the Eric Johnston mission, see cable, Lourie to U.S. Embassy, London, 11 Oct. 1953, *FRUS, 1952–54*, 9:1345–46.

43. Cable, Shiloah to Eytan, 25 Oct. 1954, Shiloah Papers, 4373/17, ISA.

44. Cable, Shiloah to Etyan, 25 Oct. 1954, Shiloah Papers, 4373/17, ISA; on the Cairo and Alexandria fiasco, see Bar-Zohar, *Ben-Gurion*, vol. 2, chap. 21.

45. Cable, Byroade to Caffery, 28 Oct. 1954, 684A.85/10–2854, NAR.

46. Cable, Hughes, U.S. Consul General in Tunis, to Secretary of State, 31 Oct. 1954, 684A.85/10–3154, NAR.

47. Cable, Hughes to State Department, 8 Nov. 1954, 684A.85/11–854, NAR.

48. Cable, Caffery to Secretary of State, 4 Nov. 1954, 684A.85/11–454, NAR.

49. Cable, Caffery to Secretary of State, 6 Nov. 1954, 684A.85/11–654, NAR.

50. Cable, Byroade to Blaustein via U.S. Embassy in Paris, 6 Nov. 1954, 684A.85/11–654, NAR.

51. Memo, Rafael to Sharett, "Summary and Conclusions of Israeli-Egyptian Contacts, 1949–1955," 19 Jan. 1956, 130.20/2460.4, ISA. I am indebted to Michael Oren for his invaluable help in obtaining this document.

52. Moshe Sharett, *Personal Diary* [in Hebrew], (Tel-Aviv: Maariv, 1978), 2:603.

53. See Shamir, "The Collapse of Project Alpha," 77–78.

54. Robert Stephens, *Nasser: A Political Biography* (New York: Simon and Schuster, 1971), 135–36.

55. Cable, Caffery to the State Department, 4 Feb. 1954, *FRUS,* 1952–54, 9:2210–12.

56. Memo, Dulles to Byroade, 10 Apr. 1954, *FRUS,* 1952–54, 9:1508.

57. Miles Copeland, *The Game of Nations* (London: Weidenfeld and Nicolson, 1970), 104.

58. Memo, Rafael to Sharett, 19 Jan. 1956, 130.20/2460.4, ISA.

59. On Blaustein's involvement, see memo, Rafael to Sharett, 19 Jan. 1956, 36–37; cable, Rafael to Shiloah, 12 Oct. 1954, Shiloah Papers, 4373/17, ISA; Sharett, *Personal Diary,* 3:689–90.

60. Hal Lehrman, "Arms for Arabs—and What for Israel?" *Commentary,* Nov. 1954, 423–33.

61. Memos of conversation, Eban et al. with Byroade, 17 June 1954, *FRUS,* 1952–54, 9:1580–83; see also 9:1620–21, 9:1623–24, 9:1627–28, 9:1634–35. On Klutznick's anxiety, see memo of conversation, Klutznick with Dulles, 19 Aug. 1954, *FRUS,* 1952–54, 9:1617.

62. Eban to Dulles, 8 Oct. 1954, 93.04/40/19/b, ISA. See also *FRUS,* 1952–54, 9:1669–72.

63. Memo of conversation, Dulles-Byroade with Eban-Shiloah, 8 Oct. 1954, *FRUS,* 1952–54, 9:1667–69.

64. Cable, Eban to Sharett, 20 Jan. 1955, 130.02/2455/2, ISA.

65. Cable, Dulles to Hoover, 12 May 1955, *FRUS,* 1955, 14:185–86; cable, Dulles to Macmillan, 5 Dec. 1955, *FRUS,* 1955, 14:821. On Dulles's deviousness, see Townsend Hoopes, *The Devil and John Foster Dulles* (Boston: Little, Brown and Co., 1973), 113.

66. Cable, Lawson to State Department, 1 Mar. 1955, *FRUS,* 1955, 14:75–76. See also Sharett, *Personal Diary,* 3:799–800.

67. Cable, Byroade to State Department, 1 Mar. 1955, *FRUS,* 1955, 14:73–74.

68. Memo of conversation, Blaustein with Allen, 18 Mar. 1954, 611.84A/3–1855, NAR.

69. Ibid.

70. Memo, Shiloah to Eban, 21 Mar. 1955, Eban private papers.

71. Memo, Blaustein to Shiloah, 21 Mar. 130.02/2456/15; memo, Shiloah to Yaacov Herzog, 25 Mar. 1955, Shiloah Papers, 4374/20, ISA.

72. Cable, Hart to Byroade, 5 May 1955, 784A.5274/5–555, NAR.

73. Memo, Rafael to Sharett, 25 Apr. 1955, 130.02/2456/15, ISA.

74. Memo, Hoover to Eisenhower, 20 July 1955, White House Central Files, box 329, DDEL; Blaustein to Eisenhower, 2 Aug. 1955, White House Files, box 329, DDEL; Blaustein to

Dulles, 3 Aug. 1955, box 90, Dulles Papers, Princeton Univ. Library; memo, Nathaniel Goodrich to Slawson, 31 Aug. 1955, box 22, AJC Papers, YIVO.

75. Abba Hillel Silver to Adams, 24 May 1955, folder "Eisenhower, 1954–55," AHSA.

76. Abba Hillel Silver to Dulles, 2 Sept. 1955, folder "US State Department, 1955–56," AHSA.

77. Memo of conversation, Blaustein with Allen, 22 Aug. 1955, 784A.5/8–2255, NAR.

78. Cable, Eban to U.S. Division, 23 May 1955, 130.02/2456/15, ISA.

79. Cable, State Department to Dulles, 19 Sept. 1955, *FRUS*, 1955, 14:481.

80. Ibid., 618.

81. Dulles's comments, cabinet meeting, 30 Sept. 1955, Sherman Adams Papers, box 16, Dartmouth College.

82. Memo, Armstrong to Dulles, 22 Sept. 1955, *FRUS*, 1955, 14:507–8. For a more complete list of arms, see Mordechai Bar-On, *Challenge and Quarrel: The Road to Sinai, 1956* (Sde Boker: Ben-Gurion Univ., 1991), 12–13.

83. Cable, Lawson to State Department, 17 Nov. 1955, *FRUS*, 1955, 14:784–86.

84. Numerous references to American awareness of the preventive war idea are to be found in *FRUS*, 1955, 14:578, 591, 606, 609, 742, 768, 812, 821, 879.

85. Memo of conversation, Goldmann with Allen, 6 Dec. 1955, 784A.00/12–655, NAR.

86. Memo of conversation, Dulles with Blaustein, 26 Jan. 1956, 784A.5/1–26, NAR.

87. On the Anderson mission, see *FRUS*, 1 Jan.–26 July 1956, 15:1–346; Saadia Touval, *The Peace Brokers* (Princeton, N.J.: Princeton Univ. Press, 1982), chap. 5.

88. Memo of conversation, Dulles with Blaustein, 26 Jan. 1956, 784A.5/1–26, NAR.

89. Memo of NSC discussion, 20 Oct. 1955, *FRUS*, 1955, 14:616–30, in particular 629.

90. Blaustein to Dulles, 26 Feb. 1956, Dulles Papers, box 100, Princeton Univ. Library.

91. Memo of conversation, Dulles with Blaustein, 26 Apr. 1956, 784A.5/4–2656, NAR.

92. Memo, Dulles to Eisenhower, 24 Apr. 1956, 611/84A/4–1056, NAR; memo of conversation, Dulles, Eisenhower with Abba Hillel Silver, 26 Apr. 1956, Dulles Papers, box 4, DDEL.

93. Abba Hillel Silver to Dulles, 27 Apr. 1956, Dulles Papers, box 104, Princeton Univ. Library.

94. Blaustein to Dulles, 29 June 1956, 784A.56/6–2956, NAR.

95. Dulles to Blaustein, 13 July 1956, 784A.56/6–2956, NAR.

96. Memo of conference, Engel with Dulles, 9 Aug. 1956, box 199, AJC Papers, YIVO.

97. Author's telephone interview with General (ret.) Dan Tolkowsky, Commander, Israel Air Force during that period.

98. Minutes of meeting, Ben-Gurion with American Jewish Committee delegation, 18 June 1957, Ben-Gurion Papers, 230/72/656, IDFA.

99. Cables, Eban to Ben-Gurion, 30 and 31 Oct. 1956 (and to Golda Meir), A. Z. 1301, IDFA.

100. Liebman, *Pressure Without Sanctions*, chap. 5.

101. Memo of conversation, Dulles with Shaikh Yusuf Yasin, Saudi Arabian Deputy Minister of Foreign Affairs, 7 Feb. 1957, *FRUS*, 1957, 17:101–5.

102. Memo of telephone conversation, Dulles with Senator William F. Knowland, 16 Feb. 1957, *FRUS*, 1957, 17:187–88.

103. Memo of telephone conversation, Dulles with Henry Luce, 11 Feb. 1957, box 6, Dulles Papers, telephone call series, DDEL; *FRUS,* 1957, 17:136–37.

104. Memo of conversation, Dulles with delegation of the American Council for Judaism, 18 Jan. 1956, 784A.56/1–1856, NAR.

105. Eisenhower, phone call to Barney Balaban, 15 Feb. 1957, box 21, Eisenhower Diaries, DDEL. Quotation taken from memo of conversation, Eisenhower with Dulles, Humphrey, and Lodge, 16 Feb. 1957, *FRUS,* 1957, 17:178–80; ee also 17:195.

106. *New York Times,* 22, 23 Feb. 1957; Herman Finer, *Dulles over Suez* (Chicago: Quadrangle Books, 1964), 477–84.

107. Memo of conversation, Dulles with the Balaban group, 21 Feb. 1957, 674.84A/2–2157, NAR. On Blaustein's role, Eban to Golda Meir, 21 Jan. 1958, Shiloah Papers, 4374/29, ISA.

108. Memo of conversation, Dulles with the Balaban group, 21 Feb. 1957, 674.84A/2–2157, NAR.

109. Ibid.

110. Ibid.

111. Aide-memoire from the State Department to the Israeli embassy, Washington, 11 Feb. 1957, *FRUS,* 1957, 17:132–34.

Bibliography

Primary Sources

Manuscript Collections

Abba Hillel Silver Archives (AHSA), The Temple, Cleveland, Ohio.
American Council for Judaism Archive (ACJA), State Historical Society of Wisconsin, Madison, Wisconsin.
American Jewish Committee Archives and the Blaustein Library (AJCA), New York City.
Clark M. Clifford Papers. Harry S. Truman Library, Independence, Missouri.
Central Zionist Archives, Emanuel Neumann Papers, Jerusalem, Israel.
David Ben-Gurion Papers, Ben-Gurion Research Institute for the Study of Israel and Zionism, Sde Boker; and his papers at IDF Archives near Tel-Aviv.
David K. Niles Papers, Harry S. Truman Library, Independence, Missouri.
Dwight D. Eisenhower Library, Abilene, Kansas.
Eliezer Livneh Papers, Yad Tabenkin, Ephal.
Hadassah Archive, New York City.
Harry S. Truman Library, Independence, Missouri.
Israel Goldstein Papers, Central Zionist Archives, Jerusalem, Israel.
Israel State Archives, Jerusalem, Israel.
Jacob Blaustein Papers, Baltimore, Maryland (just the available portion).
John F. Dulles Papers, Seeley G. Mudd Manuscript Library, Princeton University.
Minutes of the Jewish Agency Executive, Central Zionist Archives, Jerusalem, Israel.
Nahum Goldmann Papers, Central Zionist Archives, Jerusalem, Israel.
Reuven Shiloach Papers, Israel State Archives, Jerusalem, Israel.
Sharett Archives, Society to Commemorate Moshe Sharett, Tel-Aviv Zionist Archives, New York.

Public Documents

Medzini, Meron. *Israel's Foreign Relations: Selected Documents, 1947–74.* Jerusalem: Ministry for Foreign Affairs, 1976.

State of Israel. *Documents on the Foreign Policy of Israel, May-Sept. 1948.* Vols. 1–8 (1981).

———. *Documents on the Foreign Policy of Israel, Oct. 1948-Apr. 1949.* Vol. 2 (1984).

———. *Documents on the Foreign Policy of Israel, May-Dec. 1949.* Vol. 4 (1986).

———. *Documents on the Foreign Policy of Israel, 1950.* Vol. 5 (1988).

———. *Documents on the Foreign Policy of Israel, 1951.* Vol. 6 (1991).

———. *Documents on the Foreign Policy of Israel, 1952.* Vol. 7 (1992).

———. *Documents on the Foreign Policy of Israel, 1953.* Vol. 8 (1995).

U.S. Department of State. *Foreign Relations of the United States, Diplomatic Papers.* Vol. 5, 1948 (1976).

———. *Foreign Relations of the United States, Diplomatic Papers.* Vol. 6, 1949 (1977).

———. *Foreign Relations of the United States, Diplomatic Papers.* Vol. 5, 1950 (1978).

———. *Foreign Relations of the United States, Diplomatic Papers.* Vol. 5, 1951 (1982).

———. *Foreign Relations of the United States, Diplomatic Papers.* Vol. 9, 1952–54 (1986).

———. *Foreign Relations of the United States, Diplomatic Papers.* Vol. 14, 1955 (1989).

———. *Foreign Relations of the United States, Diplomatic Papers.* Vols. 15, 16, 1956 (1989–90).

———. *Foreign Relations of the United States, Diplomatic Papers.* Vol. 17, 1957 (1990).

World Zionist Organization. *Political Documents of the Jewish Agency, Jan.-Nov. 1947.* Vol. 2 (1998).

Minutes and Reports

American Council for Judaism, Executive Committee, 1948–57. (Mimeographed)

American Jewish Committee. Minutes of Meetings of the Administrative, Steering and Executive Committees, 1948–57. (Mimeographed)

American Zionist Emergency Council. Minutes of Meetings of the Executive Committee, 1949. (Mimeographed)

Jewish Agency for Palestine. Minutes of Meetings of the Jerusalem and American Executive, 1948–57.

Stenographic Report. Twenty-third Zionist Congress. Jerusalem: Zionist Executive, 1951, Hebrew.

Divrei Ha-Knesset. Official Record of the Israeli Parliament, 1952.

Contemporary Periodicals and Newspapers

Commentary (American Jewish Committee), 1947–57.
Davar (Israel), 1948–57.
Haaretz (Israel), 1948–57.
Jerusalem Post (Israel), 1948–57.
JTA (Jewish Telegraphic Agency) Daily News Bulletin, 1948–57.
The New York Times, 1948–57.
The Reconstructionist (Jewish Reconstructionist Foundation), 1948–57.

Interviews and Correspondence

Abramov, S. Z., numerous occasions in Jerusalem, 1980s.
Evron, Ephraim, Tel-Aviv, Oct. 1991.
Gazit, Mordecai, numerous occasions in Jerusalem, 1980s and 1990s.
Gelb, Saadia, numerous occasions in Kibbutz Kfar Blum, 1980s and 1990s.
Gold, Bert, New York, Sept. 1990.
Harman, Abe, Jerusalem, July 1990.
Herlitz, Esther, Tel-Aviv, Sept. 1991.
Herman, Zvi, Haifa, Nov. 1992.
Hertzberg, Arthur, New York, Sept. 1990.
Himmelfarb, Milton, White Plains, New York, Sept. 1990.
Hirsh, Selma, New York, Sept. 1990.
Judge Rifkind, Simon, New York, Sept. 1990.
Lerner, Natan, Kriyat Ono, Sept. 1991.
Shamir, Shlomo, Tel-Aviv, Dec. 1992.
Torczyner, Jacques, New York, Sept. 1990.
Zak, Moshe, Tel-Aviv, Dec. 1990.

Secondary Sources

Abramov, S. Z. *Perpetual Dilemma: Jewish Religion in the Jewish State*. Rutherford, N.J.: Fairleigh Dickinson Univ. Press, 1979.

Adler, Frank J. *Roots in a Moving Stream: The Centennial History of Congregation B'nai Jehudah of Kansas City, 1870–1970*. Kansas City: The Temple, 1972.

Almog, Doron. *Weapons Acquisitions in the U.S., 1945–49*. Tel-Aviv: Ministry of Defense, 1987, Hebrew.

Alteras, Isaac. *Eisenhower and Israel, U.S.-Israeli Relations, 1953–60*. Gainesville: Univ. Press of Florida, 1993.

Alterman, Natan. "An Unfounded Assumption." In *The Seventh Column*. Tel-Aviv: Davar, 1954, Hebrew.

Ambrose, Stephen E. *Eisenhower, the President.* New York: Simon and Schuster, 1984.

The American Jewish Year Book. Vols. 49–58. New York: American Jewish Committee, 1947–57.

Auerbach, Jerold S. *Rabbis and Lawyers.* Bloomington: Indiana Univ. Press, 1990.

Bar-On, Mordechai. *Challenge and Quarrel: The Road to Sinai, 1956.* Sde Boker: Ben-Gurion Univ., 1991.

Bar-Zohar, Michael. *Ben-Gurion.* 3 vols. Tel-Aviv: Am Oved, 1977, Hebrew.

Begin, Menahem. *Ha-Mered.* Jerusalem: Achiasaf, 1950, Hebrew.

Ben-Gurion, David. *The War of Independence Diary.* Tel-Aviv: Ministry of Defense, 1982, Hebrew.

———. *Yihud Veyeud.* Tel-Aviv: Ministry of Defense, 1972, Hebrew.

———. *The Restored State of Israel.* Tel-Aviv: Am Oved, 1969, Hebrew.

Berger, Elmer. *Memoirs of an Anti-Zionist Jew.* Beirut: Institute for Palestine Studies, 1978.

Bialer, Uri. *Between East and West: Israel's Foreign Policy Orientation, 1948–56.* Cambridge, UK: Cambridge Univ. Press, 1990.

Blaustein, Jacob. *The Voice of Reason.* Presidential Address. New York: American Jewish Committee, 1950.

Brecher, Michael. *Decisions in Israel's Foreign Policy.* London: Oxford Univ. Press, 1974.

———. *The Foreign Policy System of Israel.* London: Oxford Univ. Press, 1972.

Campbell, John C. *Defense of the Middle East.* New York: Harper and Brothers, 1960.

Clifford, Clark. *Counsel to the President.* New York: Random House, 1991.

Cohen, Michael J. *Truman and Israel.* Berkeley: Univ. of California Press, 1990.

Cohen, Naomi W. *Not Free to Desist.* Philadelphia: Jewish Publication Society, 1972.

Copeland, Miles. *The Game of Nations.* London: Weidenfeld and Nicolson, 1970.

Davis, Moshe, ed. *With Eyes Toward Zion.* Vol. 2. New York: Praeger, 1986.

Dayan, Moshe. *The Story of My Life.* Jerusalem: Edanim Publishers, 1976, Hebrew.

Divine, Robert A. *Eisenhower and the Cold War.* Oxford, UK: Oxford Univ. Press, 1981.

Eban, Abba. *An Autobiography.* London: Futura Publications, 1977.

Eilts, Herman F. "Reflections on the Suez Crisis: Security in the Middle East." In *Suez,* edited by William Roger Louis and Roger Ower, 347–61. Oxford, UK: Clarendon Press, 1989.

Elam, Yigal. *The Jewish Agency.* Jerusalem: Hassifriya Haziyonit, 1990, Hebrew.

Elath, Eliahu. *The Struggle for Statehood.* Tel-Aviv: Am Oved, 1982, Hebrew.

———. "Samuel I. Rosenman's Role in Israel's Creation." *Molad* 37–38 (1976, Hebrew): 448–54.

Elazar, Daniel. *Community and Polity.* Philadelphia: Jewish Publication Society of America, 1980.

Feintuch, Yossi. *U.S. Policy on Jerusalem*. New York: Greenwood Press, 1987.

Finer Herman. *Dulles over Suez*. Chicago: Quadrangle Books, 1964.

Fink, Reuben. *America and Palestine*. New York: American Zionist Emergency Council, 1944.

Fishman, Hertzl. *American Protestantism and a Jewish State*. Detroit: Wayne State Univ. Press, 1973.

Frisch, Daniel. "The ZOA at the Crossroad." *The New Palestine*, 13 Jan. 1949.

Gal, Allon. *David Ben-Gurion and the American Alignment for a Jewish State*. Bloomington: Indiana Univ. Press, 1991.

Ganin, Zvi. "Activism versus Moderation: The Conflict Between Silver and Wise." *Studies in Zionism* 5, no. 1 (Spring 1984): 71–95.

———. *Truman, American Jewry, and Israel, 1945–1948*. New York: Holmes and Meier, 1979.

Gazit, Mordecai. "Israeli Military Procurement from the U.S." In *Dynamics of Dependence: U.S.-Israeli Relations*, edited by Gabriel Sheffer, 83–123. Boulder, Colo.: Westview Press, 1987.

Ginzberg, Eli. *My Brother's Keeper*. New Brunswick, N.J.: Transaction Publishers, 1989.

Goldmann, Nahum. *Le Paradoxe Juif*. Ramat-Gan: Massada, 1978, Hebrew.

———. *Autobiography*. New York: Holt, Reinhart and Winston, 1969.

Goldstein, Israel. *My World as a Jew*. New York: Herzl Press, 1984.

Gorny, Yosef, *The Quest for Collective Identity*. Tel-Aviv: Am Oved, 1990, Hebrew.

Halperin, Samuel. *The Political World of American Zionism*. Detroit: Wayne State Univ. Press, 1961.

Halpern, Ben. *A Clash of Heroes: Brandeis, Weizmann, and American Zionism*. New York: Oxford Univ. Press, 1987.

———. "The Anti-Zionist Phobia: Legal Style." In *The Arab-Israeli Conflict*, edited by John N. Moore. Princeton, N.J.: Princeton Univ. Press, 1974.

———. *The Idea of the Jewish State*. Cambridge, Mass.: Harvard Univ. Press, 1961.

Hertzberg, Arthur. *The Zionist Idea*. New York: Atheneum, 1969.

———. "American Zionism at an Impasse." *Commentary*, Oct. 1949.

Hoopes, Townsend. *The Devil and John Foster Dulles*. Boston: Little, Brown and Co., 1973.

Isaacs, Stephen D. *Jews and American Politics*. Garden City, N.J.: Doubleday, 1974.

Joseph, Bernard. *British Rule in Eretz Yisrael*. Jerusalem: Mosad Bialik, 1948.

Kaplan, Mordecai M. "The Need for Diaspora Zionism." In *Mid-Century*, edited by Harold U. Ribalow. New York: Beechhurst Press, 1955.

Kaufman, Menahem. *Non-Zionists in America and the Struggle for Jewish Statehood, 1938–48*. Jerusalem: Hassifriya Haziyonit, 1984, Hebrew.

Kenen, I. L. *Israel's Defense Line*. Buffalo, N.Y.: Prometheus Books, 1981.

Kollek, Teddy. *One Jerusalem*. Tel-Aviv: Maariv, 1979, Hebrew.

Kolsky, Thomas A. *Jews Against Zionism: The American Council for Judaism, 1942–48*. Philadelphia: Temple Univ. Press, 1990.

Kubowitzki, A. Leon. *Unity in Dispersion: A History of the World Jewish Congress*. New York: Institute of Jewish Affairs, 1948.

Lehrman, Hal. "Arms for Arabs—and What for Israel?" *Commentary,* Nov. 1954, 423–33.

Lewis, Bernard. "The Middle East Crisis in Historical Perspective." *The American Scholar,* Winter 1992, 33–46.

———. "At Stake in the Gulf." *New York Review of Books,* 20 Dec. 1990, 44–46.

———. *The Arabs in History*. New York: Harper and Row, 1966.

Liebman, Charles S. *Pressure Without Sanctions*. Rutherford, N.J.: Fairleigh Dickinson Univ. Press, 1977.

Louis, William Roger. *The British Empire in the Middle East, 1945–1951*. Oxford, UK: Clarendon Press, 1984.

Maslow, Will. *The Structure and Functioning of the American Jewish Community*. New York: American Jewish Congress, 1974.

Meyer, Michael A. *Response to Modernity*. New York: Oxford Univ. Press, 1988.

Millis, Walter, ed. *The Forrestal Diaries*. New York: Viking Press, 1951.

Nadich, Judah. *Eisenhower and the Jews*. New York: Twayne Publishers, 1953.

Neumann, Emanuel. *In the Arena*. New York: Herzl Press, 1976.

———. "Towards the World Zionist Congress." *Zionist Quarterly,* June 1951, 5–15.

Niv, David. *Battle for Freedom: The Irgun Zvai Leumi*. Parts 1 and 6. Tel-Aviv: Klausner Institute, 1975, Hebrew.

Oren, Michael B. "Secret Egypt-Israel Peace Initiatives Prior to the Suez Campaign." *Middle Eastern Studies* 26, no. 3 (1990): 351–70.

Orian, Noah. "The Leadership of Abba Hillel Silver, 1938–1949," Ph.D. diss., Tel-Aviv Univ., 1982.

Patai, Raphael, ed. *Encyclopedia of Zionism and Israel*. New York: McGraw-Hill, 1971.

Proskauer, Joseph M. *A Segment of My Times*. New York: Farrar, Straus and Co., 1950.

Raphael, Marc L. *Abba Hillel Silver*. New York: Holmes and Meier, 1989.

———. *A History of the UJA, 1939–82*. Providence, R.I.: Brown Univ., Scholars Press, 1982.

Reznikoff, Charles, ed. *Louis Marshall*. 2 vols. Philadelphia: Jewish Publication Society, 1957.

Scholem, Gershom. *Explications and Implications, Writings on Jewish Heritage and Renaissance*. Tel-Aviv: Am Oved, 1989.

Selah, Abraham. *From Contacts to Negotiations: The Jewish Agency and Israel's Relationship with King Abdullah, 1946–1950*. Tel-Aviv: Tel-Aviv Univ., 1985.

Shaham, David. *Israel—Forty Years*. Tel-Aviv: Am Oved, 1991, Hebrew.

Shamir, Shimon. "The Collapse of Project Alpha." In *Suez 1956,* edited by William Roger Louis and Roger Owen, 73–100. Oxford, UK: Clarendon Press, 1989.

Shapira, Anita. *Land and Power.* Tel-Aviv: Am Oved, 1992.

Sharett, Moshe. *Personal Diary.* Tel-Aviv: Maariv, 1978, Hebrew.

Shimoni, Yaacov. *The Arab States.* Tel-Aviv: Am Oved, 1988, Hebrew.

Shimshoni, Jonathan. *Israel and Conventional Deterrence.* Ithaca, N.Y.: Cornell Univ. Press, 1988.

Shuckburgh, Evelyn. *Descent to Suez: Diaries, 1951–1956.* New York: W. W. Norton, 1986.

Silver, Abba Hillel. "The Case for Zionism." *Reader's Digest,* Sept. 1949, 57.

Silver, Daniel J., ed. *In the Time of Harvest.* New York: Macmillan Co., 1963.

Slater, Leonard. *The Pledge.* New York: Simon and Schuster, 1970.

Spiegel, Steven L. *The Other Arab-Israeli Conflict: Making America's Middle East Policy, from Truman to Reagan.* Chicago: Univ. of Chicago Press, 1985.

Stephens, Robert. *Nasser: A Political Biography.* New York: Simon and Schuster, 1971.

Stock, Ernest. *Chosen Instrument.* New York: Herzl Press, 1988.

———. *Partners & Pursestrings: A History of the United Israel Appeal.* Lanham, Md.: University Press of America, 1987.

Teveth, Shabtai. *Ben-Gurion: The Burning Ground.* Boston: Houghton Mifflin Co., 1987.

———. *Moshe Dayan.* Jerusalem-Tel-Aviv: Schocken, 1971, Hebrew.

Touval, Saadia. *The Peace Brokers.* Princeton, N.J.: Princeton Univ. Press, 1982.

Urofsky, Melvin I. *We Are One.* Garden City, N.Y.: Doubleday, 1978.

Voss, Carl Herman. "Christian Friends of the New Israel." *Congress Weekly* 17, no. 24 (9 Oct. 1950): 6–8.

Waldman, Morris D. *Nor by Power.* New York: International Universities Press, 1953.

Weizmann, Chaim. *Trial and Error.* New York: Harper and Brothers, 1949.

Index